Dr. Greenfingers'
Rx for
Healthy, Vigorous
HOUSEPLANTS

D1305626

Dr. Greenfingers'
Rx for
Healthy, Vigorous
HOUSEPLANTS

Andrew Bicknell

Illustrated by
Fiona Almeleh
Marion Mills
George Thompson

A HERBERT MICHELMAN BOOK

CROWN PUBLISHERS, Inc.
New York

Dr. Greenfingers' Rx for
Healthy, Vigorous Houseplants
by Andrew Bicknell
was conceived and produced
by Imprint Books Limited, London

Designer: Andrzej Bielecki
Editor: Penelope Grant
Editorial Assistant: Catherine Davies
Illustrators: Fiona Almeleh
　　　　　　　Marion Mills
　　　　　　　George Thompson
Consultant: George Seddon

First published 1980 in the United States
by Crown Publishers, Inc., New York
Published simultaneously in Canada by
General Publishing Company Limited

Library of Congress Cataloging in Publication Data
Bicknell, Andrew.
　　Dr. Greenfingers' Rx for healthy, vigorous
　　houseplants.
　　Includes index.
　　1. House plants　2. House plants — Diseases
and pests.　I.　Title.
SB419.G73　635.9'65　79-1036
ISBN 0-517-53821-0
ISBN 0-517-53822-9 pbk.

Printed in Belgium
by H. Proost & Cie, Turnhout

Contents

This book has been written by a British gardening authority and great care was taken to avoid the use of any word or term that would be unfamiliar on either side of the Atlantic. Throughout the text, however, the word compost, which in Britain is the equivalent of potting soil, is used. The text explains, too, that the insecticide derris is known as rotenone in the United States.

Introduction

"Out of the everywhere into here" was the Victorian poet's explanation of where babies came from. He could have said the same of houseplants. There is hardly a part of the world, except the polar regions, which was not originally the home of a houseplant. The history of how these plants got from everywhere to here is far more exciting than most conventional adventure stories. But what concerns us is the practical problem of how far the plants can adjust to the change.

Of course, our plants have not come straight from the desert or rain forests to our living rooms. Although we describe them as natives of Brazil or China or New Guinea, they have been domesticated for a long time, some of them for centuries. Strains have been developed, especially in recent years, to cope better with their new environment, which itself has changed dramatically in only a few generations; our homes are warmer, lighter and drier than they were. Not all these changes are better from the plants' points of view. Those which flourished in once uncomfortably cold houses are now expected to put on similarly good performances in the perpetual warmth of central heating. Better lighting in houses

is all to the good, if only because we always underestimate how much light a plant needs. The dry air of hot rooms, however, is even worse for plants than it is for the humans and furniture sharing it. And if the energy crisis forces us to accustom ourselves once again to cooler rooms our plants, willy-nilly, will be expected to follow suit. Some of them will be able to make the adjustment and others will not.

No plant, however long it has been away from its native haunts, loses altogether the physical characteristics evolved over millions of years. To appreciate this is the beginning of wisdom for plant owners. A plant in a living room needs, to some extent, to be treated in the way Nature treats its compatriots in the wild. It is, therefore, helpful to know from which part of the everywhere your plants originally came and what conditions are like there.

Almost all houseplants come from one of the four climatic zones shown on the map. Conditions vary within each zone, depending on altitudes, winds and proximity to the sea. Consequently, only broad generalizations can be made.

The tropical summer rain zone has hot and humid summer days, which often

end in thundery rain, with slightly cooler nights. Winter is dry if the prevailing winds have blown off hot deserts, but moist where winds blow off the sea. Most of the houseplants which come from this zone need summer temperatures in the range of 65 to 70°F (18 to 21°C), and winter temperatures between 55 and 60°F (13 and 16°C). The temperatures recommended for individual plants are given in the You and Your Plants section of this book.

The subtropical winter rain zone has summer temperatures between 68 and 82°F (20 and 28°C), except near the sea where the temperature is lower. Here the winter temperature is between 43 and 50°F (6 and 10°C). Houseplants from this zone come mainly from the cooler parts and need a summer temperature around 55°F (13°C) and a winter temperature around 45°F (7°C).

The subtropical dry zone includes the world's famous hot deserts where the temperature during the day may soar above 100°F (38°C) to be followed by ground frost at night. On western coastal areas conditions are clammier, cooler and less variable. Most plants from this zone require a summer temperature above 60°F (16°C). They need to be cool in winter—in general about 45°F (7°C).

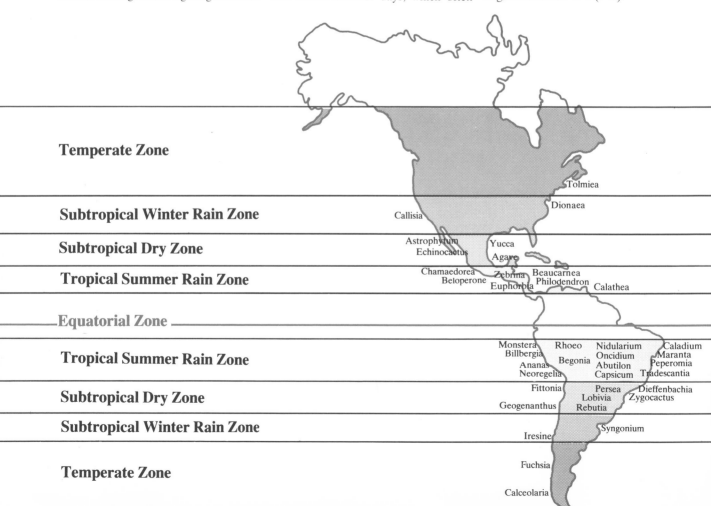

Temperate Zone

Subtropical Winter Rain Zone

Subtropical Dry Zone

Tropical Summer Rain Zone

Equatorial Zone

Tropical Summer Rain Zone

Subtropical Dry Zone

Subtropical Winter Rain Zone

Temperate Zone

The temperate zone, which lies in the belt of westerly winds, has a great variety of weather. It is mild on western coasts of continents, but inland there may be extremes of cold and heat between winter and summer. Most houseplants from the temperate zone come from its cooler areas and need summer temperatures ranging between 55 and 60°F (13 and 16°C), or a little lower or a little higher. Winter temperatures should, generally, be in the region of 45 to 50°F (7 to 10°C).

Plants which belong to the equatorial zones are hothouse plants rather than houseplants. There are three very beautiful examples—the calatheas, *Codiaeum variegatum pictum* and *Philodendron andreanum*, the velour philodendron—which people are seduced into buying and then discover how difficult it can be to keep them in the environment to which they are accustomed.

It would be absurd to choose a plant whose ingrained temperature needs cannot be met in your home. It is better to refuse resolutely to buy a beautiful, highly desirable plant that will die and to settle for a second choice that will live to give you pleasure and satisfaction.

Within each climatic zone there are endless regional or quite local variations

and the native flora in each area will, therefore, differ not only in their temperature requirements, but also in the levels of rainfall, humidity and light needed.

No matter where a plant comes from, there is no real problem about providing it with the amount of water to which it is accustomed. (How well we do it in practice is another matter.) Water requirements, therefore, do not need to be considered in the choice of a plant, although they must be attended to meticulously when looking after it.

Humidity is another matter; as an extreme case, a plant from the steamy tropics would be a dead loss in the dehydrated air in which we tend increasingly to live. There are ways to make life more acceptable for plants in such surroundings (see page 13), but for many these palliative measures are not enough. They need a warm greenhouse, which is not the atmosphere in which you want to sweat your life away.

The amount of light a plant needs continues to be affected by the environment in which its ancestors lived. As with temperature, however, plants have developed a considerable tolerance—but this should not be taken for granted.

Plants whose natural habitat is open ground need a far better light than they will get in a basement room; plants which once grew in the shade of trees may still need what passes for good light indoors, but will not be able to tolerate direct sunlight.

Compromise is necessary. Plants may go part of the way, but you will have to meet them, or decide that it is not possible, or not worth the trouble, to satisfy the needs of some particularly demanding specimen.

Northern Hemisphere		Southern Hemisphere
January	Winter	June
February	Late Winter	July
March	Early Spring	August
April	Spring	September
May	Late Spring	October
June	Early Summer	November
July	Summer	December
August	Late Summer	January
September	Early Autumn	February
October	Autumn	March
November	Late Autumn	April
December	Early Winter	May

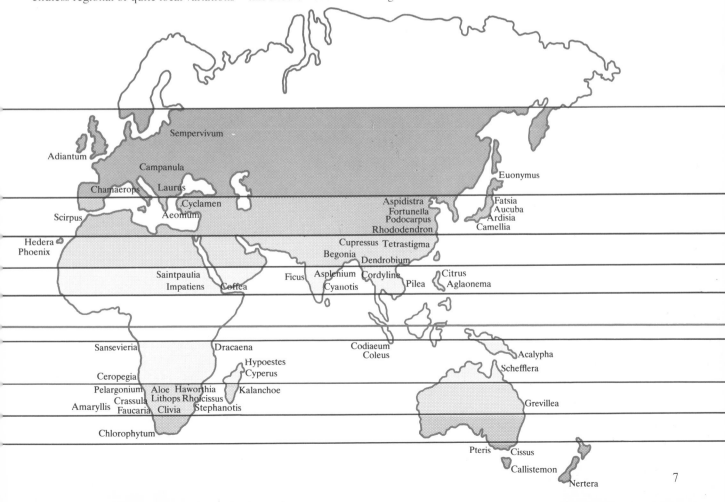

7

Choosing the Right Plant

Plants have no insuperable difficulty keeping alive in their natural surroundings; if they had they would be extinct. So when people talk about a "difficult" plant, what they mean is that it is a plant unlikely to survive in the environment they can provide for it; in other words, they have chosen the wrong plant.

Since we can never hope to re-create in our homes the conditions of, for example, a tropical rain forest, it is fortunate that so many houseplants have developed a tolerance for living alongside us in conditions we can enjoy. By the breeding of more adaptable varieties and hybrids from original species, the area of tolerance has been enormously widened. But there are still limits.

Falling in love with a plant at first sight and buying it just because it would look

The plants illustrated here are among the most popular. They are quite easy to care for and are recommended for the less experienced indoor gardener.

marvellous on a table in the hall is foolish. Before choosing a plant it is necessary to ascertain how much light and warmth it needs in summer and winter. You must then ask yourself how light and warm is the area where you want to keep the plant. When the answers to these two questions match you are halfway to successful indoor gardening. The other half depends on your continuing, intelligent care of the plant—on watering and feeding it properly and spotting trouble in time.

Skill in caring for plants increases with experience. When you buy your first houseplants you are paying not only for the plants but for the apprenticeship as well. To cut down the potential rate of failure it is best to choose from among the most popular plants; they are popular because of their strong will to live. It is also best to buy plants when they are young. Not only are they cheaper, but they will adapt more readily than older plants to the change from the nursery conditions in which they have been bred to life with you.

It is a good idea, too, to buy plants in the spring, for this gives you and them time to adjust to each other before winter begins. Bargains in plants are more likely to be picked up in the autumn, however, when nurseries tend to clear out their surplus plants rather than keep them through another winter of expensive heating.

One vital consideration when choosing a suitable plant is the range of temperatures it will enjoy (or have to suffer) in your home. There is the minimum winter temperature below which the plant is likely, or certain, to die and the maximum winter temperature above which the plant will go on growing instead of resting as, in most cases, it should. The summer temperatures it will tolerate will, of course, be higher, but each plant has a comparatively limited range within which it will grow best. The temperatures appropriate for more than two hundred and fifty plants are set out in the entries in the You and Your Plants section of this book. They should be heeded before you go shopping for plants.

The other vital consideration is whether you can give the plant all the light it needs, for without adequate light it cannot process sufficient food and will certainly languish and possibly die. Variegated plants need more light than green foliage plants and the less green there is in their variegations the more light they will need. Plants with coloured leaves need even more light and, generally speaking, flowering plants need most of all.

There are considerable variations in the temperature in different parts of even a centrally heated room, as a little research with a thermometer will demonstrate. A light meter will show even more dramatic variations in the intensity of light in a room. Sometimes the warmest, or the coolest, part of the room may be too dark, or too bright, to satisfy a particular plant. It's best to know this before you buy a plant.

We are all tempted at times to buy on impulse a pot plant already smothered in blooms. Most of these plants have a short flowering life and are then thrown away because they are difficult or impossible to get to bloom again. They may be a pleasant, although possibly extravagant, alternative to cut flowers. But real houseplants, and those from which you'll get the most pleasure, should be able to survive for at least several years, and the longer they live the better buy they are.

Before choosing a plant find out how tall, and how bushy, it may ultimately grow. The modest little plant in a small pot may become an unmanageable six feet (1.80 m) within a few years.

Obviously, the decision about which plant to buy is best made with forethought at home rather than on impulse in a shop. And when you do get there do not be seduced by another plant, handsome stranger though it may be.

The plant you take home must be healthy, free from pests and diseases, and hardened off, which means acclimated to life outside the greenhouse where it was raised and pampered. There is no mistaking a plant which is sick for one which is rudely healthy, but there are times when the appearance of a plant can be deceptive. It is therefore better to go to a reliable specialist shop or garden centre, than to a shop where houseplants are just a sideline and there is no expert to advise you. Supermarkets often buy good plants and if they have been newly delivered they may be bargains. But plants deteriorate rapidly in the atmosphere of most supermarkets.

Hardiness is difficult to judge, but it is important; a plant taken straight from the cossetting environment of a nursery greenhouse to a shop and then home is bound to suffer. On the other hand, the fact that a plant is standing in a searing wind outside a shop is no sign of its hardiness; it is more likely testimony to the foolhardiness of the shopkeeper. This is another reason to go to a reliable shop or

to buy a plant bearing the label of a well-known nursery which cannot afford to risk its reputation.

Avoid any plant with leaves that are brown, mottled or otherwise blemished; these are possible indications of either disease or neglect. Inspect a plant as closely as you can before you buy it for any evidence that pests are present. If in doubt, don't buy it.

When you have chosen a plant insist that it is well wrapped to protect it from cold or wind while you are taking it home. Never leave a plant in an airless car, and if you are driving take the corners carefully so that it does not fall over.

Once you have the plant at home do not water it unless it is obviously dry; you probably need a drink more than it does. Then inspect the plant with greater care than was possible in the shop. If you discover any sign of pests or disease take it back immediately. Even if you decide your new plant is in the best of health do not let it mix with other plants for a few days. Give it a chance to adjust by keeping it by itself, in the shade, in a fairly cool room.

Seasonal Care

After you have, with forethought and common sense, chosen the plants most likely to succeed in the conditions which you can provide in your home, you have to learn how to care for them, help them to grow, and respect their necessary periods of dormancy. Eventually silicon chips will doubtless take over the job of looking after houseplants. They may even be better at it than we often are, but they will take a lot of pleasure out of indoor gardening. That is some time off, however, and in the meantime we shall have to blunder happily on.

Everyone blunders to some extent, but you will make fewer mistakes if you have some understanding of the way in which plants grow. But there is no more need to know the complicated processes by which a plant lives than it is to have an intimate knowledge of anatomy and physiology to look after children. The basic facts are sufficient.

To grow, a plant needs nutrients, water, air, light and warmth. The nutrients, which are mineral salts, and the water are taken up through the roots, but they can also be absorbed through the leaves. Light is the most vital ingredient, for it enables the plant to turn these raw materials into the food necessary for its

During their growing period, different plants need different amounts of light. The sampling of plants illustrated below shows some which require direct light, some indirect light and others shade.

growth. By a process called photosynthesis, the plant manufactures its own food, which is sugar, in its leaves with the aid of light. The food is then used immediately by the plant or stored as starch in its roots. The temperature of the plant's environment regulates its growth.

Each plant has a range of temperatures which are most favourable for its growth; if the temperature rises somewhat higher growth may slow down and if it rises much higher the plant will wilt. Below the optimum range for growth there is a band of temperatures in which the plant will be healthily alive, but not actively growing; these are the temperatures which are suitable for the plant during the dormancy period, when it is taking its annual rest. Lower still are the temperatures at which the plant will die. Here we are concerned with growth.

For the sake of convenience, plants can be divided into three groups according to whether they need cool, temperate or warm conditions. The comparatively limited number of plants in the first and hardiest group, which need cool conditions, will grow as long as the temperature does not fall below 45°F (7°C). The majority of our houseplants, those in the second group, will not grow if the temperature falls below 55°F (13°C). The more demanding and delicate plants, some of which are the most desirable, will not grow if the temperature is below 65°F (18°C). Roughly speaking, optimum growth will take place if the temperature

is as much as 10°F (−12°C) above these minimum figures.

The night temperatures should be at the lower end of the scale and the day temperatures at the higher end. This fits in with the natural daily rhythm of most plants. In daylight the leaves, using the sun's energy, are busy manufacturing food for the plant to live on. When darkness falls this process stops, and although other processes continue the plant slows down. A slight drop in temperature is one element involved in this daily period of rest and recuperation.

Obviously, the temperatures most beneficial during the growing period for plants which need cool conditions are unrealistic because they take no account of human comfort or of the likelihood that during the summer months average temperatures, both indoors and outdoors, will be higher. (Even with air conditioning you are unlikely to set the thermostat just to please the plants.) Fortunately, most plants adjust better to periods of temperatures above their needs than they do to temperatures which are too low. A danger point is reached, however, when the temperature is high and more water is evaporated through the leaves than the roots can draw up from the compost, or potting soil. The plant may then wilt dramatically.

Whatever the season of the year, comparatively few houses have the same temperature throughout; it is a good in-

vestment to have a thermometer in every room to cut out guesswork (not least if you are trying to conserve fuel). In winter the variation in temperature from room to room may not be so great in centrally heated houses, but in summer, when the heating is off, temperatures will vary. The deciding factor is the amount of sun a room gets. The plants can be arranged accordingly. Plants needing the coolest conditions can be put into a room which faces north, the plants which need temperate conditions could go into rooms facing east or west, and the plants which need warmth will be content in a room which faces south.

During a really hot spell all the plants might be given refuge in the coolest room available. If that is impractical there are a few things that you can do to help. When the sun is scorching, remove the plants from window sills, even when they normally flourish there, for glass creates a heat trap. Drawing the curtains before the sun begins to stream through the window will prevent a violent rise in temperature. Spraying the leaves will help to prevent wilting, but do not spray while the sun is on the leaves and use water at room temperature, not cold water. Provide good ventilation, but, although you may enjoy sitting in the breeze of an electric fan, plants do not.

Although all plants must have light to manufacture food some need more light than others. It is not possible, however, to say precisely how much light a plant requires because there is simply not enough information. In any case, while you can provide, within reason, the temperatures to which a plant is accustomed in nature you cannot produce the same light. Outdoors, even the plant we regard as shade-loving gets light from all sides and, more important, from above. Indoors a plant may well get light from only one window. Even if the plant is close to the window there will be a great variation in the intensity of the light during the day as the sun moves from one side of the house to the other. Even more dramatic are the variations in light in the same room. Although these variations can be measured with a light meter, most people go by rule of thumb.

One simple rule is that a plant which is more than eight feet (2.40 m) from a window is getting only about 10 per cent of the light it would receive if it were next to the window, but not in direct sun. That means that at least half of a room may not have enough light for plants to do more than languish. A plant that is short of light has definite symptoms. These include spindly growth, leaves far smaller than they should be, pale young leaves and yellowing old ones, variegated leaves reverting to green, and refusal to flower.

Light, as well as heat, varies according to which way the windows of a room face and according to the season of the year. In a room with east-facing windows, the sun, while still low on the horizon, may fill the whole room with sunshine, but neither the light nor the heat is fierce. In a west-facing room, the sun in summer remains hot and bright as it moves across the sky. When the sun sinks it may fill the whole room, but the light is less brilliant. In a room which faces south in the northern hemisphere—and north in the southern hemisphere—the brightest position, and potentially the most dangerous for plants, is near the window. But because the midsummer sun is high in the sky, much of the direct sunlight falls on a comparatively small area of the floor near the window—and that is the danger area for many plants. The rest of the room is bright with indirect light.

In a room which faces north in the northern hemisphere—and south in the southern hemisphere—the setting sun in the summer may sneak across one wall, but it will be weak and potentially harmless. At other times the light is less variable than in other rooms. A place near the window is good for hardy plants which need direct light.

Houses are not necessarily built facing due south, north, east or west, however, and rooms may be shaded by other houses or trees. But when you have lived in a house all year you will know which are the bright and which are the shady parts of each room. Plants need far more light than human beings do—their very existence depends on it—but in summer you must take care that they are not exposed to too much sun. You can move out of the glare—they cannot.

Seasonal Care • The Growing Period

In the nature of things a plant will get the warmth and light it needs during its growing period, in the summer months, but for growth it also requires extra nutrients and water. Proper feeding and adequate watering are your responsibility.

All that feeding entails is giving the plant the nutrients it must have to grow. In the wild it gets these nutrients from the soil, but in a pot the nutrients in the compost, or potting soil, are quickly depleted and you must supply them.

The nutrients which a plant requires for healthy growth are mineral salts—nitrogen, potassium, phosphorus and various trace elements—and these are available, already mixed, in general-purpose proprietary fertilizers. There are many brands available. Some are organic, others have chemical additives, about which you may feel negative. It matters little to the plant which one you choose. There are, however, a few plants which require special feeding and this is explained in the individual plant entries.

A plant can absorb nutrients through both its root hairs and its leaves, but root feeding is the more usual method. Fertilizers for root feeding are available in solid form, either as pills, one of which is, periodically, pushed into the compost, or as a powder which is spread on the surface of the compost. Normal watering then washes the fertilizer down to the roots.

Most people find it easiest, and most successful, to use a liquid fertilizer. Proprietary mixes are available with which you can make a suitable solution. A liquid feed should be given only when the compost is moist; if the compost is dry the root hairs may be damaged. Never give a liquid feed in stronger doses than the manufacturer recommends.

You need not follow so unquestioningly the manufacturer's instructions about the frequency of feeding. Weekly feeding may be all right for very vigorous plants, but for most plants a feeding every two weeks is sufficient. Some plants need to be fed only once a month. Instructions about the frequency of feeding for individual plants are given in each plant entry. Overfeeding encourages lush growth with no stamina in the stems and it discourages the production of flowers.

A sure symptom of underfeeding, on the other hand, is the noticeably small size of the new leaves. If you have neglected to feed your plants for some time and they are obviously underfed, it is best to begin with a foliar feed, using a fertilizer solution which is sprayed on the leaves, because this works quickly. When the

mineral salts are fed to a plant in solid form they will be taken up by the roots in two to three weeks. When they are fed in solution they are taken up by the roots within a few days. If the fertilizer solution is sprayed on the leaves it is absorbed immediately.

Never feed an ailing plant; its roots cannot cope with the nutrients already available. All feeding should be stopped by early autumn when growth begins to slow down.

There are two instruments which can help you to decide if your plants need watering. One is a moisture meter, You stick it into the compost and then wait for a reading—a tedious chore if you have many houseplants. The other is a finger, quicker, and, with practice, just as effective. Your eyes can tell you only if the surface of the compost is dry, so it is important to stick your finger a little way into the compost and not just touch the surface with it.

Gardeners tend to underwater their gardens and to overwater their houseplants. The best way to avoid overwatering is to water thoroughly when you do water, but to let the plant use up most of the moisture before giving it any more. A plant can only be overwatered by watering it too often. It cannot be overwatered too much at any one time.

It is important to understand that the pot in which your plant is growing is not full of compost, but is half empty because of the spaces between the particles of solid matter. When the compost is dry these spaces are filled with air.

This is vividly demonstrated when a pot of dry compost is immersed in a bucket of water. Bubbles of air escape to the surface as the water soaks in to take their place. If the pot were left in the

bucket the spaces in the compost would stay filled with water. If a plant were in the pot it would then die, for roots need air as well as water. As soon as the pot is removed from the bucket, however, water escapes through the drainage hole—that is why it is there—and air presses in through the surface of the compost to fill the spaces from which the water has drained. But the compost itself has absorbed a proportion of the water—a loamy compost absorbs more than a sandy one—so the plant has both the water and the air it needs.

The best method of watering a potted plant is to immerse it in tepid water in the kitchen sink, in the bathtub, or in a large

bucket. However, the pot's drainage hole must not be blocked, the compost must drain well, and the plant must never be permitted to drain in a saucer, and left

standing in water. There are a few plants, however, which do like to have their feet in water. In these cases, this is noted under their entries in the You and Your Plants section.

If the pot is too large or the plant too awkward for immersion watering and you have to water it from the top, be sure that it gets enough water. You should not stop until water appears through the drainage hole. There is one important thing to watch for when watering from the top. Peat-based compost shrinks away from the sides of the pot as it dries and the water may sneak out that easy way. Check that it has not bypassed most of the compost. If the pot stands in a saucer or a dish, empty the surplus water as soon as it drains through. Roots left to stand in water become waterlogged and airless.

As compost dries out it becomes more difficult for the roots to absorb what moisture is left and a point is reached when the plant cannot draw up any more water even though some is left. Consequently, the compost must not be allowed to get really dry, and can be watered again thoroughly when it still feels slightly moist.

The compost will dry out most rapidly in hot weather and when the plant is growing vigorously. It dries out more quickly in a clay pot than in an impervious plastic pot. A sandy, peat-based compost will dry out more quickly than a loam-based compost.

With all these variables, the information about watering which appears under the individual plant entries in the You and Your Plants section cannot be taken as being precise instructions, but must be accepted merely as advice. Some plants are described as needing to be watered very frequently, frequently or, on the other hand, only fairly frequently, during the growing period. The difference is not in the amount of water you should give them each time—each watering should be thorough—but how often you will probably have to water them. If you merely dampen the surface of the compost frequently, the roots at the bottom of the pot are going to suffer. In summer, the rate at which the compost dries out may involve watering once a day, once a week, or anything in between. This is where you must depend on your finger in the compost.

Almost all houseplants do better if they are watered with soft water. Although many will tolerate hard water, some lime-hating plants, such as the popular azalea, are very sensitive. Rain water, even in the countryside, may contain some pretty noxious substances picked up in the atmosphere over industrial areas. For precious plants distilled water can be used. Houseplants should never be watered with cold water. Always use water which is tepid, that is, at a warm room temperature.

Moisture in the air is as vital for many houseplants as moisture in the soil, but high humidity is not easy to provide indoors. There is, of course, always some humidity in the air. The warmer the air the more moisture it is able to hold. When it can hold no more the moisture condenses and falls as rain or dew.

The relative humidity is the amount of moisture actually in the air compared to the maximum amount the air could hold at that temperature. In general, a relative humidity of 50 to 60 per cent is acceptable to humans and plants. But on hot, dry, summer days the relative humidity may fall far below that. The air then absorbs moisture from whatever source it can, including plants, which give off water through the innumerable stomata, or pores, of their leaves—the process known as transpiration. The lower the relative humidity the more water the plants lose, often to their detriment.

The usual and simple methods of compensating for this loss aim at creating a slightly more humid atmosphere just around the plant—a microclimate. A mist spray does this, but the effect lasts only for a short time. Pots of plants, either in a group or individually, can be placed in larger containers and surrounded by peat

which is kept constantly moist. Or the pots may be set on a dish or tray of pebbles which are always covered with water; but on no account should the bottoms of the pots ever touch the water.

For many plants these methods may be sufficient, but they are scarcely adequate in hot climates or for plants which are emigrants from tropical rain forests. In these cases, an electric humidifier is the only real solution. The most suitable one for a home is a steam evaporation humidifier, which works silently. It heats water, but not to boiling point, and gives off the vapour into the dry air. The humidifier should be placed a few feet (a metre or so) away from the plants because the rising vapour is warm, but not warm enough to affect the overall temperature of the room. An atomization humidifier, which throws out a fine mist of cold water, is excellent for a greenhouse, but not for a living room; the motor is noisy and the spray will spread limy deposits over the furniture.

Plants also need water to keep clean. In nature this is done by rain, but houseplants rely on you. Use a wet sponge to wipe the dust off both sides of large shiny leaves; a dirty top surface cuts down the light which the leaf needs for photosynthesis and a dirty under-surface clogs the stomata. Use only water, not beer, vinegar, oil or a proprietary leaf cleaner. Spray leaves which are too small or too fragile to handle. Hairy or velvety leaves should not be washed; instead brush them gently with a very soft brush.

Seasonal Care • The Dormant Period

As well as a daily rest, plants need a prolonged dormant period during the year. Shorter or colder days, the onset of heat, or a period of drought are among the natural phenomena in the wild which will cause a plant to become dormant.

During the dormancy period growth slows down. Then, when the conditions are favourable again, there is a great surge of growth. Outdoors the signs of this cycle may be obvious. Deciduous trees drop their leaves in autumn, remain dormant during the winter, and burgeon in the spring as the sap starts rising freely again. Although the growth of evergreen trees also slows down, the change is less dramatic.

Most houseplants are evergreen and it is, therefore, easy to miss the signs that they need rest. Indeed, if they are insulated from the seasons in a room that is always cozy and bright they will have no opportunity to become dormant and will continue to grow. No plant has the stamina to keep that up year after year. If you want to keep your beloved plants in radiant health you must recognize when they should rest, provide the conditions in which they can do so, and refrain from forcing them back into growth before they are ready for it.

The levels of warmth, light and moisture are just as important and interdependent when a plant is dormant as when it is growing. The winter environments which should be provided for the plants included in this book are described in the

Some plants require good light even during their dormant period. These include the cereus, opuntia, mammillaria, blechnum, dieffenbachia, hypoestes, enonymus, agave, crassula, iresine, coleus, peperomias, euphorbia and faucaria illustrated below.

individual entries, so it is a simple matter to discover each plant's requirements.

A few hardy houseplants can tolerate frost for a short period, but it is unwise to put them to the test for too long. In any part of the world where frost is possible, it would be thoughtless to leave even the hardiest plant on the window sill of an unheated room. If by accident this should happen and the leaves are touched by frost do not move the plant into a warm room; the leaf cells are liable to burst if they thaw out rapidly. Instead, spray the leaves with cold, not tepid, water, leave the plant in a cool room and hope for the best.

In a house which is only partially heated or is kept cool all winter, plants can be rearranged around the house, avoiding rooms which are bitterly cold, so that the required minimum temperatures are met as nearly as possible. A plant adjusts more easily to a lower temperature which is steady than to one which changes violently during the day. Do not, therefore, put a plant near an open fire or an electric heater.

In a well-heated house the problem is finding a place cool enough for the plants to be lulled into dormancy. The best that can usually be done is to move plants into rooms with temperatures closest to those they need. If all the rooms in the house, with no regard to expense or energy-saving campaigns, are kept at subtropical temperatures the plants will go on growing, but because it is winter there may not be enough light to ensure adequate photosynthesis to meet the plants' nutritional needs. As a result, the plants will grow because of the warmth, but the growth will be weak and stunted. The most obvious symptoms are lanky stems and small leaves.

If your home is so warm that you have

no option but to keep your plants growing, you must provide adequate light. It is easier, however, to provide adequate and suitable light for humans than for plants. Levels of light are measured in candlefoot or lux, the scientific metric unit. There is no point in going into the intricacies of these measurements, but it is helpful to use them to compare summer and winter, or outdoor and indoor, levels of light with the estimated needs of a plant.

At noon on a cloudless day in midsummer the intensity of light outdoors might be 100,000 lux, but only 10,000 lux on a window sill indoors and down to 2,000 lux three feet away from the window. In winter the intensity drops indoors to only a few hundred lux—below the requirements of even such shade-loving

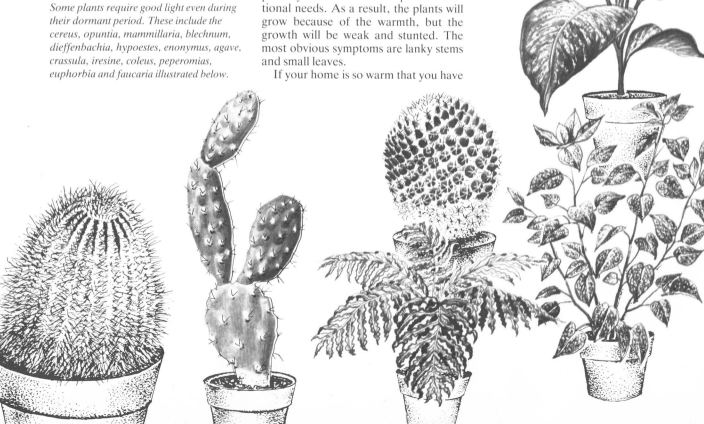

plants as fatsias and ivy. Many plants need about 1,000 lux for healthy growth, and twice that if they are in flower. Others, including some of the bromeliads, cacti, crotons and peperomias, need more than 2,000 lux and twice as much when they are in flower.

There are some enthusiastic indoor gardeners who spend a lot of money on equipment to keep all their plants bathed in light, but most of us will be content to satisfy at most a few precious plants. In that case, the most practical light fixture consists of two four-foot (1.20 m), 40-watt, fluorescent tubes, one warm white and one cool white, with a reflector above them. This should be hung eighteen to thirty inches (45 to 76 cm) above the top of the plants. Higher than that the light ceases to be of much use; lower, and the

heat may be more than the plant can stand. Trial and error will establish the best height if you have no lux meter.

To maintain healthy growth, all plants, except short-day plants (which flower only after a period when nights are longer than days), need at least twelve hours of light each day. It does not matter, however, when they get their quota. To avoid having to suffer bright fluorescent light at about eye level, you can install a time switch so that the light is on when you are out of the house or in bed.

Even during the dormancy period some plants need brighter light than others, just as some need more warmth. In winter, in more northerly or more southerly latitudes not only will there be fewer hours of daylight but the light will also be weaker. A room that is light in summer may be dark in winter, especially for a plant, hence the frequent advice in the You and Your Plants section that a plant should be put in a good light in winter. This may involve nothing more complicated than moving the plant near the window, although that position would be too bright for it in summer.

A plant not only needs less warmth and light when it is dormant, it also needs less water. The three elements are inextricably connected. If the plant is kept warmer than it should be in winter it will be encouraged to grow. It will then need more light and water in order to produce the food it needs to grow. On the other hand, if it is kept a little below the temperature at which it stops growth, it needs less light and less water. Moreover, if the compost is kept quite dry the plant will tolerate lower temperatures than it would in wet compost.

There is more risk of overwatering a plant in winter than in summer. When the plant is dormant not only is less water

taken up by the roots and less given off through the leaves, but there is less evaporation through the surface of the compost and through the sides of a clay pot. The plant is unlikely, therefore, to need frequent watering. Avoid getting into a routine of watering a plant on the same day every week just because that way it is easier to remember to do it or because you happen to have the time. Certainly your plants need regular attention, but not regular watering. Plants should be watered only when they need watering.

A plant given enough heat and light to go on growing through the winter months will be living in a continuous summer, or the equivalent of a tropical climate, with one important difference; the air in a heated room in winter is drier than it is in the natural warmth of summer. In summer, relative humidity of 50 to 60 per cent is a feasible and desirable target. But relative humidity in a heated room in winter may fall as low as 10 per cent, making the room as dry as the Sahara Desert, too dry for humans or plants. Wet pebbles and moist peat cannot bridge such a humidity gap and the only certain solution is a humidifier. Both the plants and you will be all the better for it.

Plants do not look their best when they are dormant, any more than people do when they are asleep. But just as we may look better in the morning for the rest so will the plants in spring. A plant itself is the best judge of how long its dormancy should last and unless you have any reason (such as wanting to bring it into flower by a particular date) do not impatiently hurry it along. Of its own volition it will start showing faint signs of growth. Then, and only then, is the time to start giving it more water and bring it back into the warmth.

Seasonal Care • Special Cases

So far we have been considering the varying seasonal needs of the general run of houseplants, but some plants need somewhat different care. Among these are the succulents, whose name indicates that they are able to store water, a characteristic they developed to avoid death during dry periods. Even when they are taken into our care they continue to react at certain times of the year as though they were threatened by drought. It is as well to humour them, particularly cacti.

Cacti

In summer, the desert cacti do best on a window sill that gets full sun. Turn the plants around from time to time so that they grow evenly. The epiphytes are accustomed to more shade, so put these on an east-facing window sill which gets sun only early in the day.

The best way to water cacti, not unlike other plants, is to immerse the pots in water and then let the compost drain. A cactus must never be left standing in a saucer of water. Terrestrial cacti should dry out more between waterings than most houseplants, but epiphytic cacti should not be allowed to dry out quite so much. In late summer, begin to reduce the frequency of watering in readiness for the dormant period, which cacti must have in order to set their flower buds. If the plants overwinter in an unheated room (minimum temperatures are given under individual plant entries) they may not need watering at all from autumn until early spring. If they are kept in warmer conditions they may need watering once a month; epiphytes in any case are likely to need a monthly watering. When watering is restarted in late winter or early spring, begin by giving only a little, not a soaking, increasing it gradually over three weeks or so as the plant comes into growth again.

Other Succulents

In summer the other succulents need very frequent watering, perhaps daily in hot weather. Any shrivelling of the leaves is a sure sign that water is needed. When growth is obviously slowing down reduce the frequency of watering, but during the dormant period virtually all succulents, other than cacti, need some water. How frequently you water them will depend on the warmth of their surroundings, but in a cool room watering may be necessary only once a month. When there are signs of new growth begin watering again, but with restraint until the plant is in full growth.

Bromeliads

Most of the bromeliads which are cultivated as houseplants are epiphytic; in their natural state they grow on the branches of trees in American and Caribbean tropical rain forests. Two of the most popular bromeliads, however—*Billbergia nutans* and *Ananas comosus*—are terrestrial and need much the same treatment as foliage houseplants.

The typical feature of most epiphytic bromeliads is a rosette of leaves which collects and holds water to supply the plant's needs, for the main function of their roots is to anchor them to the tree. In pots, bromeliads develop stronger root systems which will also absorb water from the compost. Nevertheless, throughout the summer months the rosette must be kept filled with water, preferably soft.

In the wild, epiphytic bromeliads also get much of their nourishment from the decomposing bodies of insects drowned in the water in the rosette. Indoors, only limited feeding is needed during the summer, when a very dilute solution of fertilizer may be poured into the rosette no more frequently than once a month. In winter no feeding is necessary for bromeliads, but plenty of light, air and warmth are essential. The temperature should not fall below 55°F (13°C) and watering should be very restricted. Empty the water from the rosette to avoid the risk of rotting, and water the compost sparingly from the top if it is drying out in a warm room.

After flowering, the rosette dies slowly, ungracefully and, eventually, malodorously, but it leaves new young plants as offspring. Do not be in a hurry to remove the dying parent. Wait until these offsets are well established because at the start they are largely dependent on the parent for food and water.

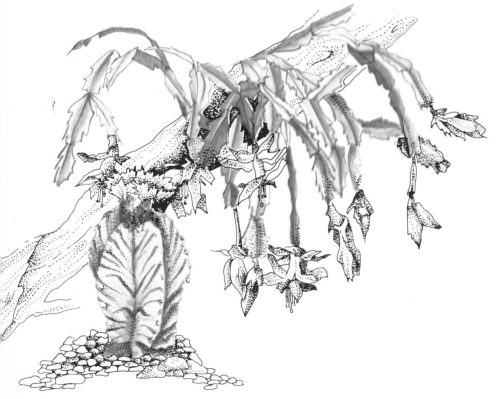

Orchids

There are about fifty thousand different orchids in cultivation, but only a few are grown as indoor plants. The eight chosen as fairly easy to grow on pages 142 and 143 may be divided into three groups. Those in the first group, naturally sun-loving, drought-resistant, xerophytic orchids—cattleyas, cymbidium, dendrobium, odontoglossum and oncidium—need warmth (above 60°F, 16°C) and light (close to a south-facing or southwest-facing window). The shade-loving orchid—paphiopedilum—would be satisfied with rather less warmth and a north-, northwest- or northeast-facing window. Those in the third group—vanda and miltonia—need light (a south-facing window), warmth (65°F, 18°C, or more when growing) and a humid atmosphere; they flourish in a well-ventilated terrarium, or so-called Wardian case, but can succeed outside. They need fresh air, but must never be in a draught.

In summer, an orchid is best watered by putting the pot in water—not totally immersing it, but submerging it to about two-thirds of its depth—and letting the water rise to the surface of the compost by capillary action; if only the surface of the compost is kept wet the roots are reluctant to travel down to the bottom of the pot. The orchids will need frequent watering when the new roots are growing; always water them only when the compost has dried out considerably since the last watering, but is not bone dry.

During the dormant period, avoid frequent watering or the old roots may rot and will not be replaced by new ones.

Hydroponically Grown Plants

Plants grown hydroponically—in water and without soil—usually need less constant attention than plants grown in compost, but how much less depends on the method used. In one method the plant is grown in an inert aggregate—pebbles, gravel or some manufactured granules—instead of the usual compost. This growing medium has to be watered with a nutrient solution, frequently in summer and less so in winter, and flushed with clean water once a week. This is a tedious method.

The least laborious method utilizes a hydropot, which consists of an inner pot

that holds the plants in an inert aggregate and an outer pot containing the nutrient solution. The plant's roots grow through the drainage hole of the inner pot into the solution below. A meter shows the level of the solution and indicates the maximum and minimum levels. At the maximum level the plant pot will be immersed to one-third of its depth in the solution. At the minimum level, the solution will be a little below the bottom of the pot and, only at that point, more must be added through the tube at the top of the container. This will involve watering at intervals of two to four weeks.

The level must be allowed to fall to the minimum before more solution is added, to allow air to reach the roots. Occasionally the growing medium has to be flushed out to prevent a build-up of mineral salts. Even this chore can be avoided if the plant is fed twice a year with ion exchange fertilizers. These are synthetic resins which slowly release the nutrients as they are used by the plant. When the meter has fallen to the minimum level, only water has to be added to raise it to the maximum. This is the least taxing and the most foolproof method of looking after houseplants, as well as the most expensive, yet devised.

Short-day and Long-day Plants

A period of dormancy is necessary for many plants to induce them to flower. Cacti, for example, require a dry, cool period if they are to form flower buds. With the so-called short-day plants the determining factor for the formation of flower buds is the amount of light they receive. They will flower only after a period when their nights have been longer than their days, roughly fourteen hours of darkness to ten hours of daylight. The opposite is true of the long-day plants; they form their buds only when the days are longer than the nights. Because of this plants can be fooled into flowering out of their normal season; the short-day plants by being shut up in darkness while it is still light outdoors, and the long-day plants by being put under artificial light after darkness has fallen.

Absent Care

For some people, worrying about their plants is almost a way of life. They are haunted by the prospect of every conceivable disaster—from overwatering to mealy bugs. Their fears are dire enough even when they are surrounded by blatantly healthy plants, but worry and guilt reach a peak when plants and overfond owners have to be parted. Pre-vacation panic sets in. This kind of concern is enough to deter some people from starting to keep houseplants—just as other people would not clutter their lives with pets, children, lovers, husbands or wives.

There are people who accept the responsibility of a garden and take it so seriously that they may refuse to go away in spring, summer and autumn because of the demands of their outdoor plants. But indoor gardening enthusiasts are not free of their plants even in winter so a vacation then is out of the question. Some people try to solve the problem by taking their plants with them—a sign of affection which may not altogether be appreciated by the plants on the move.

Going away and leaving plants does create problems, but they can be solved. One approach is to dodge much of the problem by confining your indoor gardening to growing plants in bottles or terrariums, also known as Wardian cases. This

would allow you to go on a world cruise without a care—except the cost of the cruise. In a terrarium, as the moisture evaporates through the plants' leaves it condenses on the inside of the container, seeps back into the compost, and is thus continually recycled. This form of cultivation is suitable only for small plants

which enjoy a humid atmosphere, and eventually you would have to return home to remove any plants which had grown too large. Feeding is not a problem. The aim is to keep the plants small for as long as possible.

Another similar approach is to cultivate your houseplants hydroponically. You can then grow a normal range of plants and you do not have to imprison them. Before leaving on vacation you need only make sure that the nutrient solution in which the plants are growing is topped up to the correct level and strength and the plants moved to a cool place out of direct sunlight. A plant grown hydroponically uses up as much water through evaporation as a plant grown in soil or compost. There is no recycling as with a terrarium. On the other hand, there is a larger reserve of water available to the plant than there is in a pot. The length of time you can stay away without worrying depends on how much water the container holds and how much the temperature—and the plant's transpiration rate—rises.

If you intend going away for several weeks and there is a danger of the water supply becoming exhausted, a friend can be asked to top up the container. This is less of a responsibility than having to water plants in the ordinary way since modern hydroponic containers have indicators showing how much water to add.

Neither terrariums nor hydroponically grown plants appeal to most indoor gardeners, but, fortunately, there are several ways to ensure that plants are watered while their owners are away. One way is to buy some relatively inexpensive equipment that can take over the job; the other is to enlist the help of a friend.

There are two basic and effective automatic watering systems. One, which is known as trickle irrigation, drips water onto the surface of the compost. The other supplies water from below by capillary action. Although permanent trickle irrigation is widely used both indoors and in greenhouses, there is a very important difference between the two systems, which makes the capillary system far better for occasionally unattended plants.

A typical greenhouse trickle system consists of lengths of narrow tubing leading from a water supply to each pot. By adjusting the nozzle at the end of each tube it is possible to regulate the amount of water dripping through. While this system can be adapted to indoor use it is tricky, for you have to decide before you go away how much water the plants will

need. If the weather turns hot and sunny in your absence the rate of drip may not provide enough water; if it turns dull and cold the drip may be more than the plants need and the compost will stay constantly and dangerously sodden.

With a capillary system, the plants themselves regulate the water they need. As water evaporates through the leaves, the roots draw up moisture from the compost to replace it. As the compost dries out, water will be drawn up from below by capillary action—if water is available there. Your responsibility is to ensure that it is. There are many ways in which this can be done and one way in which it must not—that is to leave the pots actually standing in water; there are very few houseplants which like their feet wet.

There are a number of capillary self-watering devices on the market, but the performance of many of them is poor or their cost excessive. Rather than waste money on these you can settle for a do-it-yourself capillary system which can be made to work satisfactorily. If you go away fairly frequently, however, a less makeshift approach could save a lot of trouble.

The vital factor in choosing a watering device is to make sure that it can keep up a supply of water for as long as you will be away. Few individual self-watering pots meet this requirement. A self-watering pot has one pot in which the

plant grows. This is suspended in a larger pot which has an inch or two (1.25 or 5 cm) of water at the bottom. A capillary wick dangles from inside the plant pot into the water and draws moisture up into the compost as the plant needs it. (Such a wick is used in many systems and works well.) The fault of the individual self-watering pot is that the water is likely to be used up in a few days. Depending on the plant's size, how vigorous its growth, and how warm the weather, it will need between ten and forty fluid ounces of water a week—and that is only for one plant.

A far better arrangement is to collect all your plants together in a shady bathroom or kitchen and pack them fairly closely together on a tray lined with sand or commercially available capillary matting. Using a trickle irrigation system, water can then be fed to the tray through a piece of tubing, which has an adjustable nozzle at the other end attached to a large plastic tank, ideally one which is fitted with a ball valve and connected to a tap for a never-ending supply of water. The water supply can be adjusted so that only a trickle comes through the nozzle and, of course, you must try to determine how much water the plants will need in your absence. To ensure that enough water is drawn up by each plant from the sand or matting, stick a piece of capillary wick into the compost through the drainage hole of each pot and press the other end firmly against the wet sand or matting.

Large plants often need individual treatment. One simple device is a commercially available earthenware cone attached to small-bore rubber tubing. The cone, first primed with water, is pushed into the surface of the compost and the other end of the tube is put into a bucket of water (which must be at a lower level than the pot). As water slowly seeps through the cone into the compost more water is sucked up from the bucket. To provide enough moisture for a large plant in a large pot, at least two cones, each leading to the bucket, will be needed. There is certainly no danger of overwatering because the plant will only take as much water as it needs.

Many people manage to keep their plants watered while they are away, however, by putting capillary action to work in simpler ways.

19

Absent Care

Other do-it-yourself methods depend on capillary action and, since they need running water, are best set up in a bathroom or kitchen, The kitchen sink or the area around it may be large enough if you have only a few plants, but if there are many plants use the bathtub. It will hold quite a number of plants since they can be put in close together, keeping each other humid.

The simplest and most effective method is to cover the bottom of the bathtub or sink with synthetic capillary matting; it is sold in various sizes and may be used again and again. The mat must extend right to the foot of the tub, so that dripping water will fall on it. Cut a hole in the mat above the outlet to allow excess water to drain away freely. Soak the mat thoroughly; it is so absorbent that it will hold about thirty ounces of water to one square yard (1 sq m) and will be kept moist by letting cold water drip slowly on it.

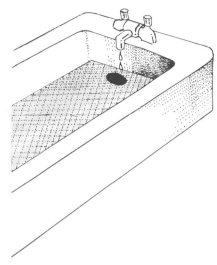

To ensure, when the pots are in place on the mat, that water does seep upwards into the compost, push a piece of capillary wick through the drainage hole of each pot up into the compost; the other end will press against the wet mat.

The Plastic Bag Method

Plastic bags, the twentieth century's answer to almost everything, can take over plant watering when you are away. The principle is that of the bottle garden or terrarium—recycling back into the compost the water which evaporates through the leaves.

The method is simple, but can be tedious to organize if you have a lot of plants. First, you must water the plant well. Then into the compost push four bamboo stakes, taller than the plant, at equal intervals around the rim of the pot and

angled outwards so that the plastic bag which is to envelop the plant will not touch the leaves. Carefully lower the plant, pot and all, into the plastic bag; it must not have holes in it and must be large enough to completely enclose the

plant. Tightly seal the open end of the bag with adhesive tape.

Is is essential that the framework of stakes holds the bag clear of the leaves. If the plastic touches the leaves they will become mouldy. It is equally important that the plant be entirely free from pests when it goes into the bag, because in that humid greenhouse atmosphere they would multiply prodigiously. Take care, too, that the plant is not left where the sun will shine on it at any time, for the heat inside the bag would be overpowering.

The plastic bag method of absent care is impractical for plants which are tall or of considerable girth. It is sometimes recommended in such a case that only the pot should be enclosed in a plastic bag, but this is of only minimal use since the major loss of water is through the leaves.

Some plants take up enough moisture without a wick, but it is a sensible precaution to fit all the pots with wicks.

Have a trial run for a day to satisfy yourself that the water will not perversely stop dripping as soon as you close the front door behind you. But remember, all you need is a drip, not a torrent.

A variation on this theme is to put the pots in the bathtub and pack sodden newspaper around them. If you are afraid that the water will not go on dripping there is another frequently recommended method you can try if you happen to have a few dozen bricks handy. Put a layer of newspaper on the bottom of the bathtub, to avoid scratches, and build a platform of spaced-out bricks, two or three bricks high. Spread a capillary mat over the construction, with the ends weighted down on to the bottom of the tub. Plug and seal the outlet in any ingenious way you can think of to prevent any water from draining away. Fill the tub almost to the top of the bricks and arrange the plants on the capillary mat. Of course, the water must be turned off completely or you may return to a flood.

A far simpler method, which is best for cool weather, is to put a group of plants in a large container and surround them with moist peat. They should survive for a couple of weeks if the peat is left considerably wetter than usual, but much will depend on the weather staying cool.

When the plants have to be left in the winter, lack of warmth may present a greater threat than lack of water. All you can do is to move the plants into the warmest room in the house. This is often the kitchen. The most delicate plants can be put on top of the refrigerator or the freezer so that they get the benefit of the warmth from the mechanism of the appliance.

The care of plants may also be carried out by proxy. For some people this is the first choice, but for others it is the last resort. This is understandable, because human beings can be either totally dependable or utterly unreliable.

If you have a conveniently situated friend who is devoted to plants as well as to you—and also knows something about them—you are indeed lucky, for a well-meaning, obliging friend with no understanding of plants can create devastation in a remarkably short time. Either the plants may be left to wilt in hot weather or be drowned; the results of overwatering may not be immediately apparent, but are a legacy you inherit on your return. On the other hand, a friend who is far better at looking after plants than you are may leave them in better health—and you with a feeling of great inferiority.

Professional plant-sitters are available, but it's advisable to employ one only on the recommendation of a friend, or after checking with other clients, for there are charlatans around. Even when you are satisfied with the professional's credentials the plants may prove not to be, for plants can be inexplicably uncooperative with some people, however expert they are. Professionals are also expensive and the money might be better spent investing in a fairly sophisticated self-watering system. Plants seem to accept a change of routine to a capillary system fairly readily, perhaps because they would rather be in control of their water supply than to have a stranger fidgeting over them.

Repotting

The leaves, stems and flowers of our houseplants may become as familiar to us as the backs of our hands, but the roots are a hidden mystery. What is really going on down there?

Roots are as diverse in structure as the parts of the plants we can see, but they all have the same fundamental role. They act as anchors for the plant whether it is terrestrial (growing in the ground) or epiphytic (growing on another plant, but not parasitically living off it). A plant also depends on its roots to supply the raw materials it needs to make its food—phosphorus, potassium, calcium and other mineral salts—as well as water to dissolve the salts and to provide hydrogen. In nature the epiphytes are less dependent on their roots for nutrients than the terrestrial plants are, but when an epiphyte is planted in a pot its roots adapt to take in more nutrients from the compost.

The compost in the pot gives the roots something on which to anchor and provides a reservoir for nutrients and water. When a plant is first potted it has the benefit of fresh, sweet-smelling compost which contains a reserve of nutrients. As these become exhausted we replace them by applications of fertilizer, usually in liquid form. There is always a risk of giving too much fertilizer and if this happens a surfeit builds up and sours the compost. This excess may reveal itself as a white deposit on the outside of a clay pot; an impervious plastic pot gives no such warning. The compost may also deteriorate by the very action of watering, let alone overwatering. Although the compost starts off being free-draining and well-areated, constant watering during the year inevitably compacts the compost, making it capable of holding far less air. If, in addition, the compost is watered too frequently it will become sodden and sour.

These are among the reasons why regular replanting—once a year or every other year—is generally advocated. A plant which grows outdoors is able to spread its roots into fresh soil, but in a pot the roots cannot go far and we have to supply the new soil. Putting a plant in fresh compost in a new pot is a kind of spring cleaning which gives the plant a fillip for the coming year.

When the intention is only to provide a fresh supply of compost, a plant is put into a pot of the same size and the operation is simply called repotting. When, on the other hand, the plant needs to be put into a larger pot because the old pot is chock full of roots, or because the old pot is too small to be in balance with the plant's size, the operation is known as potting on.

Roots grow to keep pace with the growing plant's increasing demand for nutrients and water. As the roots proliferate the compost is displaced and pushed up to or over the rim of the pot. Not enough compost is left around the roots to hold much moisture, the compost dries out rapidly, and the root hairs are left without adequate supplies of nutrients.

Signs that the roots are getting too big for the pot are the unusually rapid drying out of the compost and, without a doubt, the appearance of roots through the drainage hole of the pot. A plant may

need potting on, however, without showing these symptoms. The simplest way to find out what is happening to the roots is to sneak a look at them in the spring. Many houseplant owners seem afraid to do this, but a healthy plant will take such an inspection in its stride.

Before taking a plant out of its pot, water it well and leave it for two or three days. Then take the pot in one hand and press the fingers of the other hand against the surface of the compost, while supporting the stem of the plant between two fingers. Tap the rim of the pot against the edge of a table. The compost and

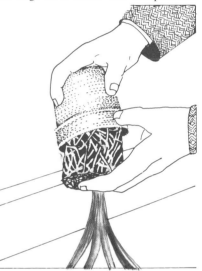

roots should come away cleanly. If they are obstinate, run a knife around the inside of the pot to ease them away. If the roots obviously still have plenty of room in the pot and the compost is sweet and well-aerated put the pot back over the compost, turn the plant the right way up and gently press the compost into place again. Look again next spring.

When, on inspection, you decide that the pot is big enough for the roots, but that it would be a good idea to freshen up the compost, do not hesitate to repot the plant. If the same pot is to be used again wash it thoroughly, inside and out. It is better, however, to have another clean pot of the same size all ready; the quicker the changeover the less the plant will suffer. (If you are using a new clay pot soak it in cold water for several hours beforehand.) Gently tease out some of the old compost from the roots. Gentleness is essential because, even if the main

roots look tough, the fine root hairs that absorb the nutrients and water are easily damaged.

The usual advice is to put crocks—small, curved pieces of a broken clay pot—over the drainage hole of a pot, but you may regret doing this if later you try to push the capillary wick through the hole. (See Absent Care watering, page 21.) Small amounts of loam-based compost may fall through an uncrocked drainage hole, but coarse, peat-based compost is less likely to do so.

When repotting try to use the same kind of potting soil as that in which the plant is already growing. Generally that means choosing either a loam-based compost or a peat-based compost. Proprietary, ready-mixed composts are sold at garden centres and plant shops. A typical loam-based compost consists of seven parts, measured by bulk, of sterilized loam, three parts of granulated peat, and one part of sharp (coarse) river sand. To these are added fertilizers to provide nitrogen, phosphate and potassium.

Supplies of good loam are becoming scarcer, however, and peat-based composts are increasingly used. They are made of granulated peat and such soil lighteners as coarse sand, vermiculite or perlite. These materials are without nutritional value, and that has to be provided by adding fertilizers, including trace elements, which the loam would have contributed.

All plants need a free-draining compost. How well compost drains depends mainly on how much soil lightener it contains. The more there is the less water the compost is able to retain after watering. Some plants do better with special mixes, possibly incorporating leaf mould, but in general the well-established proprietary brands are perfectly acceptable as they are, or with additional soil lightener. Recommendations are given in the entries for individual plants.

Because proprietary potting mixtures have been prepared to satisfy the needs of houseplants, the indoor gardener is at an advantage over the outdoor gardener who has to cope with soil which is variable, particularly in its pH value. The pH factor is the scale which defines the acidity or alkalinity of a soil. Above pH 7 it becomes increasingly alkaline. Most houseplants are happy in composts with a pH factor between 5.5 and 6.5, and this is what most prepared composts, whether peat-based or loam-based, will provide. A loam-based compost may be a little more alkaline than a peat-based compost, depending on where the loam has come from. It is therefore recommended for certain plants and not advised for others. Azaleas, cyclamen, camellias, heathers, many ferns and a large number of plants which come from tropical rain forests, for example, like an acid soil and should be potted in a peat-based compost. Orchids, which demand a particularly acid soil, need special composts. So, as far as the choice of composts is concerned the pH factor is not a problem. Constant watering with hard (limey) water will, however, make an acid soil alkaline. It is therefore important when repotting to replace as much of the old compost as possible with fresh compost.

When you are repotting, the compost must be moist, but not soaking wet. Spread a layer of it at the bottom of the pot, as much as is needed when the plant is put on it to put the soil mark on the stem to within half an inch (1.25 cm) of the rim of the pot. Allow more space, between one and two inches (2.5 and 5 cm), for large pots. This space is left to allow

adequate room for water when supplied from above and to allow for the level of the compost rising as the roots take up more room. When you have this height

correct fill the pot with compost, firming it down with your fingers. Go easy around the stem itself. Be sure that the soil mark on the stem is not exposed above the level of the compost.

Water the plant, filling the pot to the rim. Let it drain and put it in a shady and not very warm place for a few days. Daily spraying of the leaves will help the plant to recover more quickly from the shock of repotting. If a large proportion of the compost has been replaced in repotting, fertilizers should not be necessary for several months, but feeding can begin sooner if the plant's growth is vigorous.

Potting On

A time comes when a plant has to be moved to a larger pot because the vigorously growing roots need more room or the plant has become top heavy, or for both reasons. This operation is known as potting on.

A plant will usually have to be potted on several times during its life, each time moving into a pot that is only slightly larger. The first few times the move is into a pot one inch (2.5 cm) greater in diameter than the one before. When you get to a pot which is ten inches (25 cm) in diameter you can go up by two inches (5 cm). Potting on cannot, obviously, go on forever, and at some point you will have to start holding the plant in check instead.

The actual operation of potting on can be done in the way in which repotting has already been described. The pot into which the plant is to go should be thoroughly cleaned. (A new clay pot should be soaked in cold water for several hours beforehand.) The larger pot will need additional compost and this must be moistened in advance, but not made sodden. If at all possible the new compost should be of the same type as that in which the plant has been growing.

When potting on it is particularly important that the plant be at the same depth in the new pot as it was before and that the new compost be firmly pressed down the sides of the pot.

There is another way of potting on which does not disturb the roots as much, Take the plant out of its pot and put it carefully on one side without removing any of the old compost. In the bottom of the new pot put a layer of compost; an inch (2.5 cm) will probably be enough.

Centre the old pot on it and pack compost firmly all around it. Then remove the smaller pot and you have a hole custom

made to take the root ball of the plant. Press the new compost down firmly; a little more may have to be added. After potting on, water the plant, put it in a shady place for a few days, and spray it occasionally. Before long the roots will begin to spread into the new compost, but until they are well-established there they will be taking up little moisture from it. This is the reason potting on is done in small steps, not in one leap. While young plants will rapidly grow into new compost in a pot which is only one inch (2.5 cm) larger, they will take their time filling a pot three or four inches (7.5 or 10 cm) larger. Without roots in it the compost stays sodden and becomes unaerated and sour—a death trap for the root hairs when they eventually try to penetrate it. Tedious as regular potting on may be, do not try to skip a few stages. Shortcuts lead to disaster.

When a plant is too large to be taken out of its pot all that you can do is to remove the top layer of compost and replace it with new compost. Although the roots will not suddenly start growing upwards into the new compost, the nutrients it contains will be washed down to them by watering. Replacing heavily compacted compost with compost of a more open texture also helps with aeration.

When, for aesthetic reasons, you want to change from a clay pot to a plastic pot or the other way around, the time to do it is when repotting or potting on. It makes no difference to a plant's health which kind of pot it grows in. In a clay pot, however, water escapes through both the bottom of the pot and its porous sides; the roots follow the water in both direc-

tions. In a plastic pot the water cannot seep out through the sides so the direction of the water and the roots is downwards.

After changing a plant to a pot of different material, new roots will soon develop to follow the moisture. But the change may set the plant back a little until it becomes accustomed to its new way of life.

The result of potting on is that the plant is encouraged to grow, having been given more space in which additional roots can develop and new compost to nourish them. But a point will come when you do not want to encourage a sizeable plant to grow any more, even if there is a larger pot to put it in. One course of action is root pruning, which encourages the renewal of root hairs—vital for maintaining the health of the plant—but discourages top growth by not allowing room for extra roots to provide the necessary additional nutrients.

Root Pruning

To prune the roots, remove the plant from the pot as you would when repotting. Using an extremely sharp knife,

shave away the roots and compost evenly all around the root ball, removing about one inch (2.5 cm) if the plant has been in a pot which is seven inches (18 cm) in diameter or larger. Wash the pot thoroughly and put the plant back into it, packing the space around it with fresh compost. Water well and keep the plant out of bright light for a week or two.

A plant inevitably suffers a setback after the roots are pruned and the operation should be performed only in spring when the roots are actively growing and will recover most quickly. It is probably wise not to prune the roots of a plant more than two or three times in its lifetime.

Soilless Culture

Converting a compost-grown plant to soilless culture involves more than changing it from a clay pot to a plastic pot, for the plant has to develop a different root system, one which is better able to absorb nutrients and oxygen from the water. The most obvious difference is that the root hairs grow much longer. If you are making such a change, go all the way and buy a container with an inner pot and a water-level meter.

Take the plant out of the old pot and gently remove as much of the compost as

you can by hand without damaging the roots. Wash away the rest in a bowl of tepid water. Using synthetic granules, repot the plant in the inner pot. Place the pot in the outer container and fill it with tepid water to the maximum level marked on the meter, bringing the water about

one-third of the way up the plant pot. Change the water at least twice a week to be sure that the plant has adequate oxygen. After a few weeks long root hairs should develop. Replace the water in the outer

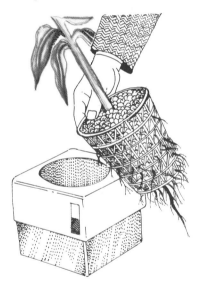

container with an appropriate nutrient solution or with water and ion exchange fertilizers.

Unlike a compost-grown plant, a hydroponic plant does not need repotting to be provided with a new source of food. Occasionally it may need potting on, changing it to a pot which is only slightly larger. The change is less likely to be forced on you by growth of the roots—this is usually less vigorous than that of plants in compost—but because the plant begins to look, or actually is, absurdly top heavy. You then replant in granules—the old ones washed well and added to the new—in a larger pot which will go into a larger container.

Pruning and Training

There are three Ps which trouble many houseplant owners—potting, pruning and propagation. Pruning, however, seems to cause the most concern. This is understandable since it would seem that when you prune what is, after all, an investment, you are making it smaller. Actually, when you prune a plant, even though this involves cutting it back, the effect is to make it grow.

When roots are pruned, a healthy plant responds by vigorously growing new root hairs, the means by which it obtains nutrients from the soil. The plant responds to any cutting back above ground by putting out extra shoots. This response is exactly what you want in a houseplant, for it will make it bushy and lush with foliage instead of lankily tall.

Outdoors, crude pruning is carried out by winds which break stems and by grazing animals which eat them, but this is fortuitous. In our homes we deliberately prune plants to shape them to our taste, handsomely we hope. There are, of course, some plants—including cacti, ferns, palms and marantas—which cannot be pruned because of the nature of their growth.

For those plants which are prunable there are three degrees of pruning—stopping (or pinching out), which is the gentle way, soft wood pruning, and hard wood pruning.

Pinching Out

Stopping involves pinching out the growing tip of a stem. This causes the pair of dormant buds below to break into growth and you then have two shoots growing

outwards instead of one growing upwards. After these shoots have grown a bit their growing points can be pinched out so that for each one another two

essential to begin this kind of pruning before the plant has become tall. To do it effectively is an art, for it involves envisaging what will happen to the plant afterwards. You may make a few mistakes before you become thoroughly skilled, but the plant may well co-operate with you in covering them up.

Pruning

With most prunable plants a pinch in time will save more drastic action later. If you let that time pass, soft wood pruning will be required. This involves not just

removing a growing point, but cutting away some new wood below it. After you have done this, shoots will appear from normally dormant leaf axil buds; these lie in the upper angle formed where the leaf stalk is joined to the stem. Before

shoots will appear. So you can go on during the growing season, the plant becoming increasingly bushy, but more manageable and more attractive than it would have been if it had been left to grow upwards in its own sweet way. It is

letting these new shoots, too, get out of hand, pinch out the growing tips and then keep on with the pinching as required. The new wood which has been cut away can usually be used as cuttings to produce new plants.

The third degree of pruning is hard wood pruning which involves cutting

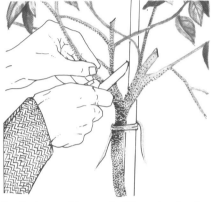

back into old wood. The aim is the same—to stir dormant buds on the bare stems into growth. Unlike axil buds, which are often visible, these stem buds are hidden under the bark of the stem and take a while to break through. The plant suffers a serious setback when pruned in this way, looks pathetic until it has grown new leaves, and seldom achieves the stateliness it would have had with regular pinching.

Before pruning a flowering plant study it carefully when it is in flower to see whether the flowers are on stems which have grown that year or on stems which grew the year before; the difference in the colour of the stems will tell you—new wood is green. The flowers of fuchsias, for example, grow on new wood. Cutting this back after flowering has finished will encourage new vigorous growth of flowering shoots the following year. If a plant flowers on the previous year's wood, that can be cut back. But do not cut back the new wood or you will be throwing away next year's flowers.

In general, the time for radical pruning is in early spring when growth is starting. Do not repot a plant which has been or is to be radically pruned; one shock is quite enough. Stopping should be done throughout the growing period, particularly when growth is most vigorous. The only equipment you need is a good set of fingernails. For soft wood pruning a small, very sharp kitchen knife will do. Only for hard wood pruning of the tough stems will you need pruning shears. These, too, must be sharp; a mangled wound lays a plant wide open to disease.

Air Layering

Hard wood pruning is not successful with some popular plants which in growing tall have, for whatever reason, lost their lower leaves. Air layering, also called Chinese layering, is the way to make such plants as *Ficus elastica*, dracaena and dieffenbachia presentable again.

A few inches (about 5 cm) below the lowest leaf make a clean, upward slanting cut not less than one-third and not more

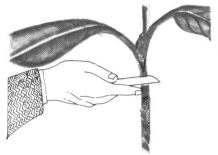

than halfway into the stem. Dust a little hormone rooting powder into the cut. Insert a matchstick or a strand of sphagnum moss into the cut so that it will not heal and roots will grow from it. Tie a handful of wet sphagnum moss around

the stem to cover the cut. Over the moss tie a piece of clear plastic, sealing it top and bottom with adhesive tape. Water and feed the plant in the usual way. In

about two months you should see plenty of new roots in the moss. Remove the plastic covering, but not the moss. Cut the stem just below the moss and pot the plant, with the moss, in a pot two inches (5 cm) larger in diameter than the root ball. Water it well.

Training

In addition to being pinched or pruned into shape, plants may need either support or discipline to persuade them to grow as you would wish. Such training is all you can do with plants which are unprunable.

Plants grow one-sided if they always face the light in the same direction. Indoors they can never be cured of the habit, which is called phototropism, because they are sensibly reaching out for all the light they can get. Outdoors the sun conveniently moves around and over them in the sky, but indoors you have to turn the pots if you want upright plants with leaves growing all around. Many plants resent a sudden turn around, so do it slowly, a little each day. Never turn them, however, while they are in flower.

When a plant is against a wall and is not seen from all sides, it makes sense to let it grow all its leaves towards you. It can be prevented from bending over by loosely tying it to a stick inserted in the pot.

Many tall plants will need such staking. It is best to stake a plant while it is still young and small and before the roots have filled the pot; there is less risk of damaging them. Put the stake near the edge of the pot and keep the ties loose.

They are there to support the plant, not to strangle it.

Such climbing plants as philodendrons are best supported with a moss stick or moss column into which the aerial roots can be pushed. If the moss is frequently sprayed the plant will have an extra source of water through the aerial roots and there will be a bonus of humidity for the leaves.

Many climbing plants may be trained up trellises or allowed to trail. Whichever they do they should also be encouraged to grow bushy by some pinching out.

Trailers are liable to deteriorate rapidly into scraggly sprawlers. If they do they should be· hard pruned. Monsteras sprawl rather than climb and the stems need to be firmly staked while they are young and malleable. Later the restraints can be removed. An untrained monstera is totally lacking in style, besides taking up too much room.

Always remove from all plants any leaves which are dead or dying or have been attacked by pests or disease.

Painless Propagation

Do-it-yourself plant propagation costs little, is far easier than building reproduction furniture, and can be very satisfying. There is nothing fundamentally mysterious about propagation. Like all living things, plants have a fierce urge to reproduce. What is remarkable is the number of ways in which we can encourage plants to reproduce themselves. We can divide them, making two or more plants out of one large one. We can take bits of the stems or leaves and induce them to grow roots. Some plants do most of the work for us by producing offsets, bulblets, suckers or plantlets. They may be attached to the parent plant itself or appear on runners (overground) or stolons (underground) and they can be removed and replanted.

The conditions for carrying out all these forms of vegetative, or asexual, propagation can be provided fairly easily. Raising plants from seeds, or spores in the case of ferns, may be more difficult. This is the common method of reproduction in nature and it is simple even with exotic plants, provided there are greenhouse conditions with adequate warmth and humidity. Indoors it is a considerable gamble, but many people enjoy the challenge. Each plant entry, in the You and Your Plants section, tells you which method of propagation is suitable for that plant and when to use it.

Division

Plants which send up several stems can be divided. Plants which send up one stem, or a plant with leaves which grow from a rosette, cannot be divided. While division is the simplest form of propagation to carry out it is nevertheless a considerable shock to the plant.

Divide only young healthy plants. An exception to this rule may be made if you have a beloved ageing plant; remove and throw away the old part of the plant and repot the younger stems and roots to take over from their ancestor. Most plants are best divided in early spring when growth is starting again. Flowering plants, however, should be divided when they are dormant or when they have finished flowering.

To divide a plant remove it from the pot as described for repotting (page 22). To know how to divide the plant you will have to remove much of the compost so that you can see the roots. It is most important to share out the roots between each division of the plant or you may finish up with one part of the divided plant having a mass of foliage and not enough roots capable of feeding it. Avoid

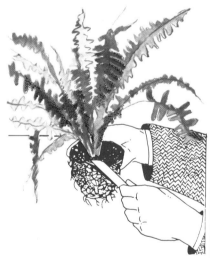

multiple division which can result in your owning too many plants, all of which look pathetic.

The roots of some plants are very easy to divide—they almost fall apart in your hand. Others will need a sharp knife to cut through the tangle; some long-established ferns may need a saw. Cut cleanly; avoid bruising. Repot promptly since root hairs dry out quickly. Use pots which are about two inches (5 cm) larger in diameter than the balls of the roots so that each plant is surrounded by an inch (2.5 cm) of new compost. The divided plants should be planted to the same depth as they were before division, with the compost well firmed around the roots. Then water the plants well and keep them out of direct sunlight until they have obviously recovered from the operation. Do not be alarmed if at first the leaves flop over. A light spraying will help to revive them, but do not water again until the compost has begun to dry out; with fewer roots this will take longer than before.

Offsets

The easiest natural form of propagation depends on the co-operation of the plant in producing small copies of itself. These can be removed from the parent plant and potted, preferably when they have started to develop their own root systems.

Some of these young plants, or offsets, are attached to their parent. There are many examples among the bromeliads. Others appear on runners, the commonest example being the chlorophytum, or spider plant. Its offsets can be pinned

down with a bent piece of wire into a pot of compost alongside the parent. When

the young plant is well established the runner is severed. *Saxifraga sarmentosa* is treated in the same way.

Sansevieria have creeping rhizomes, and these, if given enough room and

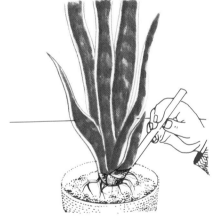

enough time, perhaps a couple of years, will put up new leaves. When a new leaf is six inches (15 cm) high the rhizome to

which it is attached can be cut away from the parent plant, potted and kept warm and humid while it puts down roots.

Tolmiea menziesii, yet another plant called mother of thousands, grows a plantlet at the base of each leaf. To propagate, remove a leaf with its stalk.

Cut the stalk down to two inches (5 cm) and push it into a pot of compost so that the leaf lies on the surface. Within a short time the plantlet will have put down its roots and the old leaf will die away.

Bulbs grow bulbets alongside themselves and these can be removed when repotting and planted separately. It will usually be several years, however, before they

flower. Some lilies reproduce bulbils on their stems. These are minute replicas of the lily bulb and may be carefully removed and grown on to maturity.

In general, ferns are reproduced sexually from spores, but a few can be propagated vegetatively. *Asplenium bulbiferum*, the hen and chick fern, grows bulbils on its fronds and these can be planted. From the basal fronds of the *Platycerium bifurcatum*, the staghorn

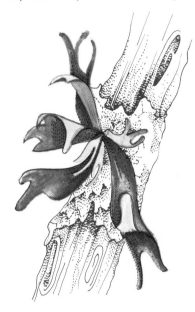

fern, new plants, called pups, emerge and can be removed and potted. *Nephrolepis exaltata*, the Boston fern, produces masses of trailing runners. If pinned down in compost these will root and produce new ferns. The runners can then be severed from the parent fern.

Painless Propagation

Bits of plants—stems or leaves—can be induced to grow roots and reproduce themselves. The most common method is to take stem cuttings, but leaf cuttings are better for some plants, particularly *Begonia rex* and African violets.

Stem Cuttings

To take a cutting, choose a stem with a growing tip which has not been pinched out. Cut it with a very sharp knife a little below a leaf joint; four inches (10 cm) is

a suitable length. Remove some of the lower leaves and dip the end of the stem in hormone rooting powder.

Some cuttings will root in water, but others will just rot. In any case it is far better to start them off in compost, unless they are to be grown hydroponically, since they will have to go into compost before long and the change can cause a severe setback.

Plant the cutting in a small pot filled with moist loam-based or peat-based compost. The simplest way to do this is

to make a hole for the cutting with a pencil and press the compost firmly

around the stem. Cover the pot with a clear plastic bag, held away from the plant with sticks, and seal the opening with adhesive tape. This will provide the

humid atmosphere the plant needs to form roots. Keep it out of the sun. Some plants will root in a few days and will soon begin to show signs of leaf growth, others will take weeks, and you must expect that some will die.

Leaf Cuttings

The simplest way to propagate saintpaulias—African violets—is to break off a leaf and its stem cleanly from the plant.

Trim the leaf stem back to one inch (2.5 cm) and push the cutting at an angle into a pot of damp sand to a depth of onehalf inch (1.25 cm). Enclose the pot in a

clear plastic bag, held away from the leaf with sticks, and seal the opening with adhesive tape. Keep the sand moist and in due course—it may take three

months—plantlets will appear at the base of the leaf. When they are large enough to handle, about one-quarter to one-half inch (0.75 to 1.25 cm) tall, sever the plantlet and pot it.

To propagate *Begonia rex* use a whole leaf. Make a few shallow cuts in the veins

on the underside of the leaf; these are points at which the plantlets will eventually grow. Press the leaf face up on the surface of damp sand in a pot and pin it

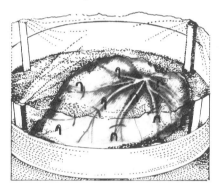

down with looped pieces of wire. Provide a temperature of 70°F (21°C) and a humid atmosphere. This can only be done by enclosing the pot in a plastic bag. After three months, and possibly

more, the plantlets will be large enough to move and pot.

To propagate sansevieria, cut a leaf into pieces about two inches (5 cm) long and plant them in a potting compost. It is vital to plant them the right way down.

When slicing the leaf make a cut on each piece to mark which was the end nearest the surface of the compost.

A sansevieria propagated this way will always have green mottled leaves, rather than the variegations of its parent.

Seed

Propagation by seed is easy, but only if the appropriate amount of warmth and humidity can be given; for many houseplants from the tropics that means a lot of both. If you have a thermostatically controlled electric propagator to satisfy those needs, the rest is child's play. Fill a pot with seed compost, either loam-based or peat-based, firming it slightly. Sprinkle the seeds very sparingly on the compost and cover them with a light layer of sand. The usual formula of a depth of twice the diameter of the seed tells you how light this layer should be. After sowing, put the pot or tray in a bowl with about one inch (2.5 cm) of tepid water in the bottom and leave it until beads of moisture appear on the surface of the compost. Let it drain before putting it into the propagator, setting the thermostat at the temperature advised on the seed packet. In temperate regions, seed which needs comparatively low temperatures to germinate may be grown without a propagator in the natural warmth of spring and early summer. Enclose the seed tray or pot in a plastic bag to provide humidity. Seedlings need good light, but must be kept out of direct sunlight. When they are large enough to handle, transplant them into small pots.

One final warning. Some people catch the plant propagation fever the way others catch colds. If you succeed you could soon be overwhelmed by your own success and neighbours may be unexpectedly reluctant to adopt your numerous unwanted offspring.

Cacti and Other Succulents

Most cacti and many other succulents are easily propagated from cuttings—cacti from late spring until late summer and other succulents either in early spring or in late summer. Since most cacti have no leaves they are propagated from stem cuttings. Even among other succulents, propagation from leaf cuttings is rare. The easiest cacti cuttings are those from plants which grow pads and long side branches. Beware of spiny cacti—hold the cuttings between several layers of newspaper. Cuttings from cacti must be allowed to dry out for several days before planting them in a mixture of half peat and half sand. They will need a temperature of 70°F (21°C), but they need not be kept in a humid atmosphere. Cuttings from other succulents need drying out for only one day. Dip euphorbia cuttings in water before letting them dry out.

What Did I Do Wrong?

It is not right to assume that every plant is healthier growing in the wild than it is indoors. Certainly a plant in the wild has the advantage of living in an environment which will better provide the levels of temperature, light and moisture it needs. But it will, at the same time, be competing with many other plants which also flourish in that environment. Moreover it will be exposed to attack from all the pests and diseases that thrive and multiply in the same conditions. Life in the wild is not as easy as it might seem for a plant.

Indoors, although a descendant of that plant may have to make do with an environment less suited to its needs, this environment is also less congenial to such enemies as insects, fungi and viruses. And the plant will not be struggling with other plants for its existence.

With these advantages it would seem easier than it is to keep houseplants in perfect health. Unfortunately, however, not all the plant's natural enemies disappear when it comes indoors and it has also acquired a new potential, although unwitting, enemy – its owner.

A plant has a comparatively limited repertoire of signals to warn that something is going wrong and most of these symptoms might just as well indicate faulty care by the owner as attacks by natural enemies. Leaves turn yellow, brown or pale, for example; they curl, droop, shrivel or wilt; they become blotchy, grow small or drop off. Any of these symptoms might occur because you yourself are killing the plant, despite your good intentions.

Consequently, when you are confronted with a plant which, without any obvious explanation – such as being smothered by aphids – begins to lose the bloom of health, the first question to ask yourself is "What have I done wrong?" and take it from there.

The symptoms shown by an ailing plant can be interpreted in a variety of ways, so diagnosis is not easy and several clues may be needed to pinpoint the problem. You can only be certain that the diagnosis is correct when the plant responds to the appropriate treatment and, in some cases, that may take time. If there is no response, be ready to revise your diagnosis and try another approach. Thus, by trial and, hopefully, not too much error, you should be able to restore the plant to health.

There are five main areas of vulnerability to consider – either when a plant is in full growth or when it is dormant. These are light, temperature and humidity, watering and feeding.

Light

A plant is a far better judge of how much light it needs than you are since its life depends on it. It is therefore important to watch for the symptoms that indicate that a plant is getting too little light or (less frequently) too much light.

A plant that is not getting enough light reaches out towards the light, grows leaves only on one side, grows unusually small leaves, or becomes lanky. Flower buds which turn brown and drop off and variegated leaves which revert to green are other symptoms of insufficient light. When a plant is getting too much light, leaves curl and turn brown or yellow and brown spots appear on the leaves. The flower buds of short-day plants will not set if there is too much light.

For further guidance on a plant's light needs see pages 13 to 15 and refer to individual plant entries.

Symptom: Leaves and flower stalks lurch in the direction of the window.
Cause: This is the result of phototropism, the natural reaction of a plant to grow in the direction from which the light is coming.
Treatment: If the plant is some distance from a window it may well be short of light and should be moved closer. But this must be done gradually. If the plant is already near the window it should be turned to face the light at a slightly different angle to correct its distorted growth.

Symptom: The flower buds of such plants as azaleas, cyclamen, fuchsia and gloxinia turn brown and die.
Cause: The plant has probably been taken from good light and put in shade; this often happens when a plant is bought in bud in midwinter and has to adjust to the poorer light in a house. Epiphyllums will often drop buds because of insufficient light when buds are forming. Aporocactus is similarly susceptible to bud drop. (A temperature which is too high, overwatering and underwatering, can, however, also cause this symptom.)
Treatment: Give as much light as possible, but not direct sunlight. All parts of the plant must have equal levels of light. This can be ensured by turning the pot regularly a little at a time.

Symptom: Failure of so-called short-day plants to produce flowers and their brightly coloured bracts.
Cause: Not enough hours of darkness to allow the flower buds to set. Some of the short-day plants, including Christmas cactus and kalanchoe, will not set flower buds unless the hours of darkness are more than the hours of daylight for two to three months. Even the weakest artificial light will inhibit a poinsettia from flowering.

Symptom: Leaves growing on only one side of the plant.
Cause: The leaves are on the side of the plant which always faces the light; the other side of the plant doesn't receive enough light to encourage growth there.
Treatment: Leaves can be induced to grow on the blind side by turning the plant around from time to time. There is little point in doing this, however, if the plant is standing against a wall; it may look better with all the foliage concentrated on the side which can be seen.

Symptom: Straggly, lanky growth.
Cause: This is a sure sign of lack of light, especially when a plant is kept in a warm room.
Treatment: Move the plant into good light and prune the weak shoots to encourage new, sturdier and bushier growth.

Symptom: Variegated leaves have lost their variegations.
Cause: Inadequate light. Chlorophyll, the green pigment in leaves, is essential for efficient photosynthesis, the process by which, with the help of light, the plant manufactures food. The less green the leaves are, the greater the need for good light to compensate for the lack of chlorophyll. Without such light the plant may grow greener leaves to prevent starvation. All variegated plants are liable to revert in this way, especially those with coloured variegations.
Treatment: Give the plant more light—and that means rather more light than is needed by green foliage plants. Variegated leaves may revert to green for other reasons. When this happens, no matter what the reason, cut off the stems which have reverted or the whole plant may turn green.

Symptom: Browning leaves and curling tips.
Cause: Light too bright in summer, leading to scorching.
Treatment: Move the plant so that it will not be in direct sunlight. A few feet away will be ideal. Calatheas and marantas are particularly susceptible to discolouring of the leaves by sunlight.

Symptom: The leaves of a *Monstera deliciosa* grow without the typical serrations and perforations.
Cause: It is natural for the first leaves of a young monstera to grow without serrations, but if later leaves do not have them, the probable cause is insufficient light.
Treatment: Move the plant into better light, but not into direct sunlight. After a time new leaves should appear with their characteristic serrations and perforations. Those which did not have them will, however, remain unadorned.

Symptom: Unusually small leaves.
Cause: In all likelihood there is not sufficient light for the plant to manufacture enough food to grow normal-sized leaves.
Treatment: Given better light the plant will begin to grow normal-sized leaves. The leaves produced while it was suffering from light starvation will, however, remain somewhat stunted.

What Did I Do Wrong?

Temperature and Humidity

The greatest mistake you can make regarding temperature is to buy a plant which needs a warmer or cooler environment than your home can provide. Short of changing homes, the plant can never be expected to flourish. But there are other problems, too, such as providing proper levels of temperature during a plant's dormant period. Likely symptoms that the temperature is too low are yellowing leaves, falling leaves, leaves which turn brown, and brown patches on cactus pads. Curled leaves and leaves which curl and then fall are possible symptoms. Likely symptoms that the temperature is too high are wilting, dropping leaves, drooping leaves, leaves which shrivel and turn brown, flowers which last only a short time, a plant which grows leggy, and fruit and leaves dropping. Possible symptoms are older leaves which drop and tips and edges of leaves which turn brown.

Temperature and humidity are intimately connected since warm air can hold more moisture than cold air—but the moisture must come from somewhere. Plant problems caused by lack of humidity are most evident in winter in heated rooms; indoor temperatures are high, but the air holds comparatively little moisture because there is little moisture in the cold air outdoors to draw upon. Instead moisture is drawn from the walls, the furniture, people, and through the leaves of plants. The drier the air, the more and the faster the plants become dehydrated, even to the point of collapse. Plants which are particularly susceptible to the havoc wrought by dry atmosphere include ferns and ivies, caladium, dizygotheca, avocado, maranta, aphelandra, scindapsus, acalypha, anthurium and gloxinia. Most plants, however, may be affected to some degree.

Wilting, shrivelling leaves, buds dropping, browning tips of leaves, and dropping leaves are all symptoms that may be displayed by a plant which is suffering from lack of humidity. If any of these symptoms are read against a background of a centrally heated room, cracks in doors and furniture, and a constant dry feeling in your mouth, you can be certain that the cause is indeed lack of humidity.

First aid for a plant which has been dehydrated to the point of wilting is to spray it. Spraying would also prevent it from reaching this stage if you see the symptoms in time.

More permanent preventive measures consist of surrounding the pot with peat which is always kept damp or standing it on a tray of wet pebbles. Far more effective than any of these measures is an electric humidifier. An alternative solution is to grow cacti and other succulents which are little affected by lack of humidity.

While excessive humidity encourages a number of diseases the problem is unlikely to arise in a home unless plants are growing in bottle gardens or enclosed terrariums.

Symptom: Buds and leaves of a cyclamen drop.
Cause: The room is too warm.
Treatment: Move the plant to another, cooler room or at least to the coolest part of the same room. Cyclamen do not like warmth; the ideal temperature range throughout the year is 45 to 55°F (7 to 13°C). A camellia will also lose its buds when the temperature is too high.

Symptom: Leaves look shrivelled and slightly translucent.
Cause: They have been touched by frost.
Treatment: Spray gently with cold—not warm—water and put the plant in a position where the leaves can thaw out slowly. Rapid thawing will damage the tissue of the leaves.

Symptom: Leaves of a *Dizygotheca elegantissima* fall all year.
Cause: The most likely cause is that the temperature is too low.
Treatment: This is a plant which needs warmth. From autumn until early spring it is best not to let the temperature fall much below 60°F (16°C) and never below 50°F (10°C). For the rest of the year provide a temperature not below 65°F (18°C).

Symptom: Leaves falling during the dormancy period.
Cause: Temperature too low.
Treatment: Move the plant to a somewhat warmer room. The range of temperatures best suited to some plants during dormancy can be uncomfortably narrow. This schefflera, for example, dormant from autumn until early spring, should have a temperature which does not fall below 55°F (13°C) or remain long above 60°F (16°C).

Symptom: Brown patches on the pads of a cactus.
Cause: Temperature too low.
Treatment: While cacti like cool conditions in winter, they should not be exposed to frost. This opuntia, for example, should have a winter temperature which does not fall below 46°F (8°C). Once on the pads, the brown patches cannot be removed.

Symptom: Leaves of a dieffenbachia turn yellow during the dormancy period.
Cause: Temperature too low.
Treatment: Move the plant into a room with a minimum temperature of 60°F (16°C). Remove affected leaves cleanly from the stem.

Symptom: Fruit and leaves of a fruiting plant drop.
Cause: Winter temperature not low enough.
Treatment: Either move the plant to a cooler room or enjoy the fruit in your living room and let them drop.

Symptom: Leaves of a *Euonymous japonicus* dropping.
Cause: Too warm in winter.
Treatment: From autumn until late winter keep the plant in a place where the temperature is around 40°F (5°C). Higher temperatures will lead not only to falling leaves, but also to weak growth later because the plant has been denied its dormant period.

Symptom: The leaves of a codiaeum have dropped.
Cause: Sudden changes in temperature.
Treatment: Try to keep a steady temperature all year—in the region of 65°F (18°C). This plant is particularly affected, too, by draughts.

Watering

This is the area of plant care in which there is the greatest risk of going astray. Waterlogged compost is an obvious sign of overwatering, Likely symptoms of overwatering are tips and edges of leaves that turn brown, leaves that turn yellow and fall, soft black or brown areas on leaves, and rotting leaves. Lower leaves that turn yellow, bloated leaves of succulents, wilting, and new leaves that are soft and poorly coloured are also possible symptoms of overwatering. Plants which are particularly vulnerable to overwatering include African violets, aglaonema, amaryllis, begonias, columnea, cordyline, dizygotheca, dracaena, fittonia, peperomia, pilea, cacti and other succulents.

It is, of course, possible to underwater plants, although most people err on the side of generosity. Hard-packed and dry compost is an obvious sign of underwatering. Likely symptoms of underwatering are limpness and wilting, all the leaves dropping off, lower leaves turning yellow and falling, brown, crisp spots appearing on the leaves, the edges of the leaves turning brown, the leaves of succulents shrivelling, leaves and buds dropping, flowers dying prematurely. Pale, washed-out leaves and older leaves which drop off are possible symptoms of underwatering. Plants likely to suffer from underwatering include aphelandra, azaleas, cissus, ferns, ivies, carnivorous plants, ficus and philodendrons.

Symptom: The leaves of a succulent look bloated.
Cause: Overwatering. The leaves of succulents, like this *Stapelia variegata*, store water and are quite likely to become bloated if the compost is kept too wet.
Treatment: Let the plant use up some of its reserve before giving it any more water. Cut down the frequency of watering in the future.

What Did I Do Wrong?

Symptom: The leaves have turned yellow and are falling.
Cause: Since the plant has been left standing in a saucer of water, this is a simple case of gross overwatering.
Treatment: Pour the water out of the saucer immediately and never let it accumulate again. Permitting the compost to drain properly after watering is as vital as getting the compost thoroughly wet in the first place. This applies to all plants, with the rarest exceptions, such as the umbrella plant, *Cyperus alternifolius*, which thrives when standing in water. Compost which has become waterlogged should be allowed to dry out until it is barely moist before you water again.

Symptom: The edges of the leaves have turned brown during the dormancy period.
Cause: This is a common reaction to overwatering during the winter.
Treatment: Let the compost dry out thoroughly and then reduce the frequency of watering while the plant is dormant. During the spring and summer months the plant may be watered frequently, but in the winter months the compost should be barely moist for most of the time—except just after watering. Don't be surprised if leaves which have turned brown as the result of overwatering soon drop off.

Symptoms: Leaves and stems wilting and space between the compost and the side of the pot.
Cause: Typically a case of serious underwatering.
Treatment: Water immediately, but be careful. If you water from above take care that the water does not merely escape through the space between the compost and the pot, leaving most of roots still dry. If you immerse the pot in water, dried compost may float to the surface of the water unless it is held down firmly until it has swelled out again in the pot. Thereafter inspect the plant more frequently and water it before it gets to the wilting stage.

Symptom: The leaves of a succulent are shrivelling.
Cause: The plant is not getting enough water.
Treatment: This can happen to succulents during the hot summer months when they may need watering every day. It can also happen during the winter dormancy period if they are not watered occasionally. Succulents which are susceptible to shrivelling are *Agave americana*, *Cyanotis kewensis*, euphorbias and haworthia.

Symptom: The lower leaves have fallen.
Cause: Almost certainly a case of overwatering during the winter months of dormancy.
Treatment: Unfortunately, nothing can be done to induce this Norfolk Island pine, or most other plants, to replace lost lower leaves. To prevent further losses keep the compost just moist from autumn until late winter. When you stick your finger into the compost and it feels dry about one and a half inches (3.75 cm) below the surface, it is safe to water again. Watering with very cold water in winter can easily put a plant into shock; use slightly tepid water.

Symptom: Edges of leaves have turned brown during the growing period.
Cause: Underwatering. Many plants are susceptible to browning. They include calatheas, chlorophytum, marantas, dieffenbachia and *Scirpus cernuus*, which is also one of the few plants which should always be kept standing in a saucer of water.
Treatment: In summer these plants need frequent watering; spraying the leaves will help to prevent browning. Browning will often occur in winter, too, when restraint in watering results in being too sparing. A thorough watering followed by a drying out period is the best solution.

Feeding

Deficiencies of the major nutrients needed by a plant will only occur if you have potted it in impoverished garden soil or in much-used and exhausted potting soil. A good loam-based compost is less quickly exhausted than a peat-based compost that depends for its nutrients on fertilizers added to the peat and sand. Fresh compost will not need further fertilizer for three or four months. Then, to renew the nutrients which have been used by the growing plant, water the compost with a solution of a balanced proprietary fertilizer devised for indoor plants. See individual plant entries for suggested frequency of application.

Symptom: Leaves turn yellow, except for the veins which remain green.
Cause: Lack of iron (Fe). (The leaves of lime-hating plants, such as the Indian azalea, may, however, turn yellow if there is lime in the compost, possibly as the result of watering with hard water.)
Symptom: Older leaves have greenish or brown blotches.
Cause: Lack of magnesium (Mg).
Treatment: Iron and magnesium are trace elements. Both of these deficiencies can be treated by using a balanced fertilizer which contains trace elements.

Symptom: Pale leaves.
Cause: Can be the result of lack of nitrogen (N).
Symptom: Weak stems, stunted growth, leaves turn very dark green, possibly with purple blotches.
Cause: Lack of phosphorus (P).
Symptom: Leaf edges turn brown and brittle; blooms are few or look pathetic.
Cause: Lack of potassium (K).
Treatment: The treatment for all these deficiencies is the same; feed the plant with a balanced proprietary fertilizer.

Symptom: Unpleasant-looking white deposits appear on the side of a clay pot or on the surface of the compost.
Cause: Too much fertilizer is being given.
Treatment: Water the plant well to get rid of excess salts. Clean the surface of the pot and then clean it again if more deposits appear. Do not feed the plant until the pot stays clear of any deposit for at least two weeks.

Other Problems

Sometimes, despite proper light, watering, feeding, temperature and humidity, a plant will develop seemingly inexplicable symptoms which challenge your powers of diagnosis. Here are some helpful hints.

Symptom: Tips of leaves become brown or wither.
Cause: This often happens if a plant has been placed so near a wall or window that the leaves touch the surface.
Treatment: Nothing can be done to restore the damaged leaves, but you can cut off some of the withered part of the leaves. Do not cut back into the green leaf or it will probably wither further.

Symptom: Leaves are tattered or torn.
Cause: People and pets. Plants standing near the floor are at risk from crawling babies and swirling skirts; at higher levels they are vulnerable to elbows and gesticulating arms. Cats tend to chew leaves and play games with the tips of trailing plants. A dog's wagging tail can wreck any plant that happens to be in the way.
Treatment: Anticipate disaster and place plants where they may expect to be undisturbed. Put them out of harm's way if you are giving a party that is likely to be lively.

Symptom: Leaves look dull and lifeless.
Cause: They are covered with dust and grease which is slowing down photosynthesis and clogging the stomata in the leaves through which the plant breathes.
Treatment: Wash large, waxy leaves with water, both top surfaces and the undersides, and spray small leaves. Brush hairy leaves and cacti with a very soft brush.

Symptom: Brown edging of leaves.
Cause: The plant may have been in a cold draught.
Treatment: Find a more congenial place for it.

Symptom: Leaves turn yellow and die.
Cause: Natural causes and, for once, in no way your fault. Leaves do age and die, as eventually the whole plant must. As Shakespeare's Macbeth said: "I have lived long enough; my way of life is fall'n into the sear, the yellow leaf." With a plant, however, you may be able to anticipate that time by propagating it before it prepares to go.

If It Isn't Me Who's To Blame?

You cannot be blamed for every ailment that besets your houseplants. They are, after all, vulnerable to attack by plant pests and diseases. There are, however, two basic ways to cope with pests and diseases. The first is to do everything you can to prevent them; the second is to get rid of them.

The most important preventive measure must be taken when you buy or are given a new plant. At that time inspect it thoroughly. To be on the safe side, spray the plant with warm, soapy water (soap not detergent), followed by warm, clear water. Keep the newcomer away from other plants for several days, or a week, and look at it frequently and carefully to be sure there are no signs of pests or disease.

If you put a plant outdoors for the summer, inspect it with even greater care when you bring it into the house again for signs of pests which may have infiltrated the compost.

When you are repotting always use a sterilized proprietary potting soil, not garden soil which may be teeming with pests so small you cannot see them.

Isolate a plant which shows the least sign of ill health; many pests and diseases spread like wildfire. Do not bring a sick plant back among other plants until you can give it a thoroughly clean bill of health.

Always keep pots clean and remove fallen foliage and flowers.

Preventive spraying with chemicals is a bad, lazy habit indoors where it is far easier to keep an eye on a plant than it is in the garden. When a particular pest or disease turns up there will be time enough then to use the pesticide, fungicide or whatever chemical is appropriate to deal with it.

Pests

When it comes to getting rid of pests and diseases remember that none of the thousands of chemical preparations sold to gardeners is safe; all are intended to kill something. In doing that, some may damage the plants themselves, or harm animals or humans. Choose carefully; impulse buying is dangerous.

Avoid overkill. Fingers are quite capable of picking off a few pests. A good spraying with soapy water will fairly readily dispose of aphids, for example, although you may have to repeat the treatment several times.

Moving up the scale, there are two pesticides which are made from plants—derris (rotenone in the United States),

which contains the poison rotenone, obtained from the derris root, and pyrethrum, from the flower heads of certain species of pyrethrum. These pesticides are favoured because they are not persistent, which means that they have a very limited life and do not go on killing insects (some of which are helpful) and poisoning the compost. Derris and pyrethrum are often used in all-purpose sprays. Nicotine sulphate, derived from tobacco, is another organic substance which effectively destroys foliage pests.

Organochlorine pesticides are the most viciously persistent and many of them (notably DDT) have been banned. The organophosphorus compounds are less persistent in the soil and in the tissues of plants and are, therefore, considered less dangerous.

Malathion is widely used against sucking insects, which make up the vast majority of houseplant pests. It kills the adult pests, but may not destroy the eggs, so several sprayings at intervals may be necessary. Cython is a new, similar insecticide which does not have the strong odour of malathion. Malathion and cython are harmful to some plants—ferns, cacti and other succulents—and an alternative is a systemic insecticide.

Systemic insecticides, which are advertised as such, work by being taken up through the roots to all parts of the plant, killing pests which are sap suckers and chewers. Systemics have a long-lasting effect and many gardeners object to them because of the buildup of poison in the plant and in the compost. Do not use them if there is danger of pets—or children—nibbling at the leaves.

Systemic insecticides are sold as granules or as a solution to add to the compost. To use the granules, scratch out a shallow trench in the compost around the plant and bury some of them, according to the manufacturer's instructions. Watering the compost gradually dissolves the granules and the insecticide spreads down to the roots.

These preparations should be enough to deal with the most common plant pests. The manufacturer's instructions for their use must be followed absolutely, for they can be dangerous to handle. Use them no more than you absolutely must. You may occasionally need to use a fungicide (such as maneb or zineb), benomyl (a systemic insecticide), a nematicide (to kill nematodes), a miticide (to destroy mites and their eggs), or a molluscicide (to kill slugs and snails), but with good management and a little good luck you may never need them.

The Sap Suckers

The most pernicious pests the houseplant owner is likely to encounter are vampire-type insects that kill plants by sucking the sap which is their life blood. The worst villains are aphids, mealy bugs, mites, thrips, white flies and leaf hoppers. They are usually fought with insecticide sprays or systemic insecticides applied to the soil.

Scale Insects

These are pernicious little sucking insects, hard to detect, which haunt the undersides of leaves. Among susceptible plants are codiaeum, dieffenbachia, *Laurus nobilis*, schefflera, stephanotis, ficus, cacti, bromeliads and the palm *Chamaedorea elegans*.

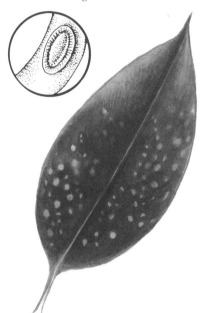

Symptoms: Yellow spots on leaves; whole leaves may yellow and fall off. Growth is stunted. Young scales are translucent and hard to see, but they can be seen and felt as immobile colonies of them build up. Sooty black mould may be found growing on their excrement, which is known as honeydew.

Treatment: If you catch them early the insects can be scraped off with a thumbnail. Then wash around the area where the scales were, to dislodge any eggs or young. If the insects are well established, spraying with malathion or cython will kill the young scales which have not grown protective shells. To kill mature scales apply a systemic insecticide powder to the compost. This treatment should also be applied to ferns, cacti and other succulents which will be damaged by malathion or cython.

Aphids

At times it seems you have only to turn your back for hundreds of aphids to appear; it has been estimated that in theory one aphid is capable of producing ten million tons of offspring in three months. Fortunately, not all aphids that are born survive, but you should assume that all plants are susceptible to attack.

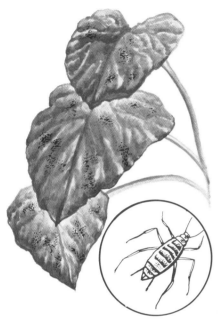

Symptoms: It's hard to miss the clusters of green, black, brown or yellow squashy insects busily sucking the sap from the tender growth of the plant—leaves, buds or flowers. Ants may be present, feeding on the insects' honeydew, which also encourages the growth of sooty mould.
Treatment: Spray with a forceful jet of soapy water (not detergent), or with malathion or cythion if it is a bad infestation. Watch carefully that no aphids have escaped to recolonize. Some aphids attack roots and these are hard to spot until it is too late to save the plant. However, if you suspect an attack—from signs of wilting—use a systemic insecticide.

Red Spider Mites

These pests are so small that only a plague of them become obvious. They flourish in a hot, dry room and given these conditions almost every plant should be considered at risk.

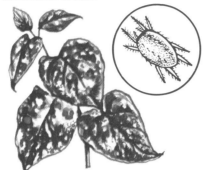

Symptoms: Tiny, straggly webs and whitish powder (the skins of dead mites) on the leaves are convincing signs of their presence. But by then the mites will have been voraciously sucking the sap and the leaves will be speckled with yellow spots and starting to fall.
Treatment: Many of the mites can be washed off with a forceful spray of tepid water, but some will survive and they readily move to other plants. A malathion or cythion spray is more effective, but cannot be used on ferns and cacti, which should be treated with a systemic insecticide in the compost. Frequent spraying of plants helps to prevent attacks, for the mites dislike humid conditions.

Leaf Hoppers

These are energetic versions of aphids with a fondness for fuchsia, calceolaria and pelargoniums.

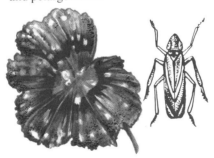

Symptoms: Yellow blotches on the leaves where, on the undersides, the hoppers have been sucking the sap. Leaves eventually turn brown and fall.
Treatment: Remove affected leaves and spray the rest, especially the undersides, with malathion or cythion. A systemic insecticide in the soil is an effective alternative.

Mealy Bugs

Related to scale insects, these pests are not as successful in concealing themselves because of their white waxy covering. Plants susceptible to attack include coleus, geogenanthus, opuntia, echeveria, hoya, stephanotis, orchids, palms and African violets.

Symptoms: The appearance of white fluff on stems and leaves is the first sign of an attack—this is the coating around the bugs. They reproduce rapidly and soon the mass sap-sucking makes the leaves turn yellow, wilt and fall. Their honeydew is a breeding ground for fungal diseases.
Treatment: Mild infestations can be dealt with by spraying with malathion or cythion once a week until the plant has been cleared of all bugs and eggs. For heavier attacks apply a systemic insecticide. (This is also the treatment for ferns, cacti and succulents which are harmed by malathion or cythion.) Attacks by mealy bugs at root level are harder to detect, but if symptoms suggest an infestation turn the plant out of the pot; your suspicions may be confirmed by the presence of masses of white eggs and bugs. Use a systemic insecticide.

If It Isn't Me Who's To Blame?

Cyclamen Mites

Even smaller than red spider mites, cyclamen mites do even more damage and flourish in cool, humid conditions which would deter red spider mites. Not only cyclamen, but African violets, gloxinia, pelargoniums, begonias, azalea, impatiens and fuchsia are prone to attack.

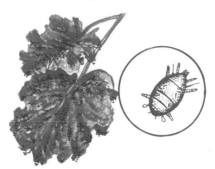

Symptoms: Leaves become scarred, shrivelled and brown; flower buds wither and drop. Growth is stunted.
Treatment: If the plant is seriously infested the wisest thing you can do is to throw it away for the sake of your other plants. A minor infestation may be dealt with by the application of a systemic insecticide. Follow the manufacturer's instructions precisely.

Thrips

These are flying insects which suck the sap of plants; their offspring at the nymph stage eat the leaves. Susceptible plants include avocado, azalea, codiaeum, begonias, citrus, fuchsia, orchids, gloxinia and stephanotis.

Symptoms: Leaves mottled with silver, and papery scars. New shoots are distorted. Flower buds drop or flowers are deformed. The insects' honeydew encourages fungal diseases.
Treatment: Spray with malathion or cythion each week if attacks persist. A systemic insecticide applied to the compost will have a longer-term effect.

White Flies

These minute moths and their nymphs are sap suckers. Plants especially susceptible to attack are fuchsia, calceolaria, pelargoniums, begonias and impatiens.

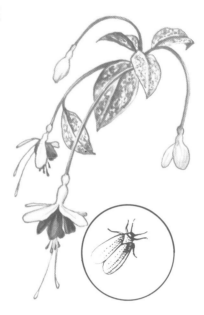

Symptoms: Small, white flies hovering around the plant, and pale green scales on the undersides of the leaves – the developing nymphs. Leaves turn a mottled yellow, wilt and finally drop off. Plant is in a general state of collapse. Sooty mould may grow on the honeydew excreted by the pests.
Treatment: Spray the plant with malathion or cythion once a week until all trace of the pest has disappeared. Put the plant in a large plastic bag when spraying, seal the bag and leave it about one hour. Applying a systemic insecticide to the compost will give longer-term protection, killing the nymphs as they emerge from the eggs laid by any female adults still flying around.

The Chewers

Another group of plants pests may be classified as chewers. They are less of a menace than the sap suckers since they are more common outdoors and if they do stray indoors they are more easily seen, since they are larger. On the other hand, most chewers tend to operate at night.

Leaf Miners

These are the most undesirable of the chewers. They are the larvae of certain moths, flies and beetles which burrow in the leaves and devour them. Plants affected by leaf miners are azaleas, African violets, begonias, pelargoniums, ficus and palms.

Symptoms: Winding trails and blisters beneath the surface of the leaves, which eventually turn brown.
Treatment: Remove the affected leaves which may still contain larvae, spray the plant with malathion or cythion or use a systemic insecticide.

Earwigs

These chewers may venture into the house on their own, but usually they arrive hidden among the petals of flowers cut from the garden. It is a wise precaution to hold cut flowers upside down and shake them before taking them indoors.

Symptoms: Petals of flowers and, perhaps, foliage have been chewed during the night; you will seldom see earwigs during the day.
Treatment: Plants may be sprayed with malathion or cythion.

Caterpillars

They are most likely to be carried indoors on cut flowers, so check carefully when you are arranging flowers. Caterpillars prefer to eat fleshy, soft-leaved plants.

Symptoms: Leaves chewed away, often during the night, the caterpillars leaving behind them piles of excrement as clues.
Treatment: Pick them off, then dispose of them. If you think you may have missed some, spray with derris or rotenone, malathion or cythion.

Woodlice

Also known as sowbugs or pillbugs, these pests like living in dark, dank places outdoors, so their intrusion into dry, well-lit rooms is usually accidental. One of their ways of entry is on the pots of plants brought back into the house after summering outdoors.

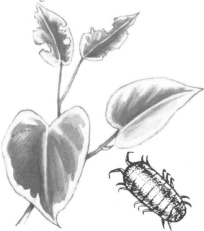

Symptoms: Their outdoor diet is decaying vegetation, but indoors woodlice may gnaw away at young shoots, leaves and roots of plants.
Treatment: Pick them off and destroy them. In the unlikely event of a major invasion, spray malathion or cythion on the compost.

Crickets

Although not universal pests, crickets are destructive night raiders, with well-developed jaws.

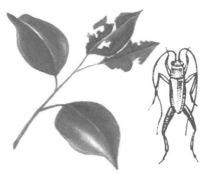

Symptoms: You may hear them clicking at night, but they hide the days away. Evidence of their presence is most likely to be the discovery each morning of severely eaten young leaves or flowers. They also gnaw at young stems at ground level or just below the surface of the compost. They are particularly attracted to plants growing in humid conditions.
Treatment: Spray with malathion or cythion. If you are seriously plagued by crickets it may be because they are laying eggs in the compost, which should be watered with a malathion or cythion solution.

Slugs and Snails

Not normal inhabitants of modern houses (where they do not feel at home), slugs and snails are usually brought in with pots which have spent some time outdoors.

Symptoms: Slimy trails on compost, and leaves which have been severely chewed during the night. Some slugs feed on the roots of plants, especially bulbous plants.
Treatment: The usual treatment is to lay down baits of methiocarb or metaldehyde. To be sure children, birds and animals can't get at them use a stone as protective covering. Alternatively, spray the plant and surface of the compost with liquid metaldehyde.

Ants

Hardly a major plant pest, ants can be a nuisance and do indicate the presence of such serious pests as aphids, white flies and other insects which excrete honeydew, a favourite ant food. Ants are a problem in their own right in two ways; they carry aphids from one plant to another and, by burrowing in the compost, they disturb roots and carry off newly planted seeds.

Symptom: Ants are gregarious and are therefore easily spotted.
Treatment: Put down ant poison or spray with malathion or cythion. It is far more important to get rid of the pests which attracted the ants in the first place.

Cockroaches

Not specifically plant pests, but if cockroaches invade your house you will find them catholic in their tastes.

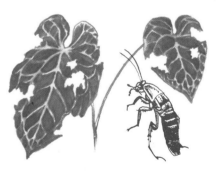

Symptom: Since they prefer to go on the rampage during the night, you are unlikely to see them at work, but in the mornings you will find the leaves of your plants chewed with holes or ragged edges.
Treatment: Sprays specifically devised for dealing with cockroach infestations are not safe to use on plants; instead, spray them with malathion or cythion (with the usual reservations about using either on ferns, cacti and other succulents).

If It Isn't Me Who's To Blame?

The Underground Movement

The soil in our gardens is full of living things, some of them of benefit to plants, some harmless and some evil. Normally, we would not expect to find these in the compost in pots indoors, and if we do we can usually blame bad management or bad luck. The best way to keep free of them is to buy plants from reliable nurserymen and never to use garden soil when repotting—only sterilized compost should be used. These underground enemies may also infiltrate the compost if plants are put in the garden for summering and the pots are left standing on soil. The risk is less if the pots are put on a hard surface.

Worms

Certainly not pests, worms are among the outdoor gardener's best friends because of their role in aereating the soil. Indoors in a pot they can be a nuisance, but there is no reason why they should be there. You may have been responsible for introducing them indoors by using soil instead of a proprietary sterilized compost for potting the plant or by permitting the pot to stand in soil outdoors during the summer months; worms then crawl in through the drainage hole.

Symptoms: Rapid drying out of the compost as a result of the burrowing habits of the worms in the pot. In such a confined space they may damage roots.
Treatment: Never use garden soil for potting. If you put plants out for the summer place the pots on a hard surface and not on soil. If you have doubts when bringing in a plant in autumn, remove the plant from the pot and if you see any worms in the compost pick them off and leave them in the garden to do their good work there.

Millipedes and Symphalids

These related insects may find their way into the house in pots which have been outdoors in summer. The rather sluggish millipedes, which curl up when touched, do sometimes attack tender roots and stems, but their main diet is decaying vegetation. Symphalids (which are often mistaken for centipedes) cause much more damage. They are very active and will burrow deeper into the compost if the surface is disturbed. They relish plants with succulent roots and eat root hairs and small roots, and damage other larger roots, making them susceptible to root rot.

Symptoms: Plants grow stunted, wilt in the sun and may eventually die.
Treatment: Both millipedes and symphalids can be destroyed by soaking the compost in a solution of malathion or cythion.

Fungus Gnats

These small, black flies are themselves probably harmless, but root-eating maggots emerge from the eggs they lay on the compost.

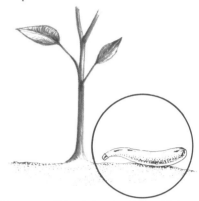

Symptom: Watch for the flies, which are attracted to moist compost.
Treatment: Soak the compost with a malathion or cythion solution to kill both eggs and larvae.

Nematodes

Also known as eelworms, these pests attack leaves and stems. But more menacing are those which destroy the roots by sucking the tissue. Susceptible plants are African violets, calceolaria, begonias, ferns, cacti and plants growing from tubers and corms.

Symptoms: Leaves turn brown and shrivel and eventually the plant collapses. By then the roots will be covered with ugly swellings.
Treatment: If nematodes are well established throw the plant away—and not on the compost heap where the pests will have every chance to spread. For a mild infestation soak the compost with a nematicide. To avoid attacks always use sterilized soil.

Springtails

These minute insects chew the roots and stems of young plants, especially those growing in damp conditions. The aerial roots of orchids growing in damp moss are susceptible to attack.

Symptom: Springtails are often seen jumping about on the surface of the compost during watering.
Treatment: Drench the compost with a solution of malathion or cythion.

Diseases

The healthiest plant may be at risk from pests but, given reasonably good growing conditions, houseplants suffer from comparatively few diseases. Overwatering, overfeeding, excessive warmth or cold, poor ventilation, and lack of light not only prevent proper growth of a plant, but may also make it susceptible to attack by various fungi, bacteria and viruses. Many diseases caused by fungi or bacteria can be brought under control, but there is no defence against a virus.

Sooty Mould

A fungus which lives on honeydew, the excrement of such pests as aphids and scale insects. Plants which are infested by these insects are susceptible to attacks.

Symptom: Black mould covers the leaves of the plant.
Treatment: Wipe the mould off the leaves with warm water. Spray the plant with an insecticide to get rid of the insects which are the cause of the trouble.

Mildew

A fungal disease likely to affect begonias, codiaeum and *Euonymus japonica.*

Symptom: White mould on leaves and stems.
Cause: Overwatering and lack of ventilation.
Treatment: Remove the mildewed parts of the plant and spray with a fungicide. Water less frequently and give the plant better ventilation.

Anthracnose

A fungal disease which may affect ficus, palms, avocado and kalanchoe.

Symptoms: The leaves develop blisters or sunken spots which are black and dry at the centre. The tips and edges of the leaves may also turn brown with small dark stripes.
Cause: Like many fungal diseases, anthracnose develops when the air is very humid and ventilation is poor. These are conditions which are more likely to be found in a greenhouse than in a home.
Treatment: Remove the affected leaves and burn them. Spray the remaining leaves with a foliar fungicide. Give the plant a rest from any mist spraying, water it less frequently, and increase the ventilation.

Botrytis

A fungal disease which may attack the flowers and foliage of many plants.

Symptoms: Grey mould appears both on the plant and on the compost.
Cause: Overwatering, overfeeding, overcrowding and underventilating.
Treatment: Act quickly, either to throw the plant away, because the disease can spread rapidly to other plants, or to effect a cure. Cut away and destroy the diseased part of the plant, remove all trace of mould from the compost, and then scratch some systemic fungicide granules into the surface of the compost and water them in gently. In the future, water less, spray less, and give the plant more air.

If It Isn't Me Who's To Blame?

Viral Diseases

These are the invisible enemies of house-plants.

Symptoms: Varied. Leaves mottled with green and yellow patches, stunted and distorted.
Cause: Infection by a virus, possibly carried by insects.
Treatment: Nothing can be done except to discard the plant to prevent infection of other plants. Also throw away the compost; never use it again, for many viruses can survive in compost for a long time.

Leaf Spot Diseases

Fungus or bacterial diseases which may affect African violets, cacti, pelargoniums, gloxinias and dracaenas.

Symptom: Brown and yellow damp spots on the leaves.
Cause: Overwatering, humid air, poor ventilation and bad light. (Brown spots may also be caused by drops of water on leaves which have been left exposed to hot sunlight.)
Treatment: Remove all infected leaves and spray the plant with a fungicide. Water less frequently until signs of infection have gone.

Root Rot

A fungal disease to which begonias, gloxinias, African violets, palms, cacti and other succulents are susceptible.

Symptoms: Plant in state of wilting collapse, with leaves shrivelling and turning brown.
Cause: Overwatering and badly aerated compost.
Treatment: If the plant is far gone throw it away. Otherwise repot it. First, remove all dead foliage and then, using tepid water, wash all compost from the roots. Cut away any roots which are brown, soft and mushy. Repot the plant in fresh compost which has been watered with a fungicide. Water sparingly and infrequently until the foliage has picked up.

Damping Off

A fungal disease which may attack any seedlings since the fungus is carried in the soil.

Symptoms: The stem is attacked at soil level, the seedling collapses and within hours is dead.
Cause: The use of unsterilized compost.
Treatment: Act when the first seedling shows signs of wilting. Reduce temperature and humidity. Dust with a fungicide. To help prevent attacks dust the seeds with a fungicide before sowing.

Crown and Stem Rot

A fungal disease which often affects African violets. Other susceptible plants are begonias, pelargoniums, philodendrons, dieffenbachias, and various cacti and other succulents, including parodias, aloes and echeverias.

Symptom: Stems and crown turn mushy. The rot can spread rapidly and kill the plant.
Cause: The disease is usually caused by overwatering or incorrect watering, but high humidity and excessive cold or heat may also trigger off an attack.
Treatment: Throw the plant away if it is badly affected. If you have spotted the disease in time remove any rotting stems and leaves and dust the compost with a fungicidal powder. Let the compost dry out and when the plant needs watering again do so from below; this is especially important with African violets. Stand the pot in shallow water and wait until the surface of the compost is glistening with moisture. Take the pot out of the water and let it drain thoroughly. This method ensures that you do not water directly on the crown of the plant, a certain recipe for disaster. By not watering from above you also avoid the risk of getting water on the leaves and causing spotting.

Rust

A fungal disease.

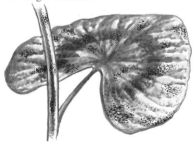

Symptom: Rusty spots on leaves and stems.
Cause: Too much humidity in the atmosphere.
Treatment: Spray the foliage with a fungicide.

How Your Plant Got Its Name

The Latinized botanical names of plants, however cumbrous they may seem, have to be used to avoid confusion. Although some plants have well-known and fairly descriptive common names, there are many plants which have been given several common names or may share a name with other plants. If you try to buy a zebra plant, for example, you could finish up with an aphelandra, a calathea or a zebrina. But no plant shares its Latin name with any other plant; by this name it can always be precisely identified.

The Latin names are in fact simple to understand. Plants are classified into different families according to their botanical similarities, although they may differ greatly in their appearance. Each family is divided into genera (the Latin plural of genus). Each genus is made up of closely related plants, although they may not necessarily look alike. Each genus is further divided into species, and these consist of very closely related plants which are recognizably alike. Yet, even within a species there may be variations; some strains may have different colours, for example, or various shapes of leaves and flowers. They are classified as varieties, if the change has taken place in the wild, or as cultivars, if the change has been brought about by breeding. ("Cultivar" is an abbreviation of cultivated variety.)

The botanical name provides all this information in two or three words, seldom more. The first word in the name shows the genus to which the plant belongs and the second word the species. These two names, which are Latin, or Latinized, are usually printed in italics. The presence of an additional word or words shows that the plant is a naturally occurring variety or a cultivated variety of the species. The name of a natural variety, often printed in italics, is Latinized, like the names of the genus and species. It may describe some distinguishing feature of the variety or be named after its discoverer or in honour of someone. If the plant is a cultivar, its name, which might be that of a royal personage or even a film star, is given not in a Latinized form but in the vernacular, printed in roman characters, and enclosed in single quotation marks. An x in the name of a plant indicates that it is a hybrid—a plant bred by crossing different species or distinct forms within a species. x *Fatshedera Lizei*, for example, is a cross between *Fatsia japonica* and a hedera.

Infuriatingly, the botanical names of plants are frequently altered as errors in classification are discovered. Because the older names are often better known they continue to be used. Sometimes they are shown as a synonym (abbreviated to syn.) of the later name. The first time a plant is mentioned the whole name is given. Thereafter the genus is abbreviated to its initial. When a cultivar is mentioned more than once, initials are used for the genus and species names.

To demonstrate how the naming of plants works out in practice, consider the large family called Acanthaceae, which is composed of two hundred and fifty related genera. (One genus is called acanthus, and the leaf pattern of one species is said to have inspired the design of the Corinthian column.) Among the genera popular as houseplants are aphelandra, beloperone, fittonia and pachystachys. The name aphelandra, which derives from the Greek words for "simple" and "male," is meant to indicate that the anthers are single-celled. The species in cultivation is named *squarrosa*, to show that the leaves overlap. The variety which established the popularity of the aphelandra was called Louisae in honour of the Queen of the Belgians, but this variety has been improved on in a cultivar from it called 'Brockfeld'. So the full name of the plant is *Aphelandra squarrosa Louisae* 'Brockfeld', although often the Louisae is dropped.

The fittonias got their generic name from two women named Fitton who wrote a book on botany and the species name *verschaffeltii* commemorates M. Verschaffelt, a Belgian expert on camellias who lived in the nineteenth century.

There is also a variety called *F.v. rubra*.

The Latin generic name of the appropriately nicknamed shrimp plant, beloperone, is created from the Greek words for "arrow" and "band." The species name *guttata* means sprinkled. *B. guttata* must, however, feel all at sea for it is only a few years since it was reclassified internationally as *Drejerella guttata* and has since undergone another change to *Justicia brandegeana*. It seems pedantic to follow suit in this and other instances until the new name is firmly established, so on page 120 you will find the shrimp plant reassuringly named *Beloperone guttata*.

In spite of such complications (and not all plants get shuffled around as much as the shrimp plant), the Latin labelling of plants is still the most certain way of identifying the plant you want. Fortunately, too, many plants now have the same botanical and common name. Begonia, coleus, fuchsia, sansevieria, dracaena, peperomia, yucca, kalanchoe, philodendron, agave and aloe are among the many Latin names which have become common names.

Knowing the botanical name is the only way to be certain of buying precisely the plant you want. Don't worry about the pronunciation; most of the words are phoney Latin and, anyway, no one knows how Latin was really pronounced when it was a living language. If you feel self-conscious about trying to pronounce Latin, just write the name on a piece of paper and take it with you when you go shopping for a plant.

You and Your Plants

One of life's golden rules is to read the instructions carefully. Here is a guide to help you make the best use of the concise instructions for the care of more than two hundred and fifty plants which follow.

Each entry begins with a description of the plant, followed by what "the doctor says" about its environmental, watering, feeding, repotting and propagating needs. Where appropriate the entry ends with special instructions for the care of the plant. In each entry, the plant named in the heading is illustrated. In many cases, however, information about the care of other related plants is included in the entry. The information given for specific plants complements the general advice on the basic routines of indoor gardening given earlier.

Environment

Under this heading recommended temperatures are given for the plant during different seasons of the year. Seasons have been chosen rather than months because plants grow according to the seasons and not according to names on a calendar. Midwinter, for example, is midwinter the world over, but in the northern hemisphere it occurs in January, whereas in the southern hemisphere it occurs in June. The table for converting months into seasons in the two hemispheres, at the beginning of this book, is repeated here for easy reference.

The range of temperatures given for the spring, summer and autumn months—the normal growing period of most houseplants—are the temperatures which the plant needs to grow well. Temperatures for the rest of the year, which is likely to include the plant's normal period of dormancy, are those which will encourage dormancy. If the temperature falls below the lower figure in the recommended ranges no damage may be done if the fall lasts only a short time, but, in general, the lower limits should be respected. Where appropriate, warnings are given that a plant will be harmed if at any time the temperature falls below a given figure.

This section also points out any special need for humidity at all or certain times of the year. An electric humidifier is the best way to increase the humidity all over a room, but alternatives are suggested for increasing humidity just around the plant. When reading the recommendations about a plant's light requirements, it is a good idea to refer to the general advice about light on pages 13 to 15.

Water

Knowing exactly when a plant needs watering can become second nature, but until it does there may be problems. Watering is the most difficult area of indoor gardening about which to give advice. It would be fine to be able to write "Give the plant ten ounces of water every three days." It would also be nonsense. The amount of water a plant needs depends on the nature of the plant, the temperature in which it is growing, whether it is growing vigorously or is dormant, and what kind of pot and compost has been used.

As a general rule, it is better to give houseplants a good soaking and then allow the compost to dry out considerably before soaking them again. This is why the emphasis in the instructions is on the frequency of watering, rather than on the amounts of water which are inevitably imprecise. After even a good watering the surface of the compost may dry out quickly and you may be tempted to water again too soon. Stick your finger down into the compost to see what is happening there. The finger test is as good a guide to watering as you can have.

The practice of watering by immersion has already been recommended (page 12). This may not always be practicable, and it would be unwise at those times when the instructions say that the compost should be kept just moist or barely moist. Instead you will have to water from above in order to limit the amount of water given at any one time as well as the frequency of giving it. Note particularly any warnings about the care needed in watering certain plants from above (lest they rot) and about the dangers to some plants of using hard water.

Above all, never, never water plants with very cold water; it can be a severe shock to the roots if the temperature of the compost is suddenly and drastically reduced.

Feed

There should be few problems about feeding your plants. The recommended intervals between feeds are on the conservative side because it is easy to over-fertilize houseplants. The heavy growth that results from excessive feeding is often weak and prone to disease and in flowering plants it often takes place at the expense of the flowers. Liquid fertilizers are most convenient, but always apply them when the compost is already moist. Never make up a feed that is stronger than the manufacturer instructs, but you can use a weaker one if you wish. Always use a balanced fertilizer—that is, one containing all the main nutrients required by the plant—made by a reputable company. See page 12 for detailed information on feeding.

Repot

The advice on repotting is basically confined to the season of the year at which it may be done, how frequently it should be done, and the type of compost to be used. (Compost and potting soil mean the same thing, but compost has been used throughout this part of the book.) The actual process of repotting (into the same size pot) and potting on (into a larger pot) and the mystique attached to these operations is explained on pages 22 to 25.

Propagate

This section indicates how the plants are usually propagated—by division, cuttings, seed or in other ways. The methods are explained and illustrated on pages 28 to 31.

The whole point in having plants in our homes is to enjoy them, This is so obvious that we often forget it and start worrying instead. This helps neither your nor the plant, for there is no evidence that plants grow any better when their owners stand over them worrying.

It might be helpful if we got rid of the idea that we grow plants; they grow themselves, because of that strong and mysterious urge that creates and maintains all life. All we have to do is give them the best chance to get on with it. Everyone can learn to do that; there is no one incapable of growing houseplants. By actually growing plants and diligently observing which die and why and which flourish and why, you would become an experienced houseplant owner, although it might take several years and a large investment in plants. But if you start with the advantage of other people's experiences—their mistakes and successes—adapting their knowledge to the conditions in your own home, you can learn faster and more cheaply.

When writing about indoor gardening, it is necessary to try to anticipate all the problems that might arise. This might give the erroneous impression that you will never be free of them, but this is no more possible than it is to be struck by every disaster you might read about in a medical book. Only a hypochondriac would imagine that. Some people somewhere can be expected to run into some of the problems that are covered in this book. Many others may escape them altogether; the unlucky few will have more than their share of troubles. If you follow the instructions for the care of your plants you will learn to avoid the pitfalls, have little to worry about, and be able to relax and enjoy your achievement.

Northern Hemisphere		Southern Hemisphere
January	Winter	June
February	Late Winter	July
March	Early Spring	August
April	Spring	September
May	Late Spring	October
June	Early Summer	November
July	Summer	December
August	Late Summer	January
September	Early Autumn	February
October	Autumn	March
November	Late Autumn	April
December	Early Winter	May

Green Foliage Plants

The core of most houseplant collections, green foliage plants tend to heighten the dramatic effect of the variegated and flowering plants alongside them. They are particularly effective as large accent plants where the emphasis is on form rather than on colour. There is also the great practical advantage that many green foliage plants will flourish in shadier conditions than more flamboyant houseplants.

Araucaria heterophylla

Once upon a time, before the days of central heating, the Norfolk Island pine was one of the most popular of houseplants. Today most homes are too warm for it in winter, and it responds by losing its lower leaves. If it is permitted to overwinter in a cool place, the plant develops into a most attractive pyramid-shaped bush. Norfolk Island, its home, lies to the northwest of New Zealand, and there it may grow up to two hundred feet (60 m) tall. Indoors it grows accommodatingly slowly to about three feet (90 cm). The woody central stem carries tiers of branches bearing bright green, needle-like leaves. The plant is usually sold under its previous name, *A. excelsa*.

The Doctor Says —

Environment: From autumn until early spring the plant should be kept in a temperature not exceeding 50°F (10°C) and not falling below 40°F (4°C). In summer the optimum temperature for growth is about 55°F (13°C), and plenty of fresh air is needed. Allow it good light in winter, but in summer it will need some shade from the sun.
Water: Frequently from spring until early autumn, and spray the leaves occasionally in hot weather. For the rest of the year water infrequently. Overwatering in winter may cause the plant to lose its lower leaves, and they will never grow again.
Feed: Every two weeks from spring until early autumn.
Repot: The Norfolk Island pine grows slowly, so it may not need repotting more than once every third year in spring. Use a loam-based compost.
Propagate: From seed in spring.
Special Instructions: Turn the pot around fairly frequently to ensure that the branches grow evenly and not just on the side facing the light.

Asparagus

Two species of asparagus make the most feathery houseplants imaginable. *A. densiflorus* (syn. *A. sprengeri*), commonly known as emerald feather, is heavily branched and has long, trailing stems which carry light green, narrow leaves called phylloclades. It is particularly effective in a hanging basket. *A. setaceus* (syn. *A. plumosus*), inevitably called the bride's bouquet fern, is even more feathery, but is more erect-growing and a richer green. The variety 'Nana', which has dense, compact foliage, is the most popular.

The Doctor Says —

Environment: From autumn until early spring *A. setaceus* needs a resting period with the temperature around 50°F (10°C). *A. densiflorus* seems able to forgo a dormant period and will tolerate a winter temperature around 45°F (7°C) or normal room temperature. For the rest of the year a temperature range of 55 to 65°F (13 to 18°C) is adequate, but higher temperatures are not harmful. Both species like plenty of light, but they must be shaded from direct sun.
Water: Frequently from spring until early autumn. Water *A. densiflorus* fairly frequently in winter if it is kept in a warm room, but for the resting *A. setaceus* keep the compost just moist.
Feed: Every two weeks from spring until early autumn.
Repot: Each spring in a loam-based compost.
Propagate: In spring, by division or from seed.

Aspidistra elatior

In the nineteenth century the aspidistra earned universal popularity because of its virtual indestructibility, lost it as the result of over-exposure, and is now fighting its way back with some success. It gained its common name of cast-iron plant from its constitution and its other name, the parlour palm, from its usual domestic habitat; it is found in the wild in the eastern Himalayas, China and Japan. The leathery, lance-shaped leaves are a deep green. The small purple flowers are produced at soil level, and often go unnoticed.

The Doctor Says—

Environment: From autumn until early spring the temperature should not exceed 60°F (16°C) and it need not go much higher during the summer months. A shady position is probably best all year round; certainly avoid direct sun or the edges of the leaves may turn brown.
Water: Fairly frequently from spring until early autumn; at other times only occasionally.
Feed: Monthly from spring until early autumn.
Repot: Since aspidistras do best if rather potbound, repotting may not be necessary more often than every three years in spring. Use a loam-based compost.
Propagate: By division when repotting.
Special Instructions: If the plant is allowed to stand in water the roots will rot.

Beaucarnea recurvata

B. recurvata, also known as *Nolina recurvata*, is a curiously shaped plant from Mexico, where it grows into a tree up to twenty feet (6 m) tall with drooping leaves three feet (90 cm) long, but less than one inch (2.5 cm) wide. The odd feature is the bulbous swelling of the stem at soil level which acts as a reservoir for water during a drought. When the plant is young the leaves grow from this base, but in time a woody trunk, grey brown in colour, develops. The form of the leaves is aptly described by one of the plant's common names—pony tail—and the swollen trunk gives it two others—bottle plant and elephant's foot. In a pot it grows slowly and presents few problems.

The Doctor Says—

Environment: From early autumn until spring the plant will tolerate a temperature as low as 45°F (7°C), but in the summer months it seems quite happy with a temperature of 75°F (24°C) or more. It likes strong light, preferably direct sunlight.
Water: Very frequently in the growing season from spring until early autumn, with regular spraying of the leaves. For the rest of the year, when the plant is dormant, water infrequently—it is a type of succulent. A sign of underwatering is shrivelling of the trunk.
Feed: Monthly from spring until early autumn.
Repot: The plant appears to do best when somewhat potbound; if repotting is necessary do it in early spring, using a well-draining compost of loam, peat and sharp sand.
Propagate: From seed in spring.

Green Foliage Plants

Cissus antarctica

The cissus make excellent climbing or trailing plants. *C. antarctica*, from Australia, hence its common name, kangaroo vine, is the most vigorous; it grows up to six feet (1.8 m). When young the leaves are light green, turning dark as they mature. *C. striata*, the miniature grape ivy from Brazil and Chile, is more delicate looking. Its red stems carry five leaflets, pinkish at first, but turning dark green on the upper surface and purplish underneath. The most striking is the variegated *C. discolor*, the rex begonia vine, from Java. The colours of its heart-shaped leaves include deep green, crimson, bronze and silvery white. It needs warmth and humidity in winter, without which it will lose either its colour or its leaves.

The Doctor Says —

Environment: From winter until early spring *C. antarctica* and *C. striata* need a temperature of at least 50°F (10°C) and in summer from 55 to 65°F (13 to 18°C). *C. discolor* needs a winter temperature between 55 and 65°F (13 and 18°C) and a minimum summer temperature of 65°F (18°C), with plenty of humidity. All need good light.
Water: From spring until early autumn water fairly frequently. *C. striata* will probably need to be watered a little more often than the others. For the rest of the year keep the compost just moist.
Feed: Every two weeks from spring until early autumn.
Repot: Every spring in a mixture of loam, peat, leaf mould and sand.
Propagate: In spring from seed (at 75°F, 24°C) or from stem cuttings in spring and summer.
Special Instructions: To encourage bushiness pinch out growing shoots. Do not let the pot stand in water or the leaves will yellow and fall.

Coffea arabica

This is the coffee plant of Ethiopia. There it grows fifteen feet (4.5 m) tall, but in a pot it will probably stay about two feet (60 cm). The best choice is the dwarf form 'Nana'. The leaves are a glossy dark green, with rather crinkly edges. The plant will not flower until it is at least three or four years old, and often not then. The small, white, fragrant flowers are followed by green berries which ripen to red. Inside them is the coffee "bean."

The Doctor Says —

Environment: From autumn until early spring when the plant is dormant the ideal temperature is around 60°F (16°C). The summer temperature should be in the range of 60 to 70°F (16 to 21°C). In its natural habitat it is accustomed to growing in the shade, but indoors all the shade it needs is to be kept out of the direct sun.
Water: From spring until early autumn water frequently; for the rest of the year be sparing. Spray during the summer months.
Feed: Every two weeks from spring until early autumn.
Repot: This plant is a fairly slow grower so repotting every other spring should be sufficient. Use a peat-based compost. with a little sharp sand added to ensure good drainage.
Propagate: In spring from seed with a temperature of 75°F (24°C) for rapid germination. Lateral stem cuttings may be taken in late summer.
Special Instructions: Pinch out the growing tips for bushiness. Watch for scale insects.

Cupressus cashmeriana

The Kashmir cypress is a tree of extraordinary grace. In its native Tibet it will grow to fifty feet (15 m) or more, but indoors it stays about five feet (1.5 m) tall. The drooping, frond-like leaves, carried on arching branches, are an unusual blue-green colour. This plant may be hard to find.

The Doctor Says—

Environment: From autumn until early spring keep the plant in a temperature around 50°F (10°C). In the summer months it thrives at about 60°F (16°C).
Water: Frequently from spring until early autumn. For the rest of the year keep the soil barely moist.
Feed: Every two weeks from spring until early autumn.
Repot: Depending on the rate of growth, either every spring or every other spring.
Propagate: From seed in spring, or by cuttings in summer.

Cyperus alternifolius

Umbrella plant, which comes from the marshes of Madagascar, will make itself at home anywhere if it is given as much water as would drown most other houseplants. It is therefore particularly successful when grown hydroponically, but will also do well if planted in a pot which is kept standing in water. It is a sedge, and the thin stalks, which are about two feet (60 cm) long, each carry a rosette of arching, green, leaf-like bracts. In summer, small, brownish-green flowers may appear from the centre of the rosette. *C.a.* 'Variegatus' has white stripes along the bracts.

The Doctor Says—

Environment: From autumn until early spring, when the plant should be dormant, the ideal temperature is between 50 and 55°F (10 and 13°C). In the summer months the ideal temperature range is 55 to 65°F (13 to 18°C).
Water: Needs a lot of water all year round. Stand the pot in a saucer or a bowl containing water, and constantly replenish it.
Feed: Every two weeks from spring until early autumn.
Repot: Every spring in a loam-based compost.
Propagate: By division in spring. It is also possible to raise the plant from seed, but germination may be slow.
Special Instructions: Never forget that you are looking after a marsh plant.

Green Foliage Plants

Dizygotheca elegantissima

The false aralia, or finger aralia, from the New Hebrides, is a tantalizing plant. It can look most elegant, as its Latin name describes it, but when it grows tall and leggy with only a tuft of leaves left at the top of the trunk it looks merely absurd. To prevent the lower leaves from falling, warmth and humidity are needed. When young the serrated leaflets, carried on a short stem, are a deep copper, but they become green with age and on an older plant, which may reach five feet (1.5 m), they grow much larger.

The Doctor Says—

Environment: From autumn until early spring the ideal minimum temperature is about 60°F (16°C). For the rest of the year the plant should have a temperature around 65°F (18°C). One of the problems is to provide it with a sufficiently humid atmosphere; during the hot summer months frequent spraying is necessary. It needs plenty of light, but not direct hot sun.
Water: Will need fairly frequent watering from spring until early autumn. For the rest of the year keep the compost just moist, never dry.
Feed: Every two weeks from spring until late summer.
Repot: This is not a fast-growing plant, so repotting every other spring is enough. Use a peat-based compost.
Propagate: From seed in spring.
Special Instructions: Lack of humidity and warmth will cause the lower leaves to drop off. If the plant grows leggy, and you have the nerve, cut the trunk back to a few inches to force the stump to sprout again. Lack of humidity also encourages red spider mites and scale insects.

x Fatshedera lizei

The birthplace of this hybrid was the nursery of the French Lizé brothers in Nantes, and the parents were *Fatsia japonica* and an ivy (*Hedera*). It takes after both, hardy and attractive, with glossy, dark green, lobed leaves, but it is not quite a shrub and not quite a climber, so it needs some support. One popular name, fatheaded Lizzie, is only a corruption, but ivy tree is more descriptive. x *F.1.* 'Variegata' has creamy white edges to its leaves.

The Doctor Says—

Environment: A suitable temperature from autumn until early spring is in the range of 45 to 50°F (7 to 10°C), but the plant will tolerate higher temperatures. The optimum growing temperature in summer is about 55°F (13°C). It will be quite happy in a light or a shady situation, but avoid the extremes of gloom and direct sunlight.
x *F.1.* 'Variegata' will need good light all year to maintain the variegation.
Water: Frequently from spring until early autumn. If kept at low temperature in winter water only occasionally, but if the temperature is higher keep the compost moist all the time.
Feed: Every two weeks from spring until early autumn.
Repot: Each spring in a loam-based compost.
Propagate: From seed in spring, or by stem cuttings in summer.
Special Instructions: Pinch out growing shoots to encourage bushiness. If the plant becomes leggy, cut it back hard.

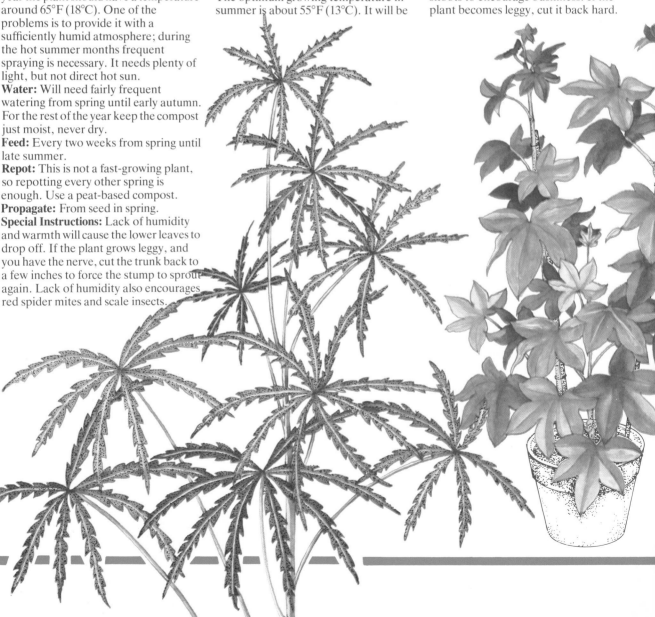

Fatsia japonica

During the century and a half this plant has been around as a houseplant it has collected many names. Botanically it is also known as *Aralia japonica* and *Aralia sieboldii* and its common names include false castor oil plant, fig leaf palm and Japanese fatsia. Whatever its name, however, *Fatsia japonica* is just as easy to look after. The large leaves, with up to nine lobes, are a glossy, dark green; those of *F.j.* 'Variegata' are tipped with creamy white. Clusters of small white flowers are more likely to appear if the plant is grown outdoors.

The Doctor Says—

Environment: *F. japonica* prefers to be cool; from autumn until early spring the temperature should be no higher than 45 to 50°F (7 to 10°C), and it will survive much lower temperatures; in summer it does best around 55°F (13°C). The variegated fatsia needs slightly higher winter temperatures. Good light is necessary all year, but do not expose the plant to direct hot sunlight.

Water: Frequently from spring until early autumn. For the rest of the year keep the compost merely moist.

Feed: Every two weeks from spring until early autumn.

Repot: Every spring in a loam-based compost.

Propagate: From seed in spring or by cuttings. *F.j.* 'Variegata' can only be propagated by cuttings.

Special Instructions: Too much warmth in winter will cause the leaves to shrivel and to turn brown. If this happens remove the affected leaves.

Grevillea robusta

The silk bark oak is a fast-growing plant; a seed sown in early spring will be a presentable plant before the year is out. Inconveniently, it goes on growing and after a few years will probably be too tall for most rooms; in its native western Australia it soars to more than one hundred and fifty feet (45 m). The feathery, fern-like leaves are particularly attractive when young, before they change from light green to dark. It is therefore best to replace the plant after a number of years or to cut it back to encourage new growth lower down the trunk.

The Doctor Says—

Environment: *G. robusta* likes cool conditions: from autumn until early spring in the range of 45 to 50°F (7 to 10°C), and 45 to 55°F (7 to 13°C) in the summer months. Good light is needed all year, but shade the plant from hot sun.

Water: Frequently from spring until early autumn; at other times keep the compost just moist.

Feed: Every two weeks from spring until early autumn.

Repot: Each spring in a loam-based compost.

Propagate: Usually by seed in spring; a temperature of 60°F (15°C) is necessary. Also by cuttings in summer.

Special Instructions: If the compost is allowed to dry out the lower leaves may yellow and fall. Watch for red spider mites.

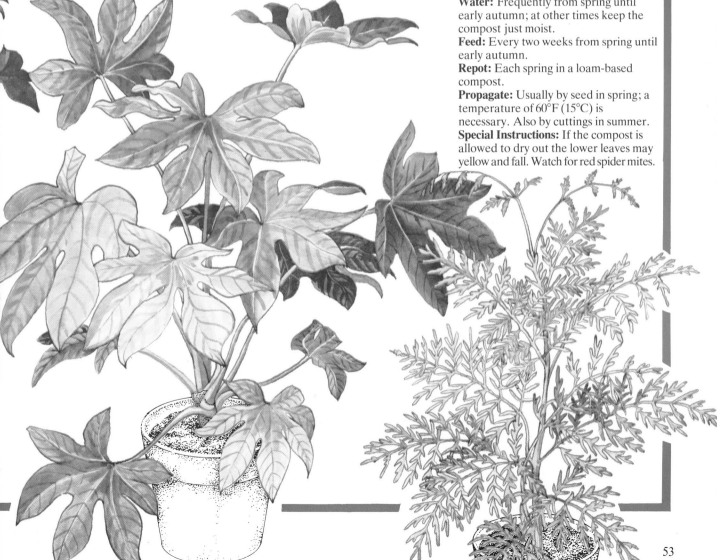

Green Foliage Plants

Hedera

Among the relatively few houseplants which originate in the temperate regions of the world, ivies are far and away the most popular. They are easy to grow (except possibly in the tropics), and the innumerable permutations in the shapes and colours of their leaves, although all unmistakably ivyish, make them attractive and amenable houseplants.

In general the most suitable ivies for indoors are those which can be induced to grow bushy rather than trail all over the place. These are self-branching ivies and will put out large numbers of side shoots if the tips of the growing stems are pinched out each year. The small-leaved *Hedera helix*, the common, or English, ivy, and some cultivars will produce only one or two shoots. There are, however, some self-branching *H. helix* cultivars. These include *H.h.* 'Chicago', *H.h.* 'Green Ripple', *H.h. sagittaefolia* and *H.h.* 'Lutzii'.

Hedera canariensis, the Canary Island ivy, has far larger leaves, is slightly less hardy than the common ivy, and is a fairly slow grower. The somewhat rounded leathery leaves are five to eight inches (12.5 to 20 cm) long. Since it is a climber it will need some support. The most attractive variety is *H.c.* 'Variegata' (syn. 'Gloire de Marengo').

The Persian ivy, *H. colchica*, is another climber with large leaves, up to nine inches (22.5 cm) long. The best forms are *H.c.* 'Dentata', which has dark green, rounded leaves, and the striking *H.c.* 'Dentato-variegata'.

The Doctor Says—

Environment: From autumn until early spring, hederas are best kept in temperatures not much above 50°F (10°C), however *H. canariensis* may be given a little more warmth. For the rest of the year they will grow well in a temperature around 55°F (13°C), although, of course, summer temperatures will often be higher. Make sure that they are not in direct sunlight; apart from that they can be in a light part of the room or in partial shade. The leaves collect dust, so spray or sponge them, using only water.

Water: From autumn until early spring keep the compost just moist. For the rest of the year water fairly frequently.

Feed: Every two weeks from spring until early autumn.

Laurus nobilis

The sweet bay, a plant of great antiquity, is often found growing in a tub on a balcony or patio or standing sentinel by a front door. But it is of Mediterranean origin and in colder regions it has to be brought indoors in the winter even if it enjoys the rest of the year outdoors. If it spends all its time indoors it must be kept in a light and airy place. Apart from the culinary uses of its dark green, pointed leaves, the bay has a mythical reputation for discouraging thunder and witches and encouraging elves and fairies.

The Doctor Says—

Environment: From autumn until early spring keep the plant in a temperature range of 45 to 50°F (8 to 10°C); if it is exposed to frost the leaves will turn brown and fall. If it is indoors in summer put it near an airy window where it will have plenty of sun.

Water: Will need frequent watering from spring until early autumn; for the rest of the year keep the compost just moist.

Feed: Every two weeks from spring until early autumn.

Repot: Every two or three years in spring, in a loam-based compost.

Propagate: By stem cuttings in summer, or from seed in spring if you have the patience to wait until the plant reaches a good size.

Special Instructions: Watch for scale insects.

Repot: Each year in spring in a mixture of loam, peat and sand, enriched with manure and leaf mould if available. *H. canariensis* is a slow grower and will probably need repotting only once every two years.

Propagate: From cuttings taken in summer.

Special Instructions: Watch for red spider mites, which will be discouraged by regular spraying or sponging of the leaves. To prevent the plant from growing spindly the tips of the self-branching varieties should be pinched out in the spring and may need to be stopped once more during the summer to keep them bushy. Ivies with variegated leaves may revert to producing green leaves. The usual reason is lack of light and the reversion is most likely to take place in the darker winter months if the plant has been kept warm enough to produce new leaves. In spring remove all the green leaves by cutting back the erring stem to the first variegated leaf. If the plant is then put in a good light it should start growing variegated leaves again.

Green Foliage Plants

Monstera deliciosa

The three or four leaves of the Swiss cheese plant standing in a small pot in a florist's window give no idea of the grandeur to come. It is a plant for a large room and ideal for a warm house. The dark green, greatly slashed leaves of a mature specimen may be twenty-four inches (60 cm) wide and thirty inches (75 cm) long. Although in its native Mexico the monstera sprawls horizontally, the only practical way to grow it as a houseplant is vertically and it will need a stake or, preferably, a moss stick for support. Indoors it is unlikely to flower or to produce the pineapple-flavoured fruit which gives it the name of Mexican breadfruit or fruit salad plant.

The Doctor Says—

Environment: From autumn until early spring minimum temperatures are within the range of 55 to 65°F (13 to 16°C) and the plant will cope happily with higher temperatures. It will not produce new leaves when the temperature is below 65°F (18°C) so the spring and summer range should be 65 to 75°F (18 to 24°C). Give it light but not direct sunlight.

Water: Frequently from spring until early autumn and spray the leaves in summer. At other times as often as necessary to keep the compost moist; if it dries out the tips of the leaves are liable to turn brown.

Feed: Every two weeks from spring until early autumn.

Repot: Every spring if growth is rapid, otherwise every other year. Use a peat-based compost.

Propagate: From seed in spring, or from stem-tip cuttings in summer.

Special Instructions: If the plant does not get enough light the new leaves may not have the attractive, characteristic holes.

Persea gratissima

Although not everybody would recognize it as *Persea gratissima*, many houseplant enthusiasts have grown it with varying degrees of success. It is the avocado, or alligator, pear. How successful you are depends on whether you stop the plant from trying to grow into a tree—in its native humid forests of Central and South America it will reach sixty feet (18 m) tall—and turn it into a well-behaved bush. This involves brutal amputation of the trunk when it is only a few weeks old. If you fail to do this you will finish up with a plant which is nothing but a long stem supporting a few leaves. Nobody ever seems to buy an avocado plant, so the real challenge is in propagating it.

The Doctor Says—

Environment: An established avocado will adjust to the usual warm temperatures of living rooms, even though they may not be the optimum temperatures for the plant. The real problem is providing adequate humidity. In summer the plant should be sprayed daily, and spraying may have to be continued throughout the winter months if the plant is then in a dry, heated atmosphere. It needs plenty of light, ideally near a sunny window.

Water: Frequently from spring until early autumn; will need fairly frequent watering for the rest of the year.

Feed: Every two weeks from spring until early autumn.

Repot: In spring every year, in a mixture of equal parts of loam, peat and sharp sand, or in a peat-based compost.

Propagate: From the pit (or stone) of the fruit. It is best to use a pit taken from a ripe pear. Put it in tepid water and leave it to soak for twenty-four hours. The pit can then be germinated either in water (where it is interesting to watch, but there is no other advantage) or in compost. To germinate in water use a jar with a narrow opening or a "hyacinth glass" and fill it almost to the top with tepid water. Stick three toothpicks into the pit—but only a little way in—to hold it in position on the rim of the jar, with the blunt end downwards and just touching the water. Temperatures between 70 and 75°F (21 and 24°C) are needed for germination. You can either use a heated propagator or place the jar near a radiator or in a warm cupboard; it is better to germinate the pit in the dark.

Keep topping up with water as it evaporates so that the base of the pit is always just in water.

The time taken for germination varies greatly, and may be weeks. Eventually the pit will either rot because it was not fertile or will grow thick white roots and a shoot from the split in the top of the pit. Wait until there is a considerable growth of root and then transfer the plant to a pot, using a mixture of loam, peat and sand, or a peat-based compost. The top of the pit should be left showing just above the surface of the compost.

To germinate in compost, plant the pit blunt end down in a peat-based compost or, preferably, in a mixture of loam, peat and sand, leaving the top just showing above the surface. Enclose the pot in a plastic bag and put it near a radiator or in a warm cupboard.

The vital operation of cutting back to ensure a bushy plant, whether it has been germinated in water or directly in compost, is carried out when the growing stem is not more than eight inches (20 cm) long. Cut it back to about five inches (12.5 cm). This removes all the leaves; all that is left is a bare stem, but before long new shoots will appear. An uncut stem grows spindly with few leaves.

Special Instructions: As the plant grows in size year by year it can be kept bushy by pinching out the growing tips.

Podocarpus macrophyllus

A member of the yew family, the podocarpus reaches massive proportions growing wild in China and Japan. In its infancy it has dense foliage and makes an agreeable if not dramatic pot plant. *P. macrophyllus*, commonly known as the Japanese yew, has long, narrow leaves which are yellow-green on the surface and slightly bluish underneath. Another species *P. gracilior*, the African fern pine, grows into a huge tree when it is mature, but indoors it does not grow quickly and its long, dark green leaves make it an attractive houseplant.

The Doctor says —

Environment: *P. macrophyllus* needs to be kept cool from autumn until early spring, with temperatures between 40 and 45°F (4 and 7°C). It does not require great heat to bring it into growth in summer; 45 to 55°F (7 to 13°C) is adequate. If possible put the plant outdoors in summer, but not in direct sunlight, even in a little shade. If it is kept indoors it should be in an airy room.

Water: Frequently from spring until early autumn. In the cool winter months water only when the compost is barely moist.

Feed: Every two weeks from spring until early autumn.

Repot: After the initial burst of growth the plant will grow quite slowly and will need repotting only every two or three years in spring.

Propagate: From seed in spring or by cuttings in summer.

Green Foliage Plants

Rhoicissus rhomboidea

The grape ivy, or Natal ivy, is a vine not unlike *Cissus antarctica* in general appearance, but it is more naturally at home in warmer rooms. The serrated leaves are light brown when young and a little hairy, but they become smooth, shiny and dark green as they age. The plant climbs by tendrils and since it may grow to six feet (1.8 m) it will need some support. *R. rhomboidea* is often sold as *Cissus rhombifolia* while *R. capensis*, the Cape grape, a vigorous, easily grown vine, often turns up as *Cissus capensis*. The large leaves are best described as squashed heart-shaped with wavy edges, and they have reddish hairs on the undersides. Older plants may produce unremarkable flowers followed by glossy red berries.

The Doctor Says—

Environment: From autumn until early spring a maximum temperature of 50°F (10°C) is desirable, while in the summer months the ideal range is 55 to 65°F (13 to 18°C). For the hardier *R. capensis* the temperatures can be lower. Provide plenty of light, but not direct hot sunlight, and an airy situation. To increase humidity, spray regularly in summer.
Water: Fairly frequently from spring until early autumn; occasionally for the rest of the year.
Feed: Every two weeks from spring until early autumn.
Repot: Each spring in a loam-based compost.
Propagate: In spring from cuttings.
Special Instructions: Pinch out new shoots to encourage bushiness.

Schefflera actinophylla

This is an elegant plant for a large room. Widely spaced branches carry long stems from which radiate from three to more than seven bright green leaves—like the rays of the sun (the meaning of *actinophylla*) or, less poetically, the spokes of an umbrella (hence its common name, Queensland umbrella tree). Although it is slow growing, the plant can reach eight feet (2.40 m) indoors, while in its Australian habitat it grows to one hundred and twenty feet (40 m).

The Doctor Says—

Environment: From autumn until early spring, while the plant is dormant, the temperature should not fall below 55°F (13°C) or stay above 60°F (16°C). During the summer growing period, the temperature should be within the range of 55 to 65°F (13 to 18°C) if the growth is to be sturdy. The plant also needs plenty of light, but not direct sunlight.

Water: Frequent watering will be necessary from spring until early autumn; at other times keep the compost moist and never in danger of drying out. The plant needs a humid atmosphere and spraying the leaves will help.
Feed: Every two weeks from spring until early autumn.
Repot: Every other year in spring, using a loam-based compost.
Propagate: From seed sown in summer.
Special Instructions: If winter temperatures are too low there is considerable danger of leaf fall; if the temperature is too high scale insects are encouraged.

Scirpus cernuus

The slender club rush is a modest, graceful marsh plant from southern Europe and North Africa. At first the wiry, dark green blades, about ten inches (25 cm) long, grow stiffly erect, but later they arch over the sides of the pot. This plant is at its most attractive in summer when small, rush-like flowers appear near the tips of the blades. It may be difficult to obtain.

The Doctor Says —

Environment: From autumn until early spring the plant will continue to grow if it is kept in temperatures between 50 and 55°F (10 and 13°C), but the temperature can safely fall somewhat lower. For the rest of the year temperatures in the range of 55 to 65°F (13 to 18°C) will be needed. Give the plant good light in winter, but some shade and no direct sun during the summer months.
Water: Since this is a marsh plant it obviously needs plenty of water all year round. Keep it standing in a saucer or bowl containing water and spray regularly in warm weather.
Feed: Every two weeks from spring until early autumn.
Repot: Every spring in a loam-based compost.
Propagate: By division when repotting.
Special Instructions: The tips of the blades are liable to turn brown if the air is too dry and the compost is not wet enough.

Syngonium podophyllum

The goosefoot plant (or African evergreen, although it comes from Central and South America) is a philodendron-like climber or trailer for a warm room. There are several cultivars. One of these, 'Emerald Gem', is a more compact plant and has arrowhead-shaped leaves of a rich, glossy green. There are also variegated forms. The plant likes to be supported by a moss stick into which the aerial roots can grow.

The Doctor Says —

Environment: From autumn until early spring this plant must have a temperature no lower than 60°F (16°C). For the rest of the year the range should be between 65 and 75°F (18 and 24°C). While it likes a fairly good light, it should not be exposed to direct sunlight, especially in the summer months.

Water: Frequently from spring until early autumn, keeping the compost just damp for the rest of the year. If the plant is being overwintered in a warm room the compost will dry out quickly and may need fairly frequent watering. Humidity is also important and spraying the leaves will be beneficial.
Feed: Every two weeks from spring until early autumn.
Repot: Each spring, using a loam-based or a peat-based compost.
Propagate: By stem cuttings in summer.

Green Foliage Plants

Tetrastigma voinierianum

The chestnut vine, to use its more pronounceable name, is a vigorous climber from Indo-China, suitable for a fairly warm and quite large room. It is not unlike a cissus, but the leaves are larger. They consist of five serrated leaflets, each one at least five inches (12.5 cm) long, glossy green on the surface and slightly hairy underneath. It will need long stakes to support it. Grown indoors it is unlikely to produce any flowers, which are very small and green. It may be hard to obtain.

The Doctor Says—

Environment: From autumn until early spring the temperature should be between 55 and 60°F (13 and 16°C)

rising to 65°F (18°C) in the summer months. The plant needs good light, but not direct sunlight. It is fairly tolerant of dry air, but spraying the leaves in warm weather will do it good.
Water: Very frequently from spring until early autumn, but during the rest of the year keep the compost barely moist.
Feed: Weekly from spring until early autumn.
Repot: Because of its vigorous growth it will need repotting every year in spring. Either a loam-based or a peat-based compost is suitable.
Propagate: From cuttings taken in summer.
Special Instructions: If the leaves turn yellow it may be because the plant is not being fed well enough for its size.

Tolmiea menziesii

This American plant is an oddity, popular because of the interesting way in which it reproduces itself. This it does by growing a small plantlet at the joint of the leaf and the stalk, hence the variety of its common names on the same theme — piggyback plant, mother of thousands, hen and chick. Its other attraction is that it is easy to grow. The leaves are light green and hairy, the flowers greenish brown and insignificant.

The Doctor Says—

Environment: From autumn until early spring the temperature should not fall below 45°F (7°C), and can go higher than that. Around 55°F (13°C) is a good summer temperature. The plant will tolerate a fair amount of shade, but it does better in the light as long as it is not in direct sunlight.
Water: Very frequently from spring until early autumn; fairly frequently for the rest of the year. Lack of water will cause the leaves to become limp and to shrivel.
Feed: Weekly from spring until early autumn.
Repot: Each spring in a peat-based compost.
Propagate: By removing and planting the small plantlets in spring and summer.
Special Instructions: Growth will be weak if the plant is kept in too much shade.

Yucca aloifolia

A well-grown yucca is a striking plant well worth house room—if there is room for it. The young plants are interesting enough, but only when they are mature will there be any chance of the long panicles of creamy white flowers. *Y. aloifolia* produces its sword-like, dark green leaves in a rosette. As the new leaves grow and the lower leaves die a spiky trunk develops. *Y. elephantipes* is similar in appearance, but the leaves are softer. *Y. filamentosa* reaches a height of three feet (90 cm) and the flower panicles, produced in summer, may be up to six feet (1.80 m) long. All these species come from the United States, Mexico or the West Indies.

The Doctor Says—

Environment: From autumn until early spring the plant must be kept in a cool place where the temperature is not more than 45°F (7°C); this is important. For the summer months the temperature can be 55°F (13°C) and above. If at all possible the yucca should spend the summer outdoors in order to get all the sunshine it needs. It is also more likely to flower there. If it is kept indoors it must have the best possible light. A dry atmosphere does not seem to worry it.

Water: Frequently from spring until early autumn. During the cool dormant period only occasional watering will be necessary.

Feed: Every two weeks from spring until early autumn.

Repot: Once every two or three years in spring in a loam-based compost, with added sand.

Propagate: From seed in spring.

Yucca Cane Plant

The odd-looking, so-called cane plants have become increasingly popular in recent years. They have been grown from sawn-up sections of the bare, woody stems of certain plants that have been induced to root and then sprout. The stem will always remain the same height, so the plant will never outgrow its welcome. Cane plants can be bought in various sizes, from a modest twelve inches (30 cm) tall to giants of ten feet (3 m) or more. The bare stems are imported into the United States and Europe and then cut and rooted. The plants grown in this way that are normally on sale are *Yucca elephantipes*, which has sword-like, dark green leaves and *Dracaena fragrans* 'Massangeana', which has strap-shaped, glossy, dark green leaves striped with emerald green and yellow.

The Doctor Says—

Environment: From autumn until early spring the yucca needs a temperature around 45°F (8°C), while the dracaena cane plant must have a temperature no lower than 60°F (16°C), and preferably a little bit higher. For the rest of the year the dracaena must be kept around 70°F (21°C) in a humid atmosphere. The yucca also like to be warm, but will tolerate a wider range of temperatures and is not disturbed by dry air. In summer it benefits from being outdoors with as much sun as it can get. The dracaena needs good light, but should be shaded from the hot summer sun.

Water: Frequently from spring until early autumn, but occasionally for the rest of the year.

Feed: Every two weeks from late spring until early autumn.

Repot: Every other spring using a loam-based compost for a yucca, a peat-based compost for a dracaena.

Propagate: If you have a woody-stemmed dracaena or yucca which has grown tall and leggy you can convert it into a cane plant. First, you must air layer the top section in spring. When the top part has grown roots and has been severed from the old plant and potted, you will be left with a bare trunk. Cut that into sections, according to how tall you want the cane plants to be. Put each piece of stem—bottom end down—into compost and keep it in a temperature around 70°F (21°C) until it sprouts.

Ficus

There are ficus with small leaves and ficus with huge leaves. Some ficus climb, some trail, some grow stiffly erect, some are gracefully arching, and while some remain a manageable size, others will grow tall enough to reach the ceiling.

The most graceful is *F. benjamina*, the weeping fig from India, and the taller it grows the more elegant it is. The leaves are seldom more than four inches (10 cm) long and have slightly wavy edges. When they are young they are a bright light green, but later they turn dark glossy green.

F. nitida (syn. *F. lucida*), the Indian laurel, is like a small version of *F. benjamina*; the leaves themselves are only half the size, shiny mid green, and are carried in profusion. *Ficus diversifolia* (syn. *F. deltoidea*) also has small leaves, about two inches (5 cm) long, pear-shaped, dark green and leathery. It also carries yellowish berries, hence its common name, the mistletoe fig. In India and Malaya it grows as an epiphyte on the branches of trees; in a pot it stays a small shrub, about twenty-four inches (60 cm) tall with rather formally spaced branches.

Smaller still is *F. pumila*, the creeping fig from China. The thickly growing, heart-shaped leaves, only about one inch (2.5 cm) long, are carried on long stems which can be allowed to climb or trail.

The most widely seen large-leaved ficus is undoubtedly the India rubber plant, *F. elastica*. *F.e.* 'Decora' is the usual form, and its shiny, leathery, dark green leaves may grow twelve inches (30 cm) long. Before it grows too tall – it quickly reaches six feet (1.80 m) – the stem can be cut back to turn it into a branching plant. Variegated forms are *F.e.* 'Doescheri' and 'Tricolor'.

The leaves of *F. retusa*, the glossy leaf fig, resemble those of *F. elastica*, but the virtue of this ficus is that it naturally grows into a small, branching tree.

The most dramatic ficus is *F. lyrata* (syn. *F. pandurata*), the fiddle leaf fig, and it needs a large room to perform in. The wavy-edged leaves are some twelve inches (30 cm) long, dark green and leathery, and shaped like the body of a

fiddle or, some say, elephants' ears. Almost as striking is *F. nekbudu*; like *F. lyrata* it comes from tropical West Africa, but it is somewhat more difficult to look after.

F. *diversifolia* and *F. pumila* are the easiest ficus to grow, accepting cooler and shadier conditions than are suitable for the others.

The Doctor Says—

Environment: From autumn until early spring the temperature should be in the range of 55 to 60°F (13 to 16°C). Although *F. pumila* and *F. diversifolia* will survive at 45°F (7°C) it is better if the temperature is above 50°F (10°C). None should have temperatures much above 60°F (16°C) during these months because the plants are then dormant. For the rest of the year the temperature range should be between 65 and 75°F (18 and 24°C). *F. pumila* likes shade, but the others will do better in a good light, while tolerating a certain amount of shade. They should not be in direct sun, especially when new leaves are emerging and can be easily scorched. Variegated ficus, like variegated plants in general, need better light than the plain green varieties. They like an airy situation, but loathe draughts. Sponge the leaves regularly, both the top surfaces and the undersides, so that the plant can breathe.

Water: Frequently from spring until early autumn. For the rest of the year water infrequently; in the winter months it is less dangerous to underwater than overwater. As the result of overwatering the edges of the leaves will turn brown or the leaves may drop off.

Feed: Every two weeks from spring until early autumn.

Repot: Once every two years in spring should be sufficient. Use either a peat-based compost or one made of equal parts of loam, peat, leaf mould and sharp sand.

Propagate: By cuttings in summer.

Special Instructions: If the lower leaves droop in winter it is an indication that the temperature is too high.

63

Philodendron

Central heating brought the philodendron indoors from the greenhouses to which it had been taken from the tropical regions of South and Central America. Given warmth it is one of the easier houseplants to keep alive. In the United States, the climbing heart-leaf philodendron is the best-selling houseplant of all, but there are other philodendrons which are more dramatic, and just as adaptable to indoor life. There are bushy types—although some will grow too large for most ordinary rooms—and climbers.

Of the climbers *Philodendron andreanum*, the velour philodendron, is probably the most handsome. The heart-shaped leaves have a velvety texture, are dark green on top and have purplish undersides. It is often described as *P. melanchryson*, but this is not a separate species, merely the infant version of *P. andreanum*. It is at this stage that it is usually bought as a houseplant, being then of a more manageable size. The young leaves are about six inches (15 cm) long, but grow four times the size when mature. *P. erubescens* is called the blushing philodendron, because the emerging leaves are rosy pink. Later they turn dark green with a coppery sheen while the undersides are a deep red. The leaves are shaped like arrowheads and eventually grow about ten inches (25 cm) long. *P. oxycardium* (or *P. scandens*), the parlour ivy or heart-leaf philodendron, is the best known and most tolerant. It is a vigorous climber and needs support, but it is just as effective, and less trouble, when allowed to trail. The heart-shaped leaves are a dark, glossy green and usually about six inches (15 cm) long. *P. panduraeforme* has leaves of varying shapes, as suggested by its popular names—the fiddle leaf or horse's head. They are mid green and their appearance is leathery. *P. pertusum* is now called *Monstera deliciosa* (see page 56).

The climbing philodendrons have aerial roots through which, in the wild, they absorb moisture and food. Indoors the plant will benefit if it is trained up a

moss stick (always kept damp by spraying) into which the aerial roots can be pushed to take in additional moisture.

The leaves of some of the bushy philodendrons are most striking. *P. selloum*, the lacy tree philodendron, saddle leaf or finger leaf, is very similar when young, to *P. bipinnatifidum*. The leaves start heart-shaped but later become deeply divided. They also grow very large; those of *P. bipinnatifidum* will be about eighteen inches (45 cm) long, and those of *P. selloum* up to three feet (90 cm) long. These are plants for large rooms. *P. wendlandii*, another non-climber, is totally different in appearance from other philodendrons. The dark green leaves are lance-shaped, about twelve inches (30 cm) long, and grow in the form of a rosette.

The Doctor Says—

Environment: Undemanding though philodendrons in many respects may be they do need warmth. From autumn until early spring temperatures in the range of 60 to 65°F (16 to 18°C) are ideal. For the rest of the year the range should be 65 to 75°F (18 to 24°C). They will grow in either light or partly shaded conditions, but they should not be exposed to direct sun, especially in the summer months. They do best in a humid atmosphere, so it helps to keep the pot in a larger container of moist peat or to stand it on a layer of wet pebbles, and to spray the leaves often.

Water: Frequently from spring until early autumn. At other times infrequent watering will suffice.

Feed: Every two weeks from spring until early autumn.

Repot: Every other year in spring, using an all-peat compost.

Propagate: By taking cuttings of stems or growing tips in summer.

Special Instructions: To make *P. oxycardium* grow bushy, pinch out the growing tips. Give thanks that philodendrons are remarkably free of pests and diseases.

Palms

A revival of the once supreme palms is overdue, for their appeal is unique. The leaves, which grow outward from a single, long, flexible stem, are usually in the shape of fans or feathers and divide into many leaflets. Palms must be kept moist all the time. Underwatering and dry air can cause the tips of the leaves to turn brown and these spots will never disappear.

Chamaedorea elegans

This graceful palm, with arching stalks and narrow leaves, is as elegant as its name implies, even when it is sold as *Neanthe elegans*, *N. bella* or *Collinia elegans*, or by one of its common names – parlour palm or good luck palm. Growth is slow and its height seldom exceeds four feet (1.20 m) indoors. It cannot be relied on to flower, but when it does the yellow flowers are carried on mimosa-like sprays, and may be followed by berries. A native of Mexico, in the wild it grows in the shade of taller trees and, therefore, needs moist shade indoors.

The Doctor Says —

Environment: Likes partial shade and dislikes high temperatures; the summer average should be about 65°F (18°C), but in winter not higher than 55°F (13°C).
Water: Frequently in summer, and spray often. In winter keep the soil just moist.
Feed: Monthly from early spring until autumn; never in winter.
Repot: When the plant is young every other year in spring in a peat-based compost which is one-third sand. Less frequently as the plant grows older.
Propagate: By seed in spring in a heated propagator (75°F, 24°C). Propagation is tricky because germination is very slow and the seedlings are easily broken when transplanting.
Special Instructions: Watch for scale insects and red spider mites to which this palm is susceptible.

Chamaerops humilis

Not surprisingly, this palm is popularly known as the European fan palm, for the leaves are most delicately fan-shaped and it is the only palm which grows wild in Europe, mainly in Spain and southern Italy. Its habitat has made it hardier than most palms and it can even be housed in an unheated room. The "fans" may be eighteen inches (45 cm) long and the leaves are a beautiful greyish green. *C. elegans*, which has silvery leaves, is smaller and therefore makes a particularly good houseplant.

The Doctor Says —

Environment: This is a palm which requires light in summer and winter. In summer it grows best at a temperature around 55°F (13°C), but it will, of course, tolerate a higher one. In winter a temperature of 45°F (7°C) is all right, but no harm is done if it falls to 40°F (4°C).
Water: This palm will need very frequent watering through late spring and summer; for the rest of the year water only occasionally.
Feed: Every two weeks from early spring until autumn.
Repot: The plant may need moving to a slightly larger pot in early spring every second or third year, but this must be done with great care for the roots can be easily damaged.
Propagate: Remove the suckers when repotting and plant them in a free-draining peat and sand compost.
Special Instructions: When the new leaves of *C. humilis* emerge they are covered with what looks like grey meal. This is perfectly natural, not a disease.

Chrysalidocarpus lutescens

This palm has other drawbacks besides its name. One of these is its size, for even in cultivation it can grow into a large bushy tree up to twenty feet (6 m) tall. And, since it is a native of Mauritius, it needs more heat and greater humidity than many people do in their homes. You can, however, get around the tongue-twisting name, which derives from the Greek for golden fruit, by thinking of it as the areca palm, or yellow butterfly palm, because of its yellowish stems.

The Doctor says—

Environment: The atmosphere must be humid and warm all year round—in the 70s F during the day (at least 21°C) and not lower than 60°F (16°C) at night.
Water: Will need frequent watering all year.
Feed: Monthly from spring until autumn.
Repot: Pot on every spring to keep up with the growth of this palm for as long as is feasible. When the plant is young use a compost of half peat and half loam, but as it gets older change to one part of loam and one of sand, plus horse manure or dehydrated cow manure.
Propagate: By seed in spring.

Cycas revoluta

There are a number of palms which look more like ferns and this plant, which has long, stiffly arching fronds divided into a hundred or more narrow segments, is one of them. A native of Japan and China, its common name is sago palm. Like *C. circinalis*, the fern palm, which comes from the East Indies, it is grown for the extraction of sago. While they are young, both of these plants are suitable as pot plants, but as they grow they are better transferred into tubs. The related *C. media*, the gaveu nut tree, comes from Australia where the large seeds, when rendered non-poisonous by long cooking, are eaten by aborigines.

The Doctor says—

Environment: These palms will tolerate lower temperatures than those to which they are accustomed in their native habitats. Around the 65°F (18°C) mark would be satisfactory in summer and a little lower in winter.
Water: Will need to be watered very frequently in summer, and fairly often in winter.
Feed: Every two weeks from spring until autumn.
Repot: Will need potting on each spring and should eventually be removed to tubs.
Propagate: By seed in spring.

Palms

Howea forsteriana

This droopy palm is one of the most popular and, fortunately, one of the best for growing indoors. Though widespread in captivity, it is found growing naturally only on the small Lord Howe Island in the Pacific. It is from the capital of that island that it derives the name by which it is best known—the Kentia palm. Its less prosaic name is paradise palm. A young plant, with leaves which at that stage are quite erect, looks well in a pot, but as it grows and bows with age it is more attractive standing on the floor in a tub.

The Doctor Says—

Environment: In its native jungle the Kentia palm is accustomed to growing in the shade and it will tolerate being in a room too dark for many other plants. It certainly does not like strong sunshine. Aim for a summer temperature between 55 and 65°F (13 and 18°C) and a winter temperature of 55°F (13°C).

Water: Needs most frequent watering when the new leaves appear. In winter water just often enough to keep the compost moist.

Feed: Every two weeks from early spring until autumn.

Repot: When young may need to be repotted every other spring, but when mature repotting may not be necessary.

Propagate: By seed in early spring; much warmth (75 to 80°F, 24 to 27°C) is needed, as well as patience; the seeds take up to nine months to germinate.

Special Instructions: Very hard water may cause the leaf tips to turn brown.

Microelum martianum

This small palm—the dwarf coconut or terrarium palm—might, but for one thing, seem the perfect palm for a small room since it can take twenty years to reach six feet (1.80 m). The snag is that it comes from the tropical rain forests of Brazil and it would be undesirable, if not extremely difficult, to reproduce these conditions in your home. For some years, however, it will put up with the kind of comfort you want and, if you're lucky, it may adapt to your life-style.

The Doctor Says—

Environment: In summer the plant should be in partial shade with the temperature between 65 and 70°F (18 and 21°C). Place the pot in a larger container filled with moist peat, especially when new leaves are growing. In winter a temperature between 60 and 65°F (13 and 18°C) is desirable.

Water: Frequently, with soft water, from late spring until late autumn, and spray often. Keep the compost barely moist for the rest of the year.

Feed: Every ten days from late spring until early autumn.

Repot: Every other spring, but with care, since the roots react badly to even slight damage.

Propagate: In spring, by seed. While possible, it is nevertheless quite difficult.

Special Instructions: Leaves will turn brown if the soil dries out or if hard water is used.

Phoenix canariensis

Of the various date palms *Phoenix canariensis*, from the Canary Islands, is the hardiest and easiest to grow and *P. roebelenii*, the miniature date palm or pigmy date palm from India, is the most graceful and most difficult. Naturally, therefore, *P. canariensis* is the date palm usually grown as a houseplant.

The Doctor Says—

Environment: In summer *P. canariensis* likes the sun and (perversely for an indoor plant) prefers to enjoy it outdoors. In winter it appreciates good light and does not mind the cold; 40°F (4°C) is satisfactory. *P. roebelenii*, on the other hand, needs a moist, shady spot, never cooler than 60°F (16°C).

Water: If it is growing in a free-draining compost, as it should be, *P. canariensis* can be watered very frequently in summer—but be miserly in winter.
Feed: Each week from early spring until summer.
Repot: When the palm is young, pot on every year in spring, but as it gets older repot only when it is in danger of becoming potbound.
Propagate: In spring, by seed, which take a long time to germinate, but otherwise cause little difficulty.
Special Instructions: Leaves may turn yellow because of insufficient light. The tips may turn brown because of hard water, too much water or far too little water.

Rhaphis excelsa

This palm is known contradictorily both as the large lady palm and the little lady palm, but since it is a tufty dwarf palm "little" seems more apt. It has fan-shaped leaves on quite short stems and as the palm grows older the divisions in the leaves become deeper. Native to both China and Japan, *R. excelsa* was first brought to the West from Japan by the great plant hunter Robert Fortune in the middle of the nineteenth century. *R. humilis*, also from Japan, looks much the same. Both are reasonably amenable as houseplants if they are treated properly.

The Doctor Says—

Environment: Likes partial shade and dislikes high temperatures; the summer average about 65°F (18°C), but in winter not higher than 55°F (13°C).
Water: Very often in summer and spray frequently. In winter keep the soil just moist, not wet.
Feed: Monthly from early spring until autumn; never in winter.
Repot: When young every other year in spring in a peat-based compost which is one-third sand. Less frequently as the palm grows older.
Propagate: By seed in spring in a heated propagator (75°F, 24°C).
Special Instructions: Watch for scale insects and red spider mites.

Ferns

Hardy ferns went out of favour when homes became well heated. Now ferns which need or tolerate heat are taking their place. These, nevertheless, must have a humid atmosphere and standing the pots on wet pebbles or burying them in moist peat will help. In the past, ferns were likely to fall victim to coal and gas fumes. Today the aerosol pesticide spray is the number one fern killer.

Adiantum

The maidenhair ferns are too attractive for their own good, for they are often condemned to languish and die in an environment entirely unsuited to them. They all need shade and a very moist atmosphere. Those from temperate parts of the world, such as *A. capillus-veneris*, which grows wild in the United States and Britain, need cool, moist shade. Those from the tropics must have warm, moist shade, of the kind found in a warm greenhouse. Some people, however, are luckier with them than others, for no apparent reason, and the most popular tropical species are the graceful *A. cuneatum* (syn. *A. raddianum*), the Delta maidenhair, which has fronds up to fifteen inches (37 cm) long, and *A. tenerum*, the fan maidenhair, which has fronds up to three feet (90 cm) long.

The Doctor Says—
Environment: From mid-autumn until early spring *A. capillus-veneris* requires a minimum temperature of 45°F (7°C) and a summer temperature of 45 to 55°F (7 to 13°C). *A. cuneatum* needs a minimum winter temperature of 55°F (13°C); and 65 to 75°F (18 to 24°C) in summer. In winter *A. tenerum* appreciates it if the temperature is about 55°F (13°C) and in summer ranges from 55 to 65°F (13 to 18°C). They all need some shade, especially from spring until early autumn, and must never be put in hot direct sunlight. They also need to be in a very humid atmosphere and out of draughts.
Water: Frequently from spring until early autumn; occasionally for the rest of the year to keep the compost just moist.
Feed: Every three or four weeks from spring until early autumn.
Repot: Each spring in an all-peat compost or in a mixture of equal parts of loam, peat and sand.
Propagate: By division in spring.
Special Instructions: Any dying fronds should be cut off cleanly at the base.

Asplenium bulbiferum

This is a good fern for a beginner. It is graceful, easy to grow and fascinatingly easy to propagate. Bulbils grow on long, arching fronds and in the wild—in New Zealand, Australia and India—when they touch the ground they take root. In captivity, since the bulbils cannot be expected to root in the carpet, they have to be removed and potted. This form of reproduction is responsible for the fern's two matriarchal common names—the hen and chick fern and mother spleenwort.

The Doctor Says—
Environment: From autumn until early spring a minimum temperature around 55°F (13°C) would be satisfactory although a somewhat lower temperature would be tolerated. In summer the temperature range should be 55 to 65°F (13 to 18°C). Throughout the year the plant needs a fairly light position—not in direct sunlight and certainly not in deep gloom. Plunging the pot in peat or standing it on a dish of wet pebbles will help to provide the humid atmosphere this fern requires.
Water: Frequently from spring until early autumn; fairly frequently for the rest of the year.
Feed: Weekly from spring until early autumn.
Repot: In spring, in an all-peat compost or in a mixture of equal parts of loam, peat and sharp sand.
Propagate: The bulbils which grow on the surface of the fronds can be removed and potted in a loam, peat and sand compost. Alternatively, the plant can be divided when it has grown to a good size. Either of these operations should be performed in spring.

Asplenium nidus

The bird's nest fern is an odd one out among aspleniums. It grows on the branches of trees in tropical rain forests and its fronds are not divided. In the wild it may look like a bird's nest when seen from below, but since we see it from above it is more like a glossy green shuttlecock of shoehorn-shaped fronds. It requires a fairly constant temperature all year round, so it is not the easiest of ferns to keep alive for many years.

The Doctor Says—

Environment: To stay in good condition the plant needs a temperature range of 60 to 65°F (16 to 18°C) all year. Varieties of asplenium which have leaves with black midribs will, however, tolerate rather lower temperatures. Keep the fern in good light throughout the year, but out of direct sunlight. A humid atmosphere is essential from spring until early autumn; the choice is between putting the pot in a container of damp peat or standing it on a dish of wet pebbles. Regular spraying also helps.

Water: Frequently from spring until early autumn, pouring some water on the centre of the rosette where in nature the plant collects most of its moisture. For the rest of the year water only the compost and only as often as is necessary to keep it just moist.

Feed: Once a month from spring until early autumn should be sufficient, but since this fern is epiphytic and has a small root system a foliar feed is the most effective.

Repot: Aspleniums do not make a mass of roots and therefore do not become potbound quickly, so repotting is more a question of balancing the size of the plant with the pot. Repotting, when necessary, should be done in spring, using a peat-based compost because good drainage is essential.

Propagate: The most common, and most difficult, method is by spores, which appear in rows on the undersides of the leaves.

71

Ferns

Blechnum gibbum

This is a popular fern, probably because it has the air of a palm, especially when it grows older. It then develops a small, scaly trunk which carries the crown of heavily segmented fronds which are light green and glossy. They may grow up to three feet (90 cm) long, making this a very distinguished looking houseplant. Unlike many ferns, *B. gibbum*'s home is not in damp jungle, but in a warm, temperate zone; it was discovered a century ago in New Caledonia, one of the Pacific Islands. From there it brought its need of warmth and good light all year round.

The Doctor Says—

Environment: From autumn until early spring the temperature should not fall much below 55°F (13°C), rising for the rest of the year into the range of 65 to 75°F (18 to 24°C). Good light, but not direct sunlight, is needed all year, and during the spring and summer it needs as much humidity as possible.
Water: Will need frequent watering from spring until early autumn and fairly frequent watering the rest of the year.
Feed: Every two weeks from spring until early autumn.
Repot: In spring each year, in either an all-peat compost or, preferably, in a mixture of equal parts of loam, peat and sand.
Propagate: Best to avoid, since propagation from spores is a difficult operation and division can ruin the plant's appearance.

Cyrtomium falcatum

Unfairly, the holly fern, or fish tail fern, is often made to suffer for being so easygoing, as ferns go. Although it will survive cold, draughts and poor light there is no reason why it should and it will be a far more attractive plant if it does not have to. But do not go to the other extremes—it does prefer to be cool for much of the year. It grows quickly and the dark green fronds will reach eighteen inches (45 cm) in length. *C.f.* 'Rochfordianum' is rather more compact, but the leaflets of the fronds are larger and more like holly leaves.

The Doctor Says—

Environment: Shade, humidity and a fair amount of warmth in the growing season are the main needs of this fern. From autumn until early spring the temperature should not drop much below 50°F (10°C) and it is better if it stays above that. For the rest of the year temperatures up to 65°F (18°C) will be needed to achieve sturdy growth. Regular spraying during the growing season will be of benefit. Never allow the plant to be exposed to hot, direct sun.
Water: Frequently from spring until early autumn. In the winter months water only as often as is necessary to keep the compost just moist.

Feed: Every two weeks from spring until early autumn.

Repot: This fern grows rapidly so it will probably have to be repotted every year. Do this in spring, using an all-peat compost or a mixture of equal parts of loam, peat and sharp sand.

Propagate: Division is easy and should be done in spring when repotting. Growing from spores is the hard way.

Special Instructions: The fronds when young may be covered with brown or white scales, this is the character of the plant, not a symptom of disease.

Nephrolepis exaltata

Sword fern, ladder fern, Boston fern—whatever you call it this tropical fern is fairly easy to grow and hard not to adore. It is often recommended as a hanging-basket plant because the long fronds arch so elegantly over the edge, but if you grow it this way you don't have the pleasure of watching the new fronds emerge. From *N. exaltata* numerous cultivars have been raised; among the most attractive are *N.e.* 'Whitmannii', which has finely feathered, pale green fronds, and the vigorous *N.e.* 'Rooseveltii' which is a magnificent plant, perhaps to stand in a large container on the floor.

The Doctor Says—

Environment: This fern tolerates a fair amount of light as well as a fair amount of shade, but with the proviso that it must never be placed in hot, direct sun. Unless temperatures are excessive it also tolerates living all year in a heated room. From autumn until early spring it requires a minimum temperature between 55 and 60°F (13 and 16°C) and average summer temperatures between 55 and 65°F (13 and 18°C) for good growth.

Water: Very frequently from spring until early autumn, plus regular spraying of the fronds. For the rest of the year watering should be infrequent, but of course the warmer the room in which it spends the winter the more water it will need. The compost must never be allowed to get dry.

Feed: Every two weeks from spring until early autumn.

Repot: Every two years in spring in a peat-based compost.

Propagate: By removing and repotting the plantlet-bearing runners which the fern provides. Division is possible, but will result in a less attractive plant.

Pellaea rotundifolia

Although it is called button fern, because the small leaves are round when young, or the cliff brake fern, after its home in the mountains of New Zealand, this plant hardly looks like a fern at all. The dark brown stems, barely twelve inches (30 cm) long, carry twelve or more pairs of dark green, glossy, leathery leaflets, which are downy or hairy on the undersides. Although the leaves start life rotund, they become oval with age.

The Doctor Says—

Environment: Two important requirements of this fern are plenty of fresh air all year round and protection from direct sunlight. From autumn until early spring aim at a constant temperature around 55°F (13°C). The summer temperatures can range from 55°F (13°C) to 65°F (18°C).

Water: Frequently from spring until early autumn; in winter keep the compost just moist, without letting it dry out. This fern likes lime, so there is no problem if the water is hard. Do not spray with water because this has an adverse effect on the downy undersides of the leaves.

Feed: Every two weeks from spring until late summer.

Repot: Probably necessary only once every two years. It should then be done in spring, using a peat-based compost.

Propagate: By division in spring or from spores.

Ferns

Polypodium aureum

P. aureum (syn. *P. glaucum*) is the most generally available hare's foot fern, the popular name which describes the rhizome's resemblance to furry feet. The fronds are blue-green with golden spore cases on the undersides, and they can grow three feet (90 cm) long. Another form *P.a.* 'Mandaianum' is much the same, but the leaves have crinkly edges.

The Doctor Says—

Environment: From spring until early autumn keep the fern in a temperature range of 55 to 65°F (13 to 18°C). For the rest of the year the temperature can be about 55°F (13°C) or a little higher. Do not expose it to direct sunlight. The humidity it needs is best provided by placing the pot in a container of moist peat.

Water: Frequently from spring until early autumn; for the rest of the year keep the compost just moist—it must never dry out.

Feed: Every two weeks from spring until early autumn.

Repot: Every other spring in a peat-based compost.

Propagate: By division in spring or from spores.

Platycerium bifurcatum

There is no more striking house fern than the stag's horn fern, a native of Australia and the East Indies. *P. bifurcatum* (syn. *P. alcicorne*) is the one most commonly grown. It has two types of frond: circular sterile fronds which die off each year and the fertile, forked fronds, which look like horns and are two to three feet (60 to 90 cm) long. *P. grande*, the regal elk-horn fern, which grows in the wild from eastern Australia to the Philippines, is even more magnificent. The dark green, fertile fronds can be up to five feet (1.50 cm) long, rather overpowering for a small apartment.

The Doctor Says—

Environment: The temperature range throughout the year should be 55 to 65°F (13 to 18°C). Even from autumn until early spring it is best that the temperature be above the minimum of 55°F (13°C). Shade is needed all year. Providing the humidity this epiphyte needs is something of a problem, especially if it is grown high in a hanging basket, where the air will be drier and warmer. The basket should be large, not only because the plant will grow big but also to hold enough moist compost to maintain a humid microclimate around the plant. Do not spray excessively, or you will remove the down or wax-like covering on the leaves. If the plant is grown in a pot, place it in a container filled with moist peat.

Water: Frequently from spring until early autumn; for the rest of the year only often enough to keep the compost just moist.

Feed: Every two weeks from spring until late summer.

Repot: Every three years in spring in a compost of peat and sphagnum moss.

Propagate: By plantlets from the base of the plant in summer.

Special Instructions: Many plants in hanging baskets are given less attention than those within easier reach. They need more.

Polystichum acrostichoides

The shield ferns are to be found in woods and under hedges in many temperate parts of the world, but that is no reason for not welcoming them in our homes. *P. acrostichoides*, which is also known as the holly fern, is an attractive, bushy plant, with dark green, glossy fronds up to two feet (60 cm) long. *P. tsus-simense*, from China and Japan, is a more compact and slow-growing version.

The Doctor Says—

Environment: From autumn until early spring a temperature pretty close— whether lower or higher— to 55°F (13°C) is desirable. The temperature can go up to 65°F (18°C) in the summer months for good growth. Keep the fern in a fairly shady part of the room and provide some humidity—by spraying, surrounding the pot with moist peat, or standing it on wet pebbles.

Water: Frequently from spring until early autumn, occasionally at other times. If the fern is allowed to get too dry the leaves will begin to fall off.

Feed: Once a month from spring until early autumn.

Repot: Repotting need not be done every year. Every third spring should be adequate, especially for *P. tsus-simense* which grows slowly. Use a mixture of equal parts of loam, peat and sharp sand.

Propagate: Simply by division in spring, or painstakingly from spores.

Pteris cretica

There are several hundred species of pteris in the world and almost fifty of them are in cultivation as houseplants. One reason is that they are so easygoing. The best known is *P. cretica*, the Cretan brake, which grows twelve to eighteen inches (30 to 45 cm) tall and has deeply divided, light green fronds. A particularly attractive variety is *P.c.* 'Albo-lineata', called the ribbon brake because of the broad, whitish green streak which runs the length of the leaflets. The cultivar 'Wimsetii' is a larger version of *P. cretica*, with deeply divided fronds and light green leaflets with crested edges. *P. ensiformis* 'Victoriae', the sword brake, is similar in general form to *P. cretica*, but the fronds are darker green and the leaflets have a silvery streak along the rib. *P. tremula*, the trembling fern from New Zealand and Australia, has large but less deeply divided fronds, and the stems may grow up to three feet (90 cm). It is not only larger than most pteris, it is also tougher.

The Doctor Says—

Environment: From autumn until early spring *P. cretica* and *P. tremula* will be satisfied with temperatures between 50 and 55°F (10 and 13°C), but *P. ensiformis* 'Victoriae' needs a minimum of 60°F (16°C). Summer temperatures can be in the low to mid-60sF (16 to 18°C). These ferns need partial shade throughout the year and must never be left in direct sunlight. Humidity is important in summer but, except for variegated forms, less so in the winter months.

Water: Very frequently from early spring until late summer; at all other times fairly frequently. The leaves shrivel if the compost is allowed to dry out. Hard water can be harmful.

Feed: Every two weeks from spring until late summer.

Repot: Each spring, in a mixture of equal parts of loam, peat and sand.

Propagate: From spores and, although a temperature around 75°F (24°C) is needed for germination, they are less tricky than the spores of many ferns. It may also be possible to divide the plant in spring.

Special Instructions: When a frond dies off remove the whole stalk with a clean cut at soil level.

Variegated Foliage Plants

Although some of these plants do flower, it is for their ornamental leaves that they are cultivated. Many of them are as colourful as flowering plants, with the advantage that they stay that way all year round. Always bear in mind that most variegated foliage plants need good light in winter as well as in summer if the markings are to retain their vividness.

Acalypha wilkesiana

Acalyphas are bushy shrubs which come from the tropics where they flourish in the warmth and humidity. Of the three which are most commonly seen as houseplants two—*A. godseffiana* and the more attractive *A. wilkesiana*—are grown for their brilliant foliage. *A. wilkesiana* comes from Polynesia and is known there as match-me-if-you-can because no two leaves are alike. The leaves may be margined with white or blotched with various colours. The colours include crimson, green, brown, bright red and copper, hence its common name copper leaf. Although the flowers are insignificant it rivals in brilliance *A. hispida*, or red hot cat's tail, the one acalypha grown for its flowers.

The Doctor Says—

Environment: The leaves may revert to green if they do not get enough light, but they must not be exposed to direct sunlight in summer. Acalyphas need warmth, with a winter temperature not below 60°F (16°C). They also require a humid atmosphere even when dormant, from early autumn until midwinter.
Water: Fairly frequently from early spring until late summer; occasionally the rest of the year.
Feed: Every two weeks from early spring until late summer.
Repot: In late winter each year in a peat-based compost.
Propagate: In spring using stem cuttings or basal shoots. They will root readily only if given plenty of heat.
Special Instructions: To keep the plant bushy, prune back the side shoots in its first year and the top shoots each year thereafter.

Acorus gramineus 'Variegatus'

It is hard to believe that this modest, little, grass-like plant, known as myrtle grass, belongs to a family which has provided so many striking houseplants, including monstera, dieffenbachia, philodendron, anthurium and caladium. Though not as grand as those, it is an attractive plant with the great virtue that it is hardy. The leaves, which grow in dense tufts about six to nine inches (15 to 23 cm) long, are green with white stripes. The flowers are modest to the point of insignificance. A native of Japan, it is a marshland plant and therefore has an insatiable thirst.

The Doctor Says —

Environment: Likes plenty of light, even some direct sun for part of the day. In winter it should be kept in a cold, but frost-free place.

Water: This is one of the few houseplants that is difficult to water too much in summer, but it does need considerably less frequent watering during the winter months when it is dormant.

Feed: Every two weeks from spring until early autumn.

Repot: In early spring, using a loam-based compost which will not dry out as rapidly as a peat-based compost.

Propagate: By division when repotting in early spring.

Aglaonema commutatum

That small is beautiful is certainly true of this Southeast Asian plant, the so-called Chinese evergreen. Its lance-shaped, somewhat leathery leaves are only about five inches (13 cm) long, borne on three-inch (8-cm) stems. The silver markings are striking on the dark green leaves and, as a bonus, this plant bears white spathes in summer. In the wild, *A. commutatum* grows in damp and dim tropical forests, indicating the type of conditions in which it flourishes.

The Doctor Says —

Environment: Needs a summer temperature between 65 and 75°F (18 and 24°C), not falling below 60°F (16°C) in winter. It resents sunlight and enjoys a humid atmosphere; standing the pot on a tray of wet pebbles will help. Do not spray for this may damage the leaves.

Water: Frequently, but only with tepid water, from spring through late summer; only occasionally during the dormant period from autumn until late winter.

Feed: Every two weeks during the growing period.

Repot: Every other spring in a peat-based compost.

Propagate: By division when repotting or by stem-tip cuttings in summer.

Aglaonema pictum

Although it comes from Malaya and Borneo, *A. pictum* is also called Chinese evergreen. It is larger than *A. commutatum* and has velvety leaves and blotchy variegations in different shades of green. Creamy spathes appear in summer.

The Doctor Says —

Environment: Like *A. commutatum*, during the growing period it needs to be kept warm, 65 to 75°F (18 to 24°C), in partial shade in a humid atmosphere. Surrounding the pot with moist peat or standing it on wet pebbles is helpful.

Water: Very frequently from spring until late summer, but in winter keep the compost no more than moist.

Feed: Every two weeks from spring through late summer.

Repot: In spring in an all-peat compost.

Propagate: By stem cuttings in summer.

Special Instructions: Remember, particularly in winter, that this plant needs warmth.

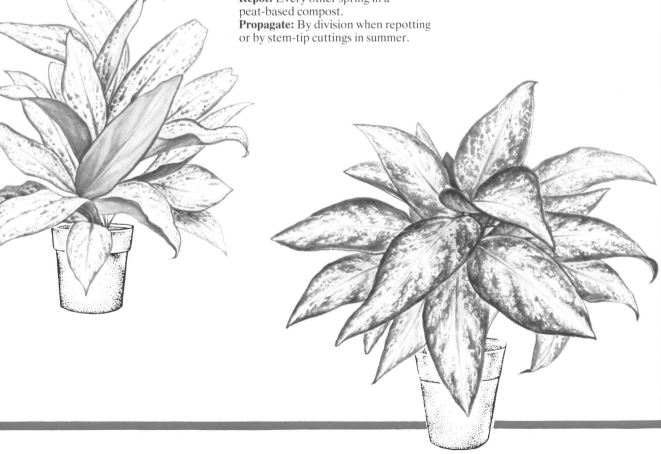

Variegated Foliage Plants

Aucuba japonica

The spotted laurel or gold dust plant is an easy-to-look-after evergreen from Japan. Its leaves are dark green, shiny (if kept clean) and spotted with yellow. The flowers, which appear in spring, have little merit, but they are sometimes followed by jolly red berries. Aucuba's great attraction is that it is undemanding and will do well even in a cool, shady room or on a stair landing. Unfortunately, it does not stay reasonably sized, but grows tall, often more than six feet (1.80 m), as well as bushy.

The Doctor Says—

Environment: Tolerates a fair amount of shade and cold; in winter it is best kept in temperatures in the low 40sF (around 7°C), but not exposed to frost.
Water: Frequently in summer, but only occasionally in the cold of winter.
Feed: Every two weeks from late spring until late summer.
Repot: In spring. When potted in a tub it can be planted in good garden soil.
Propagate: By cuttings in late summer or autumn.
Special Instructions: Sponge the leaves frequently, using only plain water. A light pruning in spring will keep the plant shapely.

Bertolonia marmorata

Appropriately called the jewel plant since it must have twenty-four carat conditions if it is to flourish, *B. marmorata* is a native of southern Brazil and demands warmth and humid surroundings. In return it grows beautiful, bright green, velvety leaves streaked silvery white on top and tinged with purple underneath. Unfortunately, even with the greatest care, the jewel plant rarely lives to a ripe old age. It is, too, often hard to find.

The Doctor Says—

Environment: Needs an even temperature around 70°F (21°C), shade and as much humidity as possible. Surrounding the pot with moist peat or standing it on wet pebbles will only be a palliative.
Water: Fairly frequently in spring and summer. Keep the compost barely moist in winter.
Feed: Monthly from spring until early autumn.
Repot: Every other year in late spring or early summer in an all-peat compost.
Propagate: By division of basal stem cuttings in summer or by seed in spring in a heated propagator.

Caladium

These showy, tuberous-rooted plants have to be coddled, for they are native to the tropical regions of America, particularly the jungles of Brazil. They have come a long way from the original few species, for there are now hundreds upon hundreds of cultivars in existence. Most of these which are generally available, however, are cultivars of *Caladium bicolor* or *C. hortulanum*, the fancy-leaved caladium. Some are less than eighteen inches (45 cm) in height while others are several feet tall. The broad, arrowhead-shaped leaves may vary from nine to thirty inches (23 to 75 cm). The colours range through white, greens, pale pinks and reds and the veins are pronounced. Caladiums, as well as being tender, are only part-time houseplants; the leaves die down in autumn and begin to grow again in early spring.

The Doctor Says—

Environment: To start the tuber into growth in early spring the temperature must not be lower than 70°F (21°C). The plant can be moved to a cooler place when the leaves are fully developed. During the dormant winter period a temperature around 60°F (16°C) is necessary. Caladiums need a fair amount of light, but never direct sunlight.

Water: Very frequently when the leaves are growing well. It is also helpful to spray the leaves at this time. Water rather less often thereafter. Gradually reduce the frequency of watering in late summer. Stop watering when the leaves have died to let the tuber dry out.

Feed: Weekly when the leaves are well-developed and continue until summer.

Repot: In late winter or early spring remove the tuber from the pot in which it has overwintered, trim off the old roots and replant in fresh peat-based compost.

Propagate: From offsets removed when repotting.

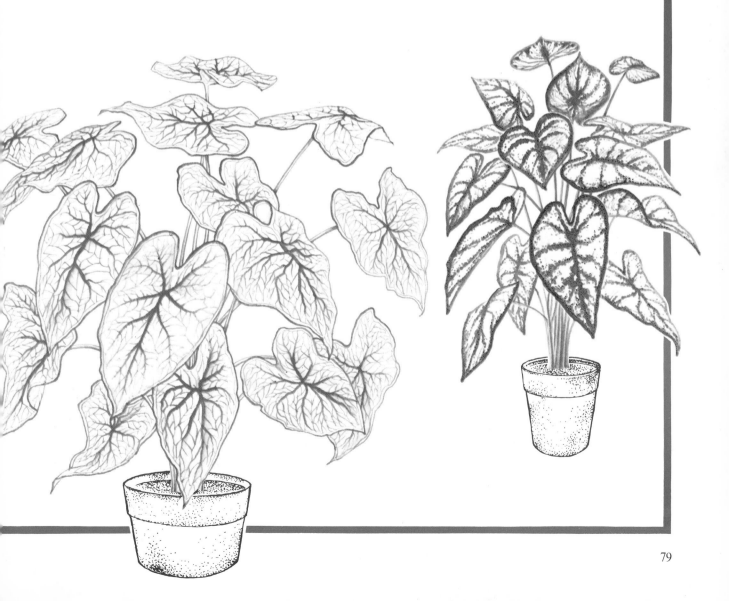

Variegated Foliage Plants

Calathea

Among the most flamboyant of variegated houseplants, almost all calatheas originate in Brazil. The Latin word *insignis*, which means "striking," could be applied to many of them. *Calathea insignis*, however, which is also known as the rattle-snake plant, has leaves which are longer and more slender than other plants in this family. The leaves are light green and the olive markings make precise patterns along the midribs. *C. insignis* grows slowly, which can be a virtue in a houseplant, and usually stops well short of two feet (60 cm).

Calathea makoyana is even more striking than *C. insignis*. The patterns on

its broader leaves look like stylized drawings of plants. The markings on the tops of the silvery green leaves are dark green and those on the undersides are purple. If confined to a small pot this plant will stay small, less than twelve inches (30 cm). It is commonly known as the peacock plant.

"Showy" is the meaning of *ornata* but, oddly, *Calathea ornata* from Colombia is one of the least showy of the calatheas. The pale pink stripes on the dark green leaves turn cream colour as the plant gets older. It can grow large, but usually stays about eighteen inches (45 cm).

Both *Calathea zebrina*'s Latin name and its common name, the zebra plant, are self-explanatory; the tops of the emerald green leaves are striped with dark green and the undersides are striped with purple. It has arching stems which give it a more graceful appearance than those calatheas whose leaves are stiffly erect. It seldom grows more than eighteen inches (45 cm) tall.

The Doctor Says—

Environment: In summer all calatheas like a humid, somewhat shady situation in a temperature not lower than 65°F (18°C). In winter the temperature should not be less than 60°F (16°C).
Water: Frequently in summer, only occasionally in winter. Soft and tepid water is preferable.
Feed: Every two weeks from late spring until early autumn.
Repot: Each year in early summer, using an all-peat compost.
Propagate: By division in spring.
Special Instructions: Calatheas must be allowed their dormant period with slightly cooler conditions and less water than when they are growing. In summer, light which is too bright and too little water will cause the leaves to brown and to curl up at the tips. Red spider mites are a threat.

Callisia elegans

The striped inch plant, indigenous to North America, is by nature a creeping plant, but it does not sprawl as much as its close relative tradescantia, which it resembles. The densely growing leaves, dark green with white stripes on top, are purplish underneath. The insignificant white flowers begin to appear in spring and continue into autumn. This plant has one drawback—as it gets older it often becomes rather bare of leaves. It is ridiculously easy to propagate, however, so it is possible to have a constant supply of young plants to replace their elders.

The Doctor Says—

Environment: *C. elegans* will prosper in a temperature range of 55 to 65°F (13 to 18°C). It enjoys good light, but not direct sunlight in summer.
Water: Will need frequent watering in summer. In winter water only as often as necessary to keep the compost just moist.
Feed: Weekly from early spring until autumn.
Repot: In spring, but it is usually worth doing only once since the plant begins to go downhill by the time it is two years old.
Propagate: Very easily, by basal cuttings in spring and summer.

Chlorophytum elatum

Its Latin name is the only difficult thing about the spider plant which originally came from South Africa, but has been known as a houseplant for two hundred years. It grows quickly, producing large numbers of arching, green and white striped leaves. In spring and summer it also puts out long, wiry stems bearing tiny, white flowers and plantlets which will hang there until given the chance to become the new generation of chlorophytum.

The Doctor Says—

Environment: This plant will grow in a warm room or a cool one, as long as the winter temperature does not fall below 45°F (7°C). It does best in bright light, but must be protected from the hot midday sun in summer. Even dry air does not worry it too much.
Water: Frequently when growing—from early spring until early autumn. Less often when dormant—from autumn until midwinter.
Feed: Weekly from early spring until early autumn.
Repot: Usually in spring, but this amenable plant will tolerate being repotted at other times, except in winter.
Propagate: By pegging down a plantlet in a small pot of loamy compost and severing it from the parent plant when it has taken root. This can be done in spring or summer.
Special Instructions: Leaves will brown if the compost is too dry and will curl if the plant is fed in winter.

Variegated Foliage Plants

Codiaeum variegatum pictum

These striking plants cannot be confused with any others and, at the same time, there is infinite variety among them. The leaves differ in shape and the many colour combinations are unpredictable and include green and pink, yellow and brown and black and orange. The markings may appear as blotches, spots or veins. Only the flowers are insignificant. The codiaeum is a native of Malaysia and although one of its common names is South Sea laurel, it is best known as croton. By any name, however, it is not the easiest plant to grow.

The Doctor says—

Environment: Needs constant warmth, with the temperature never lower than 65°F (18°C), and a humid atmosphere. It has to have bright light, but must be protected from the hot summer sun.
Water: Frequently from spring until early autumn, plus daily spraying. Somewhat less often during the rest of the year.
Feed: Weekly from early spring until late summer.
Repot: In spring in an all-peat compost.
Propagate: In summer by stem-tip or basal cuttings.
Special Instructions: Leaves will drop as the result of sudden changes of temperature or of draughts. Insufficient light causes leaves to become plain green, while hot sun can cause a general bleached-out look. Dry air may bring on mildew resulting in bare lower stems. Watch out for scale insects, mealy bugs, red spider mites and thrips.

Coleus blumei

Flame nettle, its common name, well describes this plant; its leaves are nettle-shaped and their colours—mainly reds and yellows—glow like fire. There are about two hundred species to be found in Africa and Asia, but *C. blumei*, which is a native of Java, is one of the most attractive pot plants. It is bushy and seldom grows much taller than eighteen inches (45 cm). Unfortunately, older plants tend to get bare and straggly after a year or two, but it is easy to start new plants from healthy cuttings.

The Doctor says—

Environment: Aim at a summer temperature not lower than 60°F (16°C) and a winter minimum of 55°F (13°C). Although the brighter the colours of variegated plants the more light they need to stay brilliant, *C. blumei* should not be exposed to direct sunlight at the height of summer.
Water: With fairly soft water, very often in summer plus frequent spraying in hot weather; less frequently in winter.
Feed: Every two weeks from early spring until early autumn.
Repot: In lime-free, peat-based or loam-based compost in late winter.
Propagate: By cuttings in spring or summer.
Special Instructions: The leaves will inevitably lose some colour in winter, so this is nothing about which to be concerned. Remove any flower buds which form and pinch out leading shoots to keep the plant bushy. Watch for mealy bugs.

Cordyline australis

Somewhat unfairly called the New Zealand cabbage palm or grass palm, *C. australis* depends on gracefulness for its appeal, since its variegations can be quite modest. To compensate for that, it carries clusters of small, sweet-smelling flowers in summer.

The Doctor Says—

Environment: A temperate climate plant, *C. australis* likes fairly cool conditions, with the temperature about 65°F (18°C) in summer and as low as 55°F (13°C) in winter.
Water: Very frequently in summer, but less often in winter.
Feed: Every two weeks from spring until autumn.
Repot: Every other year in spring using an all-peat compost.
Propagate: By planting the sucker shoots which appear at the base of the plant in a heated propagator (70 to 75°F, 21 to 24°C) in summer.
Special Instructions: Pests are not greatly attracted to this plant, but overwatering might encourage red spider mites.

Cordyline terminalis

Of the cordylines, *C. terminalis*, the lovely Hawaiian ti plant, is the most dramatic with its vivid red, pink and cream variegations. In the wild the plant will grow a trunk ten feet (3 m) tall and the broad leaves are used for thatching, for cattle feed and to make cloth for Samoan-style skirts. In the house the plant stays a more manageable size and is just expected to look beautiful.

The Doctor Says—

Environment: Needs a temperature around 70°F (21°C) in summer and no lower than 60°F (16°C) in winter. Needs a humid atmosphere. Likes good light, but should be protected from hot direct sunlight during the summer months.
Water: Frequently in summer, and less often in winter.
Feed: Every two weeks from spring until autumn.
Repot: Every other year in the spring using an all-peat compost.
Propagate: In summer. Plant the sucker shoots in a heated propagator or, when the plant gets too tall and leggy, by cutting the tips of the plant's central stem into sections and rooting them in the propagator. Shoots should appear from each stem joint.
Special Instructions: Watch for red spider mites which can be encouraged by overwatering.

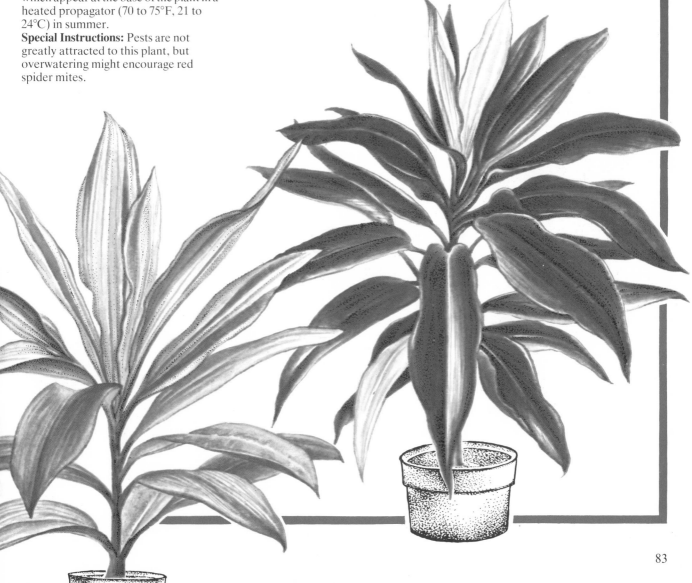

Variegated Foliage Plants

Dieffenbachia picta

This rather fleshy plant has quite large green and cream leaves. It comes from Brazil, but, according to some sources, its Latin name may commemorate a famous Austrian gardener; according to others two Germans. Its common name, dumb cane, is more easily explained: the stems of the plant contain calcium oxalate which, if it gets into the mouth, has a paralyzing effect on the tongue and throat. A rather less striking species, *D. amoena*, will tolerate poorer light.

The Doctor Says—

Environment: This plant will flourish only in a humid atmosphere. In summer it needs a temperature of about 65°F (18°C) and if the winter temperature falls below 60°F (16°C) the lower leaves may turn yellow. It requires light and in winter enjoys full sun, but in summer it must be kept out of direct sunlight.

Water: With soft tepid water, often in summer with frequent spraying; only occasionally during the dormant period from early autumn until late winter.
Feed: Weekly from early spring until late summer.
Repot: Every spring preferably in a loam-based compost.
Propagate: By tip cuttings or sections of the stem in a heated propagator (80°F, 27°C) in summer.
Special Instructions: Keep this plant out of draughts. Leaves produced in winter tend to stay small, so to discourage growth stop feeding and limit water. If the compost is allowed to dry out the edges of the leaves will turn brown. As the plant gets older the lower leaves drop off, but if it is healthy it can be given a new lease of life with major surgery. Cut the stem back to four inches (10 cm) and new shoots should appear.

Dracaena

There is such a great variety of dracaenas that it is difficult to believe that they are related. *D. deremensis*, the dragon plant from Africa, has long, strap-shaped, dark, glossy, green leaves striped with silver. The leaves of *D. fragrans* 'Massangeana' are the same shape, but they are emerald green and yellow. *D. godseffiana*, known as gold dust dracaena, is quite different for it has small, glossy, green leaves with oval, yellow spots and small, yellow flowers in spring which are followed by red berries.

The Doctor Says—

Environment: Dracaenas come from tropical Africa and Asia, but some species more than others will survive in less than tropical conditions. *D. deremensis* and *D. fragrans* do best with summer temperatures of at least 65°F (18°C) and not lower than 60°F (15°C) in winter. Slightly lower temperatures will satisfy the others. They all require light, but should be protected from the hot summer sun. They need a moist atmosphere.

Water: Frequently in spring and summer; much less often in winter.

Feed: Every two weeks from late spring until early autumn.

Repot: Every other spring in an all-peat compost.

Propagate: By tip cuttings or stem sections using a heated propagator (not less than 75°F, 24°C) in summer for *D. deremensis* and *D. fragrans*. By cuttings in early summer for *D. godseffiana*, also in a heated propagator.

Special Instructions: Leaves will lose some variegation through lack of light and will turn brown if the plant gets too dry. Watch for red spider mites, scale insects, mealy bugs and thrips.

Euonymus japonicus

Commonly known as the Japanese spindle tree, this is not one of the most dramatic of houseplants, but it is blessedly undemanding. It looks rather like a laurel, but with smaller leaves which are dark green and blotched with yellow. For a houseplant it will in time grow quite tall, even to six feet (1.80 m), but nothing like the twenty-seven feet (9 m) it achieves in its native habitat.

The Doctor Says—

Environment: In summer the optimum temperature should be about 55°F (13°C), but in winter about 40°F (5°C) is desirable,. The plant will suffer if it is denied this resting period from autumn until late winter. During that time it needs plenty of light to maintain its variegation, but in summer some shade from direct sunlight is necessary.

Water: Very often in summer, but only frequently enough in winter to keep the compost barely moist.

Feed: Every two weeks from spring until late summer.

Repot: Each year in early spring for the first two years, then every other year.

Propagate: By cuttings in summer.

Special Instructions: Pinch out the tip of the plant in spring to encourage bushiness in summer. Too much warmth in winter may cause mildew and dropping of old leaves and invite scale insects.

Variegated Foliage Plants

Fittonia argyroneura

A plant which has its home in the rain forests of Peru obviously needs special attention if it is to be at home in yours. These low-growing plants have a special attraction–the network of veins which covers the leaves. *F. argyroneura*, or the silver net leaf, has white veins on its bright green leaves, while *F. verschaffeltii*, which is somewhat easier to grow, has red veins on dark green leaves.

The Doctor Says–

Environment: Obviously, considering their background, these plants need warmth, moisture and a certain amount of shade; at any rate, no direct sunlight. A summer temperature between 65 and 70°F (18 and 21°C) and not lower in winter than 60°F (16°C) for *F. argyroneura* and 55°F (13°C) for *F. verschaffeltii*. To increase humidity keep the pot on a bed of wet pebbles.
Water: Very often in spring and summer with frequent spraying; less often in winter.
Feed: Every two weeks from early summer until early autumn.
Repot: In mid-spring, using a peat compost with one-third sharp sand, in a wide, shallow pot.
Propagate: By cuttings in late spring in a heated propagator (about 70°F, 21°C) or by division when repotting.
Special Instructions: Draughts will kill and overwatering in winter will encourage all manner of pests and diseases.

Geogenanthus undatus

The heart-shaped leaves of the seersucker plant from Peru look as though they had been run up on a sewing machine. As well as the puckered and quilted effect, the leaves are also adorned with mid and dark green wavy lines and a metallic sheen, while the undersides have a purplish-red tinge. It might seem that no other special effect was possible for a plant which grows only twelve inches (30 cm) tall, but *G. undatus* also produces blue flowers.

The Doctor Says–

Environment: This plant needs warmth, about 70°F (21°C) in winter. Good light is essential to maintain the brightness of the variegations, but it must be protected from the hot summer sun.
Water: Frequently in spring and summer, but in winter go easy. Spraying the leaves with tepid water is beneficial all year round.
Feed: Every two weeks from early spring until late summer.
Repot: In spring in a loam-based or a peat-based compost.
Propagate: By division in late spring or by stem cuttings in summer.
Special Instructions: Watch for mealy bugs and red spider mites.

Hypoestes sanguinolenta

There are some plants which beg to be pampered, but *H. sanguinolenta* looks as though it could put up with tougher conditions than it actually will, for it is a tropical plant from Madagascar and needs warmth and high humidity. It is called freckle face or the pink polka-dot plant, and it is the well-defined markings on the dark green leaves which are the plant's unusual feature. The small, pretty flowers, which appear over a long period during the summer, are usually dismissed as insignificant and removable.

The Doctor Says —

Environment: In summer provide a temperature in the low 70s F (at least 20°C) and to create a humid atmosphere, spray daily with tepid water. In winter the temperature should not drop below 55°F (13°C). The plant needs filtered sunlight or very bright light to maintain its colourful polka dots. It will grow in the shade, but the leaves will be green.
Water: Frequently in spring and summer, but in winter keep the compost just moist.
Feed: Weekly from early summer until early autumn.
Repot: Every spring in a peat-based compost.
Propagate: By stem cuttings in summer in a heated propagator.
Special Instructions: The plant will become leggy if the top shoots are not pinched out to induce bushiness. Stems which have got out of hand should be cut back in spring.

Iresine herbstii

The so-called beefsteak plant comes from South America and has bright red leaves and stems. Another species, *I. lindenii*, or bloodleaf, is darker red. The leaves of both plants are attractively veined.

The Doctor Says —

Environment: The summer temperature should be about 65°F (18°C) and the winter temperature not lower than 60°F (16°C). The essential humidity can be increased by constant spraying. Above all, full sunlight is needed to keep the colours full-blooded.
Water: Very frequently in summer using tepid water. During the winter the compost should be fairly dry, and the frequency of watering increased gradually from early spring.
Feed: Every two weeks from early spring until early autumn.
Repot: In early spring in a loam-based or peat-based compost.
Propagate: By stem cuttings in early spring or early autumn.
Special Instructions: Nip out the top shoots in early spring to make the plant grow more busy.

Variegated Foliage Plants

Maranta

There are three popular varieties of this tropical species of maranta. The largest-leaved is *M. leuconeura* 'Erythrophylla', commonly called red herring-bone because of the pattern which the crimson veins make on the dark green leaves. *M. leuconeura* 'Kerchoveana', dubbed the prayer plant because of its habit of folding pairs of leaves together at dusk, has blotches, which range from dark brown to dark green, on its grey leaves. The smallest-leaved is *M. leuconeura* 'Massangeana', commonly called rabbit's foot, which has pale green, dark green and white markings on the leaves. All grow to much the same height, no more than twelve inches (30 cm) and carry modest white flowers in spring and early summer.

The Doctor Says—

Environment: These plants need a summer temperature between 65 and 70°F (18 and 20°C) and between 60 and 65°F (16 and 18°C) in winter. Keep in a good light but out of the sun. To increase humidity surround the pot with moist peat.
Water: Very frequently in summer with soft tepid water and spray daily. Water less often from early autumn until late winter, but do not let the compost dry out.
Feed: Every two weeks, from spring until late summer.
Repot: Each year in spring in a peat-based compost.
Propagate: By division when repotting.
Special Instructions: Too much light and too little water will make the leaves curl and become brown at the tips.

Pandanus veitchii

The screw pine is not a true pine, but it acquired its common name because of the cone-shaped fruit it bears when grown outdoors. It comes from Polynesia and is more tolerant than many tropical plants, but if it is to flourish it needs warmth and humidity. The narrow, dark green, serrated leaves which grow more than three feet (1 m) long and arch, have margins and tips of creamy white.

The Doctor Says—

Environment: The summer temperatures to aim for are in the high 60s or low 70s F (19 to 24°C) and it is inadvisable, although not fatal, to let the winter temperature drop below 65°F (18°C) for long. The screw pine needs a humid atmosphere, especially when new leaves are appearing. Keep the plant in a good light, but out of direct sunlight.
Water: Very frequently in spring and summer, using tepid water. Spray daily. Keep the compost on the dry side between waterings during the resting period from early autumn through midwinter.
Feed: Every two weeks from early spring until late summer.

Repot: In early spring each year when the plant is young, into gradually larger pots until it grows too large to move. Use a loam-based compost. As the plant grows taller, larger aerial roots begin to appear on the surface of the compost and these must not be covered.
Propagate: Remove suckers from the base of the plant in summer when they have a few leaves and grow them as cuttings.
Special Instructions: Pests and diseases seldom strike. Sometimes the large aerial roots will lift the plant out of the pot. If this happens, repot the plant.

Peperomia

There are about a thousand species of peperomia, most of them from Central and South America. In the tropical wild they grow in shallow soil at the feet of trees or in the crevices of tree trunks. The handful of species cultivated as houseplants can be divided into two groups—those which send up a cluster of stalks from the roots and those which have stalks growing from the main stem. Most peperomias grow about twelve inches (30 cm) tall and produce spikes of white flowers from spring until early winter.

The most popular plant in the first group is *Peperomia argyreia* (syn. *P. sandersii*), which has two common names, the rugby football plant and the watermelon plant. The curiously shaped silver and dark green leaves are carried on dark red stems. The leaves of *P. hederaefolia*, which belongs to the same group, are smaller, heart-shaped, quilted and silver grey with dark green veins. *P. caperata* 'Emerald Ripple' is a mini version of *P. hederaefolia*, only three inches (7.5 cm) tall with small, heart-shaped, crinkled leaves that are dark green tinged with purple grey.

The most widely grown peperomias in the second group are the two varieties of *P. magnoliaefolia* 'Variegata', the young ivory leaves of which turn green with age, and 'Green Gold' which has a yellower and longer-lasting variegation.

The Doctor Says—

Environment: Peperomias need a temperature between 60 and 65°F (16 and 18°C) all year round, a humid atmosphere and good light, but not direct sunlight. In winter they require less humidity, but still good light.

Water: Only fairly frequently in spring and summer, letting the compost get quite dry between waterings. Use soft tepid water. Spray on hot days. In winter keep almost dry. Since stems which grow from the roots are quick to rot, it is best not to water from above, but to stand the pot in shallow water for a short time and then drain.

Feed: Once a month from early spring until late summer.

Repot: Each spring in a well-draining peat-based compost.

Propagate: By stem cuttings from spring until late summer, but push the stem only a little way into the compost to avoid rot.

Special Instructions: Beware of overwatering. Watch for red spider mites. *P. argyreia* cannot stand draughts; it is the fussiest of all.

Variegated Foliage Plants

Pilea cadierei

As houseplants go, this is an infant, having arrived in the West from Vietnam only in the 1940s. Its popular name is aluminium plant, because of the silvery patches on its dark green, quilted, oval-shaped leaves. Older plants become straggly and leggy, but cuttings can be easily propagated. The cultivar 'Nana' is, however, a more compact improvement.

The Doctor Says—

Environment: In summer between 55 and 65°F (13 and 18°C), in winter not below 50°F (10°C); it prefers shade and, unexpectedly, dry air, except just when growth begins again in early spring.
Water: Fairly frequently in spring and summer; and only often enough in winter to keep the compost just moist.
Feed: Every two weeks from early spring until early autumn.
Repot: Rarely necessary since pileas grow best in three- to four-inch (8- to 10-cm) pots.
Propagate: From cuttings in late spring or summer, in loam-based or peat-based compost.

Rhoeo spathacea

This striking plant (syn. *R. discolor*), looks more demanding than it is. Although of tropical origin it does not need great warmth and the vivid variegations survive a certain amount of shade. The lance-shaped leaves, which are nine to twelve inches (23 to 30 cm) long, grow from a central stem and are olive green on top and purple underneath. The clusters of tiny white flowers appear from late spring until summer in purple boat-shaped bracts, hence one of the plant's common names—boat lily. Two others are Moses-in-the-cradle and Moses-in-the-bulrushes.

The Doctor Says—

Environment: Temperature around 60°F (16°C) is adequate in summer, and a minimum of 50°F (10°C) is necessary in winter. Although *R. spathacea* likes some shade in summer, it requires a good light in winter. To increase the humidity from early spring until late summer keep the pot on wet pebbles.
Water: Very often from early spring, gradually reducing the frequency in late summer and early autumn., Water only occasionally during the dormant period from autumn until late winter.
Feed: Every two weeks, from early spring until late summer.
Repot: When necessary, in spring, using a peat-based compost.
Propagate: By basal shoots removed in the spring.

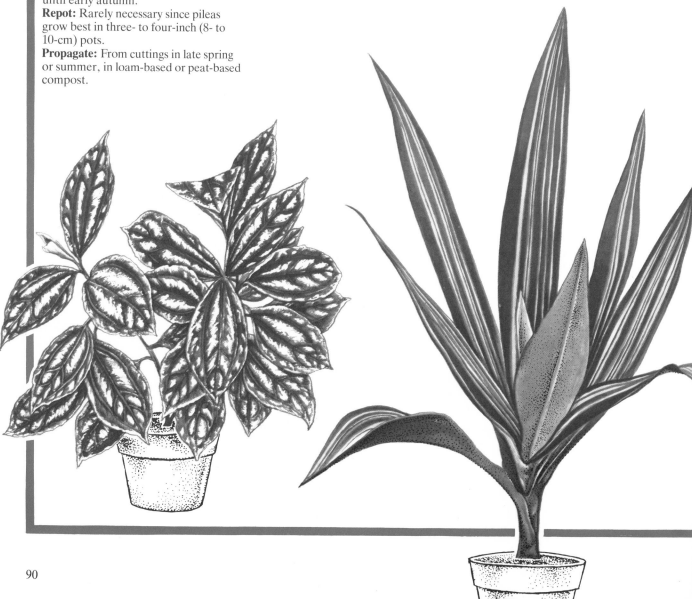

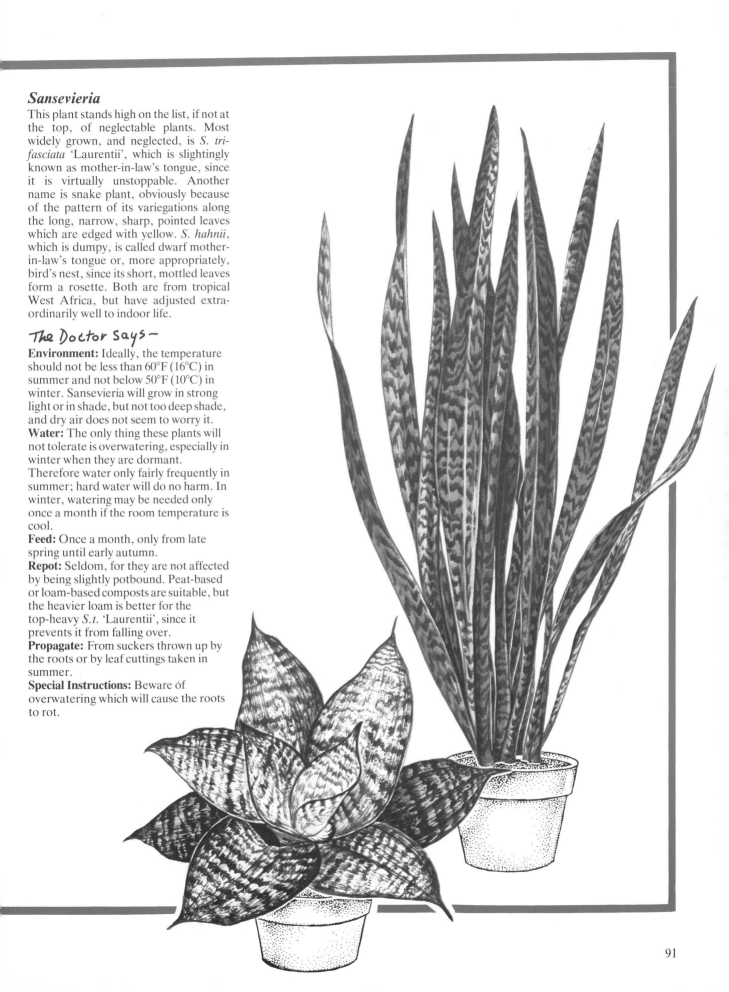

Sansevieria

This plant stands high on the list, if not at the top, of neglectable plants. Most widely grown, and neglected, is *S. trifasciata* 'Laurentii', which is slightingly known as mother-in-law's tongue, since it is virtually unstoppable. Another name is snake plant, obviously because of the pattern of its variegations along the long, narrow, sharp, pointed leaves which are edged with yellow. *S. hahnii*, which is dumpy, is called dwarf mother-in-law's tongue or, more appropriately, bird's nest, since its short, mottled leaves form a rosette. Both are from tropical West Africa, but have adjusted extraordinarily well to indoor life.

The Doctor says—

Environment: Ideally, the temperature should not be less than 60°F (16°C) in summer and not below 50°F (10°C) in winter. Sansevieria will grow in strong light or in shade, but not too deep shade, and dry air does not seem to worry it.

Water: The only thing these plants will not tolerate is overwatering, especially in winter when they are dormant. Therefore water only fairly frequently in summer; hard water will do no harm. In winter, watering may be needed only once a month if the room temperature is cool.

Feed: Once a month, only from late spring until early autumn.

Repot: Seldom, for they are not affected by being slightly potbound. Peat-based or loam-based composts are suitable, but the heavier loam is better for the top-heavy *S.t.* 'Laurentii', since it prevents it from falling over.

Propagate: From suckers thrown up by the roots or by leaf cuttings taken in summer.

Special Instructions: Beware of overwatering which will cause the roots to rot.

Variegated Foliage Plants

Scindapsus aureus

Golden pothos, or devil's ivy, native of the Solomon Islands, is a popular climbing plant for it will tolerate staying in a warm room all year round without a dormant period. The leaves, bright green with yellow splashings, change shape from oval to heart-shaped as the plant matures. The plant will need support for it grows to more than six feet (1.80 m). Alternatively, it can be put on a shelf and allowed to trail.

The Doctor Says—

Environment: *S. aureus* can flourish if the winter temperature never goes below 55°F (13°C) and is at least in the high 60s F (about 20°C) in the summer. It requires bright light even in winter if the leaves are not to revert to solid green. Stand the pot on a tray of wet pebbles to give the necessary humidity.

Water: Very frequently in summer, and spray daily. In winter allow the compost to dry out between waterings.

Feed: Every two weeks from late spring until late autumn.

Repot: In spring, no more frequently than every other year, since it demands potbound roots. Use a peat-based compost.

Propagate: By stem-tip cuttings in summer.

Special Instructions: Pinch out new shoots to encourage bushiness. Leaf curl may be caused by extremely dry air.

Tradescantia

These plants are so ridiculously easy to grow that they are too often left to get on with it with little help from their owners. A little more care makes the difference between a well-groomed plant and an unkempt one which trails lankiness all over the place. The species which are grown as houseplants come from the tropical areas of South America, but the name was first given to a hardy species found in North America in the seventeenth century. It honours the Tradescants, gardeners to Charles I. Its popular names are endless: speedy Jenny, wandering Jew, spiderwort, Moses-in-the-bulrushes and zebrina inch plant are only a few. Patterns of variegations differ, but the colours of the stripes are usually white, cream or pink. The most popular are varieties of *T. fluminensis* 'Quicksilver' and 'Variegata' which bear small white flowers, or of *T. albiflora* 'Silver' and 'Tricolor' which are shy to flower. All these are suitable for hanging baskets. *T. blossfeldiana*, a rather more erect species, has pinky purple flowers in profusion from early spring until late summer.

The Doctor Says—

Environment: Tradescantias are happy in any room that is well lit and not colder than 50°F (10°C) in winter.

Water: Very frequently in summer when the plant is growing rapidly; less often in winter.

Feed: Every two weeks from early spring until late summer.

Repot: In spring, every second or third year, in a loose loam compost or a peat-based one.

Propagate: By cuttings in spring or summer, which will readily root in water or in compost.

Special Instructions: Remove all shoots which produce green leaves; if you don't they may take over completely. The better the light (but not direct sun) the brighter the variegations. Pinch out the leading shoots at least twice during the growing season to stop the trailing stems from becoming lanky. Avoid getting the soil waterlogged in winter or too dry in summer—an encouragement to greenfly.

Zebrina pendula

Commonly called the zebra plant, *Z. pendula* looks almost like a copy of tradescantia, and confusingly shares one of its names—wandering Jew. But it makes an even better hanging plant because of the purplish colour of the undersides of its leaves. The cultivar 'Quadricolor' is the most striking, with a purple stripe on the surface of the leaf as well. The zebrina, however, which comes from Mexico, will not tolerate as much neglect as the tradescantia, since it needs rather more warmth and light.

The Doctor Says—

Environment: A summer temperature in the mid 60s F (around 17°C) and a winter temperature around 55°F (13°C) is recommended, although zebrina can survive slightly lower temperatures. While good light is needed to preserve the variegations, too much can turn the leaves an unpleasant shade of brown.

Water: Frequently in hot weather, but only occasionally the rest of the year, using soft water. Some dryness seems to bring out the colours.

Feed: Every two weeks from early spring until autumn, but only at half strength.

Repot: In spring, adding a little sand to a peat-based compost.

Propagate: With cuttings of the shoots in spring.

Special Instructions: To keep the plant bushy, pinch out the tips when vigorous growth has begun.

Cacti

Almost all cacti are succulents, which means they can store water. Cacti must store water, usually in their swollen stems, because many grow in arid areas, while others, the epiphytes, grow not in soil, but on trees in tropical forests. Their areoles, the small protuberances from which any flowers and spines grow, distinguish cacti from all other plants. For healthy cacti, gradually reduce the amount of water leading up to the dormant period and gradually increase it when the plant starts to grow. Do not water in midwinter, but watch the plant carefully. Softening is a symptom of thirst, buds dropping a symptom of insufficient light.

Aporocactus flagelliformis

This is the rat's-tail cactus and in a healthy specimen the cascades of green stems—the "tails"—are up to three feet (90 cm) long. In its native Mexico this cactus looks particularly dramatic when seen hanging from a rocky outcrop; in captivity it looks well in a hanging basket. Given the right conditions, in spring masses of spectacular, deep pink, tubular flowers will appear along the trailing stems. This is a day-flowering cactus and the flowers last up to four days. To produce flowers, however, *A. flagelliformis* must have a period of winter dormancy and adequate light when the buds appear.

The Doctor Says—

Environment: A period of dormancy is essential in winter; this involves moving the plant to a cooler room—where the temperature does not fall below 45°F (7°C)—but still giving it plenty of light.

In late winter, the period of dormancy over, move the plant back into the warmth and as much light as possible.
Water: Frequently from spring until late summer. Reduce the frequency considerably when the plant is dormant, keeping the compost barely moist.
Feed: From spring until late summer, but only once a month.
Repot: Each year after flowering is over. Use a loam-based compost with added coarse sand (one part of sand to three of compost) or a free-draining peat compost.
Propagate: By cuttings, taken from early spring until midsummer.
Special Instructions: Accept that with age, and through no fault of yours, the stems may rot back and the plant die.

Astrophytum myriostigma

Bishop's cap flourishes, appropriately, in the pure air thousands of feet up in mountainous northern central Mexico, but adapts extraordinarily well to less rarified living-rooms. It is a dark green, globular plant, spineless, but covered with small scales, and achieves a corpulence of some eight inches (20 cm) in maturity. It may have as few as three ribs or as many as eight, and the areoles are often fluffy. Flowers appear fairly reliably in summer, growing from the centre of the plant. They are yellow, and red-throated. There are other species of astrophytum, but *A. myriostigma* is the most dependable.

The Doctor Says—

Environment: From late autumn keep this cactus in a temperature of 45°F (7°C). In spring move it into the warmth and light; a window sill on which the plant will not be exposed to too much harsh sunlight is ideal.
Water: Only from early spring until autumn, and then only when the compost has become quite dry.
Feed: Only every other month during the growing period.
Repot: In spring, in a loam-based compost, adding an equal amount of fine grit or sharp sand.
Propagate: By seed in spring.

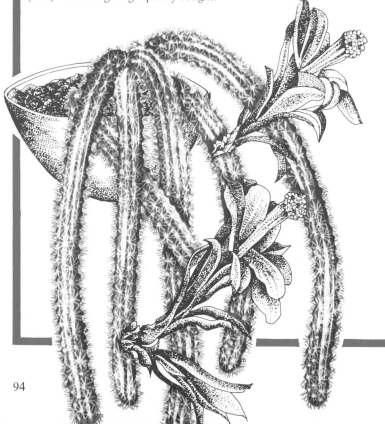

Cephalocereus senilis

This old man cactus would have been even better named the Methuselah cactus since some of those growing in the wild are more than two hundred years old. By then they have reached up to forty-five feet (13 m) in height. The cactus gets its common name from its long, venerable-looking white hairs, which grow from the areoles, but they are at their best only when the plant is young. As it ages it is prone to baldness, which spreads up the columnar stem. You are unlikely to see its white flowers; they are seldom produced before the plant is eighteen feet (6 m) tall and when they then appear in summer it is at night, when, it is said, they are pollinated by vampire bats.

The Doctor Says—

Environment: Do not let the temperature in winter fall below 45°F (7°C) and be sure the plant is always in a very good light.

Water: Keep the compost moist in summer and dry from late autumn until late winter. In summer the plant will appreciate a little humidity, but spray into the air above it so that the hairs do not get too wet.

Feed: Every two weeks from late spring until late summer.

Repot: Every spring for a young plant, but at longer intervals as it grows older. Use a porous compost.

Propagate: In spring from seed.

Special Instructions: In spite of its hairy protection the old man cactus is averse to draughts.

Cereus peruvianus

Tree cactus is an apt name for most species of the giant cereus, including the widely grown *C. peruvianus*. On the slopes of hills in many parts of southeast America they grow in profusion, reaching heights of more than forty feet (12 m)—veritable forests of bluish-green cacti. When young they grow in straight columns and then branch at sharp angles. In indoor cultivation they seldom get beyond the columnar stage, and even that may be excessive for a houseplant, for they are very vigorous growers. Branching can be induced by judiciously chopping off the top of the column, but indoors *C. peruvianus* will certainly not produce its large, funnel-shaped, nocturnal, white flowers. This cactus has two more, somewhat less appropriate, common names—apple cactus and Peruvian apple.

The Doctor Says—

Environment: This cactus is very hardy and a winter temperature of 45°F (7°C) is perfectly adequate. It needs plenty of light all year round. A window sill is a good place for the plant in summer, until it grows too large.

Water: Fairly frequently in summer, but keep dry from late autumn until late winter when it is dormant.

Feed: Not really necessary; certainly once in two months, from early spring until mid-autumn, will be enough.

Repot: Infrequently. When necessary in spring in a loam-based compost with added sand.

Propagate: By cuttings in summer or from seed in spring.

Special Instructions: As with cacti generally, the frequency of watering must be gradually reduced leading up to the dormant period and gradually increased when the plant starts into growth.

Cacti

Echinocactus grusonii

In the searing days and cold nights of the deserts of central Mexico the golden ball, or golden barrel, grows into a lethal-looking, light green sphere some three feet (1 m) in diameter. It is heavily ribbed from top to bottom and the areoles have long, golden-yellow spines. But as a house-plant, though easy to grow, it may not exceed six inches (15 cm) in diameter and will take many years to reach that. Indoors it is unlikely to produce its small yellow flowers, which appear only in the most brilliant sunshine.

The Doctor Says—

Environment: A winter temperature of about 48°F (9°C) must be provided. In summer put the plant in a sunny but airy position.

Water: From early spring until late summer water often enough to keep the compost moist. Beginning in late summer decrease the frequency of watering until autumn when it is left completely dry.

Feed: Monthly from early spring until late summer.

Repot: Every third year in early spring will probably be enough. Use a loam-based or peat-based compost with added sand or fine grit.

Propagate: In summer, by seed in a propagator with considerable bottom heat (75°F, 25°C). Be careful when handling the seedlings as their roots are extremely fragile.

Special Instructions: Too little watering in summer may be followed by red spider mites and mealy bugs. Too much moisture will cause the plant to rot and die.

Echinocereus pectinatus

The echinocereus, from Mexico and the southwestern United States, come in many shapes and sizes. *E. pectinatus* is an erect form with thick stems branching from the base of the plant. The innumerable spines—pink when the cactus is young, white as it ages—are comb-like (pectinate). The pink flowers, about three inches (8 cm) long, appear in summer. The flowers of the variety *E. p.* 'Reichenbachii' are magenta in colour, followed by edible fruit which are responsible for its common name, strawberry cactus.

The Doctor Says—

Environment: In winter provide a temperature of 45°F (7°C), but expose the plant to as much sunlight as there is. In summer give it a sunny, airy position.

Water: Keep the soil moist at all times in summer. Do not water from autumn until early spring.

Feed: Monthly during the growing period.

Repot: Every spring in a loamy compost to which fine grit has been added.

Propagate: By seed in spring or by stem cuttings during the growing period.

Special Instructions: The compost must never be allowed to become waterlogged for this will cause the roots to rot.

Ferocactus latispinus

Savage (Latin, *ferus*) the ferocacti are called and savage they look. *F. latispinus*, a globular plant with many ribs from which grow clusters of red and whitish spines, has earned itself the name devil's tongue cactus because of the colour and shape of its spines. One of each set is longer and hooked back to give a nasty surprise. This particular ferocactus comes from Mexico where it grows some ten thousand feet (3,000 m) above sea level. When it is grown as a houseplant the fragrant red flowers it produces are seldom seen on it.

The Doctor Says—

Environment: From autumn until late winter the plant should be dormant and kept in a cool room with the temperature about 48°F (9°C). In summer it should be given as much light and warmth as possible. Even direct sunlight will do it no harm.
Water: Very frequently in summer and spray occasionally. Do not water from late autumn until late winter.
Feed: Every two weeks during the growing period.
Repot: Each year in early spring, using a peat compost with one part of sharp sand added to three parts of compost.
Propagate: From seed in spring.
Special Instructions: The plant may become infested with red spider mites if it is kept too dry in summer.

Lobivia densispina

It is as easy to grow lobivias as it is to discover their native land from their anagrammatic name. They grow at heights up to twelve thousand feet (3,750 m) where temperatures fall far below freezing. They survive solely because conditions are so dry; in more humid parts of the world they should be kept safely above freezing. As well as being easy to care for they flower readily—hence their popularity. *L. densispina* is a compact, four-inch (10-cm), cylindrical plant which is covered with whitish spines. Its flowers are funnel-shaped and brilliant yellow. They appear by day, but fade quickly.

The Doctor Says—

Environment: From late autumn until early spring provide a temperature of about 43°F (6°C) and place the plant in a light position. When it emerges from its dormant period it should be kept in a sunny but airy room.
Water: Do not water from autumn until spring. The buds should then be starting to form, an indication that watering should begin. Water frequently from then on.
Feed: Every two weeks from spring until early autumn.
Repot: Each spring in an ordinary potting compost to which some leaf mould has been added.
Propagate: From seed in spring.
Special Instructions: This Bolivian cactus needs plenty of light if its spines are to stay bright.

97

Cacti

Mammillaria

The genus mammillaria with about three hundred species, mainly from Mexico, is one of the largest among cacti. Some of the most attractive are the easiest to grow; others could drive you to desperation. They tend to be dumpy plants, although some of those which grow in clusters will form sizeable cushions. They have no ribs; the distinctive feature of these cacti is the nipple-like excrescences with which they are covered (hence their Latin name). The spines grow from the tips of these so-called tubercles.

M. bocasana, known as the powder puff, is one of the easy mammillaria. It grows in a cluster of two-inch (5-cm), blue-green globes to form a quite considerable clump, which if it gets too large may have to be divided and distributed among friends. The plant is covered with silky white hairs among which lurk hooked spines. Small, white, bell-shaped flowers appear in profusion in summer and are followed by long, purple seed pods.

M. elongata also forms clumps, but its stems are cylindrical and may be up to six inches (15 cm) in length. The spines vary somewhat in colour, but leave an overall impression of pale yellow. They grow from the areoles to form star shapes, hence the plant's common name, golden star. Creamy flowers appear in spring.

Another clusterer is *M. camptotricha*, the bird's-nest cactus, and a rather untidy nest at that. The white flowers which appear in summer are not much to look at but are sweetly scented.

The Doctor says—

Environment: Place on a sunny window sill during the summer months, turning the pot now and again so that growth does not become lopsided. In winter the plant will still need plenty of light, and must be kept at a temperature of about 45°F (7°C) and not much lower.

Water: Frequently from early spring until late summer. Keep the plant dry from early autumn until late winter.

Feed: Once a month during the summer.

Repot: Every spring in free-draining compost.

Propagate: By offshoots which will root fairly readily in summer. Seed may also be sown in spring and the plant should reach the flowering stage in about three years.

Special Instructions: Use only a porous compost and do not overwater, for to do so is to risk the plant rotting below the surface.

Myrtillocactus geometrizans

Fans of Western films will be familiar with this cactus; it could well be called the cowboy cactus. In the wild in Mexico it will reach twelve feet (3.6 m), with many branches growing from a rather short, blue-green trunk. It is well-armed with long, strong, black spines, but it has its softer side—sweetly scented, small, creamy flowers which are followed by bluish berries resembling those of the myrtle after which it is named. As a houseplant it is a bit of a dude. It is shy to branch, the spines become soft, it seldom flowers or fruits and it does not like the cold. Nevertheless it remains popular.

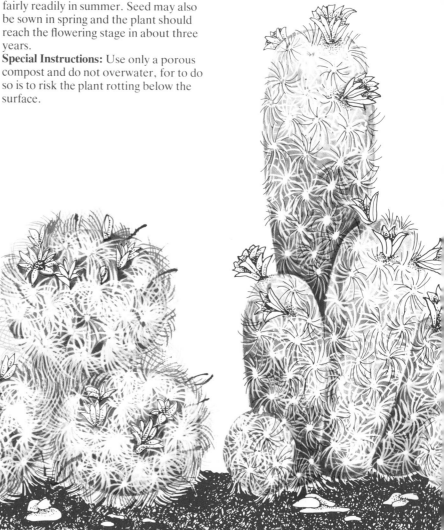

The Doctor Says —

Environment: This cactus is susceptible to winter cold; a minimum temperature of 50°F (10°C) is necessary to prevent brown patches from appearing. In summer keep it on a light, sunny window sill.

Water: Do not water from late autumn until early spring. During the summer months water fairly frequently.

Feed: Every two weeks from spring until early autumn.

Repot: Every spring in one part of sharp sand mixed with three parts potting compost.

Propagate: From seed in spring.

Notocactus leninghausii

The golden ball cactus from South America starts off spherical in shape, but loses its puppy fat to turn into a pale green, cylindrical column which in time may grow to be ten inches (25 cm) tall. It has many ribs and the golden spines grow close together. While most notocacti will begin flowering while they are still quite young this species is less precocious, but the large yellow flowers are worth waiting for. When they do appear they should do so in abundance.

The Doctor Says —

Environment: Provide a winter temperature of not less than 50°F (10°C) in a well-lit position. From early spring until autumn put the plant on a bright, sunny window sill; it will need all the sun it can get if it is to flower.

Water: In summer keep the compost moist at all times. From autumn until early spring do not water lest you encourage diseases.

Feed: Every two weeks in summer, reducing gradually as the dormant period approaches.

Repot: In spring when the plant appears too big for the pot and becomes difficult to water properly. Add sharp sand to the compost to make it more porous.

Propagate: From seed in spring in a heated propagator (about 70°F, 21°C).

Opuntia microdasys

Although an opuntia may be called bunny ears or teddy bear cactus, cuddly it certainly is not. Prickly pear is a far better description. The Mexican *O. microdasys* is one of the most commonly grown. It is easily recognizable by its branching growth of flattened, bright green stems, or pads, which look like ears. The pads are spineless but covered with areoles which bear the short, bristly hairs called glochids, typical of opuntias. Yellow flowers, when they do appear, are borne on the edges of the pads.

The Doctor Says —

Environment: This cactus needs good light while it is dormant and is susceptible to cold; if the winter temperature falls below 46°F (8°C) the pads may become blemished with reddish-brown spots. In summer it needs good light and a warm and airy position.

Water: Only occasionally in winter, but do not allow the compost to dry out, or the pads may drop off. In summer keep the compost moist at all times.

Feed: Every two weeks from spring until late summer.

Repot: In spring once every two years or as necessary, using a rich loam-based compost with added coarse sand.

Propagate: By cuttings in summer.

Special Instructions: Watch for mealy bugs.

Cacti

Parodia

The South American, globe-shaped parodias are remarkable for their fantastic, highly coloured spines. Some also have attractive flowers, which they obligingly produce while still young. Altogether these are rewarding small plants and many of the species are not difficult to cultivate. *P. chrysacanthion* grows only three inches (7.5 cm) tall and has glowing golden-yellow spines which are more striking than the small, yellow, funnel-shaped flowers which appear from the top of the plant. *P. mutabilis* has larger yellow flowers, but the whitish spines are less remarkable. *P. sanguiniflora* produces many deep-red flowers and has brown spines.

Water: Frequently in summer, but watch the neck of the plant carefully, for it is susceptible to rotting as the result of overwatering,. From early autumn until late winter, given a low temperature, no water should be needed, but as with other cacti look at the plant regularly for signs that it might benefit from a minute amount of water.
Feed: Every two weeks from spring until early autumn.
Repot: As necessary in spring in a rich compost, with one part in three of added sand.
Propagate: Plants may be raised from seed, sown in spring, but growth is slow at the start.

The Doctor Says—

Environment: It is vital to give *P. chrysacanthion* as sunny a position as possible, otherwise its spines—which are its main feature—will lose their brilliance. In winter keep the plant in a temperature between 48 and 54°F (9 and 12°C).

Rebutia kupperiana

Red crown is the common name of this cactus; it could hardly be any other. For most of the year it is a not particularly outstanding greenish-bronze globe covered with short spines. But in early spring and summer its base is totally encircled by rich orange-red flowers which form a perfect crown. This flowering is likely to happen, however, only if the cactus has been allowed quite a long cool and dry dormant period. If it has been denied that, all you can expect at best is a tiara. One of the great virtues of these cacti, which are native to the high mountains of Argentina and Bolivia, is that they start to flower when they are very young.

The Doctor Says—

Environment: From early spring until autumn the plant should have a light, sunny and airy position. It must be allowed a dormant period from late autumn until late winter, and the temperature should be about 45°F (7°C), but the plant still needs plenty of light.
Water: Frequently in summer, making sure that the compost is moist at all times. An occasional overhead spraying helps. To ensure flowering do not water from late autumn until late winter.
Feed: Every two weeks from spring until summer.
Repot: You can probably avoid doing so, but if it becomes necessary use a rich compost with added sand in early spring.
Propagate: Either from seed in spring or by division in summer.

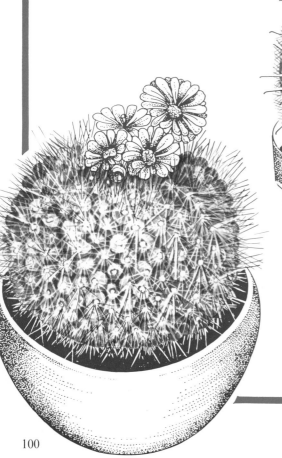

Epiphytes

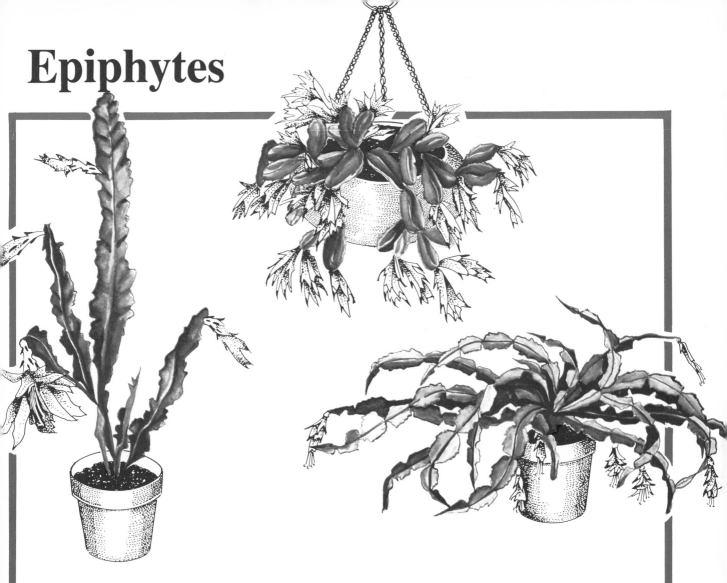

These cacti, probably the most popular of all, are not desert plants but epiphytes, which in the wild grow on the branches of trees in the warmth and wetness of tropical forests. The hybrids we grow, however, have developed considerable tolerance over a period of time; *Epiphyllum* x *ackermanii*, the orchid cactus, was first raised nearly two hundred years ago. The flowers of the original cultivar are scarlet, but there are now white, cream, yellow, orange and purple forms. The stems can grow very long, two to three feet (60 to 90 cm).

Botanists argue almost to the death whether the cactus most of us know and love as the Christmas cactus is *Zygocactus truncatus* or *Schlumbergera truncata* or *S. anything else*. There are also the alternative common names, crab or lobster cactus, suggested by the claw-like stems from which the magenta flowers hang.

A popular cactus which produces brick-red flowers over several weeks in spring is surrounded by the same confusion of nomenclature. Is it Easter or Whitsun cactus, and is it *Schlumbergera gaertneri* or *Rhipsalidopsis gaertneri*, as some would have it? Under whichever name you grow it, the flowers are just as striking.

The Doctor Says —

Environment: For much of the year these cacti will be content with whatever temperatures we ourselves enjoy, but if they are to flower well they must have a cooler dormancy period. Resting times vary according to times of flowering.

Epiphyllum x *ackermanii* flowers in late spring and then puts out new growth in summer, which it can spend outdoors in semi-shade as long as you remember to water it. In early autumn move it to a light, cool place (45 to 50°F, 7 to 10°C) and keep it as dry as possible without letting the leaves go soft—a sign of thirst. When flower buds appear in early spring move the plant into the warmth, and water it more often.

The Christmas cactus, which starts flowering in early winter, is dormant after stem growth ceases in late summer. When flower buds begin to appear in late autumn bring the cactus into the warmth. The resting period of the Easter cactus stretches from early autumn until early spring. Move the plant to a warmer place as soon as the flower buds appear; the warmer it is the more likely that the flowers will appear in time for Easter.

Water: Only occasionally when resting, increasing the frequency when flower buds appear. Spray in summer.

Feed: Only a weak feed every three weeks and only after flower buds have appeared. Overfeeding will reduce the crop of flowers.

Repot: After flowering, using a free-draining, rich, loam-based compost.

Propagate: By cuttings in summer.

Special Instructions: The critical period is when the buds have formed for they are liable to drop off. Some buds may fall off because there are so many. Other causes are draughts and underwatering and overwatering. Above all it is necessary to turn the pot around regularly so that light falls on the plant from different directions.

Other Succulents

Besides cacti, there are about ten thousand plants which are usually referred to as "other succulents." They are remarkably diverse in their habits and habitats, but they all share one characteristic—the ability to store water. While the leafless cacti store water in their stems, the other succulents store most of the reserved water in their fleshy leaves. Consequently, many succulents dry out more quickly than cacti and need to be kept barely moist during the winter.

Aeonium

The distinctive feature of the aeoniums is the way in which the leaves grow as rosettes. Those of the tree-like *A. arboreum* measure two to three inches (5 to 7.5 cm) in diameter and are borne on sturdy brown branches. As a houseplant this succulent may grow three feet (90 cm) tall, but that is only one-tenth the height these plants achieve in their native Mediterranean region. Yellow flowers on long stems appear from winter until early spring, but only on mature plants. The most widely grown variety is 'Atropurpureum', which has purple leaves.

A. *tabulaeforme*, which comes from the Canary Islands, looks like a rosette which has been turned inside out, with the leaves tightly overlapping each other like slates on a roof. This is a low plant, but the rosette may grow to twelve inches (30 cm) in diameter. Yellow flowers may appear in summer when the plant is three or so years old, and after that the rosette dies.

The Doctor Says—

Environment: *A. arboreum* needs a minimum temperature of 45°F (7°C) from autumn until early spring in a light sunny position. In summer it has a resting period before winter flowering begins so it should be put in a cool but still light room. *A. tabulaeforme* requires a similar winter temperature and normal summer temperatures but it must have semi-shade.

Water: *A. arboreum* should be watered weekly from autumn until spring and occasionally—about once a month—in summer. For *A. tabulaeforme* the programme is reversed: water monthly from autumn until spring and weekly in summer.

Feed: Every two weeks during their respective growing periods.

Repot: Each year in spring in a loam-based compost.

Propagate: *A. arboreum* by stem cuttings; *A. tabulaeforme* by seed or leaf cuttings.

Special Instructions: Grow *A. tabulaeforme* somewhat on the slant so that any water which falls on the rosette runs off easily.

Agave americana

Men, beasts and birds all find some use for the agaves as food, drink, fibre or medicine—and man has been bold enough, too, to tame them as houseplants. It is quite an undertaking, for in its native Mexico the rosette formed by *Agave americana* may reach twelve feet (3.6 m) in diameter and the leaves eight feet (2.5 m) in length. Even when domesticated the plants can be three feet (90 cm) long. They are grey-green, leathery and strap-shaped and end in a

spine. The popular *A.a. marginata* has the added attraction of yellow margins on the leaves. Its common name, the century plant, arises from the mistaken belief that it takes one hundred years to flower. In the wild it will produce green flowers on a towering stem after only a few years, but indoors it is unlikely to flower at all. But be consoled, for after flowering the rosette dies.

The Doctor Says—

Environment: From autumn until early spring a minimum temperature of 45°F (7°C) and good light are required. For the rest of the year find a warm, light spot for it.

Water: Fairly frequent watering from spring until early autumn, and thereafter water less often. If the leaves show signs of shrivelling the plant will need watering, but try not to let it get to that stage.

Feed: Only once a month from spring until early autumn unless you want it to grow prodigiously.

Repot: To keep it under control certainly no more than every two years in spring. Use a loam-based compost with additional sand mixed in.

Propagate: Either from offsets or by seed sown in spring.

Aloe

Some aloes, like the agaves, can grow to a monstrous height, but most of them stay smaller. They have one great advantage over agaves—the rosette does not die off after the plant has flowered. *Aloe arborescens* is one of the larger species, with spearhead-shaped leaves edged with sharp teeth, from which it gets its common name, the octopus plant. Other names—torch plant and candelabra plant—describe the plant's appearance when it flowers, which it rarely will in a pot. A more manageable-sized aloe is *A. variegata*, or partridge-breasted aloe, which was discovered in South Africa in the late seventeenth century. It has a striking rosette of rank upon rank of triangular green leaves banded with white. Tubular pinkish flowers are produced on twelve-inch (30-cm) stems. *A. ferox* has taller spikes of scarlet flowers and the leaves are edged with red teeth.

The Doctor Says—

Environment: Aloes will tolerate a dry atmosphere and cool conditions in winter as long as the temperature does not fall below 45°F (7°C). *A. variegata* should have a somewhat shady position, and other aloes will come to no harm if they are given the same treatment. From spring until autumn give plenty of light but shield the plants from direct sunlight.

Water: Very sparingly—about once a month—from early winter until early spring. For the rest of the year water frequently, especially in warm weather, but be careful not to water into the centre of the rosette because this may cause rotting at the base of the plant.

Feed: Monthly from late spring until early autumn.

Repot: This is not a fast-growing plant so once every two or three years in spring will probably be enough. Use a loam-based compost.

Propagate: From offsets, which can be removed in spring, or by seed.

Other Succulents

Ceropegia woodii

This very unusual South African succulent trails or climbs, as you wish. The slender stems, which may grow up to ten feet (3 m) long, carry pairs of grey-green, heart-shaped leaves—hence the plant's common names, string of hearts and heart vine. The small, purple flowers appear in summer. There are about seventy other species of ceropegia; the one to avoid is *C. cimiciodrara*. Its name means "smelling of bugs," and its foul carrion-smell attracts flies which get trapped in the hairy flowers and escape, laden with pollen, only when the flower dies.

The Doctor Says—

Environment: Take care that the temperature in winter does not fall below 45°F (7°C), and a little higher is better. On the other hand, if you keep the plant in ordinary living-room temperatures during the winter months it will become straggly and sorry-looking. Plenty of light is essential, which it can get in a hanging basket in a window, though it will soon block your view. In summer it needs some shade from the hottest sun.
Water: From spring until autumn water only often enough to keep the compost just moist; it must never become waterlogged. For the rest of the year water only about once a month.
Feed: Once a month from spring until late summer.
Repot: Each spring in a loam-based compost, with coarse sand added to it to make it more porous. Leave the top of the tuber above soil level.
Propagate: In spring the small tubers which appear on the dangling stems may be detached, along with a bit of the stem, and potted.
Special Instructions: You should have no trouble with pests, but nevertheless keep a watchful eye.

Crassula

There are about three hundred species of crassula, providing a wide variety of succulent leaves but scarcely a striking flower among them. Because most of them are easily grown, however, they are popular, as can be deduced from all the fanciful common names they have been given.

One of the most widely grown, and one of the less interesting, is *C. arborescens*, or silver dollar plant. This branching plant is tall in its native Cape Province, but can be kept relatively small in a pot. The fleshy leaves are grey-green and have red spots and margins. The pinky white flowers are seldom produced. *C. argentea* (syn. *C. portulacea*), the jade or Chinese rubber plant, is similar in form, a bushy miniature tree, but the leaves are a shiny bright green. It, too, is shy to flower; when it does the flowers are white in terminal clusters.

C. falcata is the one crassula that is by no means reluctant to flower. The large heads of scarlet flowers appear in sum-

mer, borne on long stems which may need staking to support such a weight of bloom. It gets its common name, the sickle plant, from the shape of its thick, fleshy grey-green leaves, which grow up to four inches (10 cm) long.

A complete contrast is the really tough *C. lycopodioides*, from South-West Africa. This plant has long, thin, branching fingers which are entirely covered with small, tightly packed leaves in a tile-like pattern. The greeny-yellow flowers appear from the axils, but they are insignificant.

The Doctor Says—

Environment: All crassulas need to be in a good light throughout the year. From early spring until late summer they also need plenty of sun, but should not be exposed to the hot midday sun. From early autumn until late winter the plant should have some rest, with the temperature between 45 and 50°F (7 and 10°C). If the temperature is much higher such disasters as falling leaves and greenfly may result.

Water: From early autumn until late winter water often enough to keep the compost fairly moist; for the rest of the year water only occasionally.

Feed: Once a month from spring to summer.

Repot: Every other year in spring in a loam-based compost with added sand.

Propagate: By leaf cuttings in spring and summer.

Cyanotis kewensis

At first glance this trailing plant looks like a tradescantia, and is indeed related to it, but it is a fleshy and furry version. The whole plant is covered with short, brownish-red hair, thick enough to look like fur, explaining its popular name, the teddy bear vine. Beneath the fur the surface of the leaves are dark green and the undersides purple—best seen if the plant is grown in a hanging basket. The small purple flowers appear in winter and in spring.

C. kewensis is a native of India, but another attractive species suitable as a houseplant, *C. somaliensis*, is from Somalia. The hair on its glossy green leaves is white, and the hairs which grow around the edges are long, earning the plant the name pussy's ears. The purplish blue flowers are produced in spring.

The Doctor Says—

Environment: Although these plants are actually only semi-succulent they must be treated as succulents. Plenty of light is required throughout the year and the temperature from late autumn until early spring should be no lower than 50°F (10°C).

Water: Frequently, from late spring until late summer. For the rest of the year water only occasionally, but not so occasionally that the leaves start to shrivel.

Feed: Every two weeks from spring until early autumn.

Repot: In late spring each year if growth is rapid, every other year if it is not. Use a loam-based compost.

Propagate: By taking stem cuttings in spring and summer.

Special Instructions: Like all trailing plants *C. kewensis* may become straggly. To encourage bushy growth pinch out leaf tips.

Other Succulents

Echeveria

These succulents grow as rosettes, some with almost geometric precision, while others are less tidy. *E. pulvinata*, the plush plant is so-called because its bright green leaves are covered with soft white hairs which give them a velvety appearance; in time the hairs turn brown. This plant will grow up to twelve inches (30 cm) and produces long-lasting orange-red flowers on a long stem.

The curious attraction of *E. gibbiflora var. carunculata* is that its mauve-pink leaves, carried on a long stem, are full of warts, especially in late summer and early autumn. Another *gibbiflora* variety, *metallica*, has leaves with a bronze sheen. Two echeverias with wavy-edged leaves are *E. fulgens* (syn. *E. retusa*), which produces red flowers in summer, and *E. shaviana*, whose flowers are pink outside and orange inside.

The Doctor Says—

Environment: From autumn until early spring a minimum temperature of 45°F (7°C) is desirable; frost spells death. Throughout the whole year echeverias need a lot of light with sun in summer except at midday.

Water: Occasionally from autumn until early spring; fairly frequently for the rest of the year. Be careful not to water into the centre of the rosette or the plant may rot.

Feed: Once a month from spring until late summer.

Repot: Each year in spring in a porous, loam-based compost. As the plant grows older it may not be necessary to repot so often.

Propagate: By stem and root cuttings in summer or by offshoots or seed in early spring.

Special Instructions: Do not handle the rosette or you may dislodge the waxy covering of the leaves and cause damage. Watch for mealy bugs.

Euphorbia

Euphorbias—and there are thousands of them—were being cultivated when Antony was cultivating Cleopatra. Not all are succulents, and of those which are, the most popular is only barely so. This is *Euphorbia milii*, sometimes known as *E. splendens*, but always called the crown of thorns. The slender, branching stems carry small, rounded leaves, beautiful deep red bracts from spring onwards, and vicious thorns up to three-quarters of an inch (1.5 cm) long. Another succulent member of this family, *E. obesa*, or Turkish temple, is a strikingly curious plant—a grey-green ribbed globe with purple stripes. Unfortunately, it may be hard to track down.

The Doctor Says —

Environment: This is one succulent which will not mind living in the dry warmth of a well-heated room. From late autumn until early spring the temperature must not drop below 55°F (13°C). The plant will also relish as much sun as possible throughout the year.

Water: Fairly frequently from spring until late summer. For the rest of the year water about once a month.

Feed: Every two weeks from spring until late summer.

Repot: In spring each year, using a loam-based or peat-based compost with additional sand.

Propagate: By cuttings in spring and summer, or from seed in spring.

Special Instructions: The milky sap of euphorbias can cause skin irritation, so always wear gloves—heavy ones if you are handling the crown of thorns.

Faucaria tigrina

Teeth-edged leaves give *F. tigrina* the common name tiger's jaws, but it is thoroughly domesticated, easy to grow and eager to flower. The thick, fleshy, grey-green leaves are covered with white dots and the large, yellow flowers appear on autumn afternoons. *F. felina* has fewer teeth and is, therefore, known as cat's jaws.

The Doctor Says —

Environment: From late autumn until early spring the minimum temperature should be 45°F (7°C). Plenty of sun is appreciated for as much of the year as possible.

Water: Very frequently from late spring until late autumn, or until flowering has finished. From early winter until spring do not water.

Feed: Monthly from late spring until early autumn.

Repot: When the pot has become overcrowded, using a loam-based compost, in spring.

Propagate: By seed in spring, or from cuttings in early to late summer.

Gasteria verrucosa

One of the common names of this good-natured South African succulent, ox tongue, is derived from the shape of the thick-fleshed leaves. The white warts which stand out on the dark green leaves give it another name—warty aloe. The red, bell-shaped flowers are carried on long stems from spring until early autumn.

The Doctor Says —

Environment: A temperature not lower than 45°F (7°C) should be provided from late autumn until early spring. This plant is also happiest in a slightly shaded position.

Water: Frequently from spring until early autumn. About once a month for the rest of the year.

Feed: Monthly from spring until early autumn.

Repot: Seldom, since it grows very slowly.

Propagate: By offsets in summer.

Other Succulents

Haworthia

The attraction of the haworthias is in their rosettes of fleshy, strikingly marked leaves; the flowers are forgettable. These succulents come from South Africa, but are named after the nineteenth-century English botanist A. H. Haworth. *H. fasciata*, commonly known as the zebra haworthia, has dark green, triangular leaves which are covered with white warts, and form a small, fairly open rosette. *H. margaritifera*, the pearl plant, has the dark green leaves which stand more erect, are covered in pearly-looking warts and form a rosette which is about six inches (15 cm) in diameter. In both species the small, white flowers are carried on long stems. *H. tesselata* is an oddity—one of the so-called "window" succulents. The upper surfaces of the leaves are almost transparent so that they can absorb the sunlight they need even when much of the plant is buried in the desert sand.

The Doctor Says—

Environment: Haworthias need good light, but protection from strong sun, especially in summer. If they get too much sun the leaves will turn reddish; too much shade and they may become pale green. The resting period is from late autumn until early spring, and during that time the temperature should be about 45°F (7°C).

Water: Frequently from spring until early autumn; during the rest of the year, once a month may be enough to prevent the leaves from shrivelling.

Feed: Every three weeks from spring until late summer.

Repot: Each spring in a sandy, loam-based compost. Do not be surprised if you find the roots have rotted; remove them and new ones will grow.

Propagate: Most easily by offsets when repotting, or from seed in spring.

Kalanchoe blossfeldiana

This is a cheerful, free-flowering plant from Madagascar. When in bloom its clusters of scarlet or orange-red flowers almost obscure the dark green, red-edged leaves. Left to its own devices, it will flower in late winter and early spring, but it can be tricked into flowering at other times, and, if you have a number of plants, you could have one in bloom all year. It is a short-day plant, which means that the flower buds are formed when the hours of darkness are more than the hours of daylight. Flowering can be delayed by keeping the plant in artificial light followed by a period of darkness for about fourteen hours a day during the winter months before it is brought back into normal day lengths. Conversely, the plant will flower before its normal time if the short-day treatment is imposed in the spring or summer months. Only practice will get the timing perfect.

K. tomentosa is an entirely different plant. It seldom flowers and has fleshy leaves covered with brown and white down, earning it the name panda plant.

The Doctor Says—

Environment: For *K. blossfeldiana* to flower at the normal time, it needs a minimum winter temperature of 55°F (13°C) and good light. From spring until early autumn, allow it plenty of sun, except at midday.

Water: During the dormant period before flowering do not let the plant dry out completely, but keep the compost no more than moist. Water frequently from spring until early autumn.

Feed: Every two or three weeks from spring until late summer.

Repot: Each spring in a loam-based compost.

Propagate: By stem cuttings or seed in spring.

Lithops lesleii

Lithops are brilliant impersonators from South Africa, which perfectly mimic the stones among which they grow; their common names, living stones and pebble plants, describe them accurately. The cleverly camouflaged pebbles are in fact a pair of thick leaves with only a narrow slit between them. *L. lesleii*'s leaves are reddish brown with greenish-brown grooves. Yellow flowers appear from between the split in autumn.

The Doctor Says—

Environment: Plenty of sun and air are needed with a minimum temperature of 45°F (7°C) from late autumn until early spring.

Water: Frequently from spring until autumn, but do not get water between the slit in the leaves. Do not water for the rest of the year. During the dormant period after flowering the leaves will start to shrivel and eventually a new pair will begin to emerge. At that point begin watering again, a little at first, increasing gradually.

Feed: Once a month from spring until autumn.

Repot: Only every second or third spring for these plants are very slow growing. Use a sandy loam-based compost.

Propagate: By seed sown in spring or by dividing a clump which has become large in summer.

Special Instructions: Do not try to remove the dying leaves until they are thoroughly shrivelled lest you damage the new leaves.

Sedum sieboldii

Sedums are ancient plants and, in times gone by, were grown to give protection against thunderstorms, witches and insomnia, rather than as houseplants. Some species are tender, some hardy and *S. sieboldii* 'Mediovariegatus' is halfway between and makes a good houseplant. Slender, arching stems carry rounded leaves, with red edges and yellow blotches, and pink flowers in autumn. *S. pachyphyllum*, or jelly beans, does indeed give the impression that pale green jelly beans tipped with vivid red are growing on it, but they are merely the leaves.

The Doctor Says—

Environment: Give these plants plenty of sun and air all year round. From late autumn until early spring a temperature between 45 and 50°F (7 and 10°C) is required, and it is unwise to exceed it.

Water: About once a month, from late autumn until early spring. For the rest of the year water frequently.

Feed: Once a month from spring until early autumn.

Repot: Each spring in a loam-based compost.

Propagate: By stem cuttings in summer or from seed in spring.

Other Succulents

Sempervivum

The most attractive of these beautiful, hardy succulents from the European Alps is probably *S. arachnoideum*, the cobweb houseleek. It forms one-inch (2.5-cm) rosettes of brownish-green leaves, across the tips of which stretch white silky hairs—the "cobwebs." Heads of bright red, star-shaped flowers are carried on short stems in the summer. The rosettes die after the plant has flowered, but many offsets appear to replace them, justifying the Latin name of the genus which means "to live forever." Another attractive species is *S. tectorum*, the common houseleek, which happily grows in large clumps on the roofs of houses in many parts of Europe. The rosettes are up to three inches (7.5 cm) in diameter, the leaves are tipped with red, and the flowers appear in summer on stems about ten inches (25 cm) long.

The Doctor says—

Environment: Although in the wild sempervivums are extremely hardy, indoors they become accustomed to a certain amount of pampering. So in winter do not make them sweat it out with you in hot rooms, but on the other hand do not let the temperature fall below 45°F (7°C). In summer they like an airy position, but it must be sunny if they are to keep their showy colours.
Water: About once a month from late autumn until early spring. Water frequently the rest of the year.
Feed: Once a month from spring until early autumn.
Repot: Annually in a sandy loam compost in spring.
Propagate: Either by offsets or from seed in spring.

Senecio rowleyanus

The genus senecio has more than two thousand species, of which about a hundred are succulents. Of those *S. rowleyanus*, or string of beads, is one of the oddest. The long, trailing stems carry what look like berries with pointed tips —the "beads"—but are in fact the leaves, which are made even more curious by the translucent strip on the surface; these are the "windows" found among succulents to help them to absorb sunlight. Fragrant white and purple flowers appear from early until late autumn. The trailing stems look well in a hanging basket, but their natural inclination is to spread two or three feet (60 or 90 cm) to form a mat, putting down roots as they go.

The Doctor says—

Environment: Although this plant likes plenty of sunlight all year, it must be

Stapelia variegata

The flowers of *S. variegata* are attractive, but the smell may be off-putting, at least to humans. This is the carrion flower, and the odour of rotting flesh it exudes ensures that it is visited by blowflies to pollinate it. Any fly tricked into laying eggs in the flowers, however, condemns the offspring to death for when they emerge there is no genuine carrion for them to feed on. Opinions differ about how strongly the plant smells when it is grown as a houseplant, but ordinary houseflies do seem to be attracted to it. The flowers, which appear in early autumn, look like corpulent and flamboyant starfish—greenish-yellow with brown and purple markings.

The Doctor Says—

Environment: From autumn until late winter keep the temperature around 50°F (10°C); if it is much lower there is a risk that the plant will rot. Let it have as much light as possible throughout the year, but protect it from the hot sun between early spring and early autumn.
Water: Frequently from spring until early autumn. Only occasionally for the rest of the year so that the compost is kept fairly dry.
Feed: Once a month from spring until early autumn.
Repot: Every other spring in a sandy, loam-based compost.
Propagate: By seed in spring (germination is rapid if the temperature is about 70°F, 21°C). An alternative is to take the stem cuttings in summer. Let them dry off a little before potting them or they may rot.
Special Instructions: Shrivelling leaves are a symptom of underwatering and a bloated look is a symptom of overwatering.

protected from the hot midday sun from early spring until early autumn. In its dormant period, normally from autumn until late winter, a temperature around 50°F (10°C) should be maintained; it should not drop much lower and certainly not go much higher.
Water: Frequently from early spring until early autumn. For the rest of the year a watering once a month should be adequate.
Feed: Once a month from spring until early autumn.
Repot: Each year in early spring in a sandy loam-based compost.
Propagate: By stem cuttings during the summer or by seed in the spring.
Special Instructions: Take care that the plant does not get too cold or too warm in winter; pests and dropping leaves may result.

Bromeliads

For those who live in warm climes, or who enjoy living in very warm rooms, there is nothing to beat bromeliads—the flora of tropical rain forests which have extravagantly striped leaves and fantastic flower spikes.

Aechmea fasciata

This plant was once called *Billbergia rhodocyanea*, but is more generally known as the urn plant. In its native Brazil it is an epiphyte, growing on trees and rocks, but as a houseplant it adapts itself to growing in compost in a pot. *A. fasciata* forms a rosette from which grow strap-shaped leaves, about two feet (60 cm) long, grey-green and banded with silver. The flower spike rises from the centre of the plant with a head of pink bracts which may last for many months. Tiny blue flowers appear from the bracts. When flowering stops the parent plant dies, but it throws up side shoots which make it self-renewing.

The Doctor Says—

Environment: During the dormant period, from autumn until early spring, the temperature should be in the range of 55 to 60°F (13 to 16°C); if it drops even to 50°F (10°C) the plant will be harmed. For the rest of the year a temperature around 70°F (21°C) is ideal. Good light is always needed, but not direct sunlight. Give the plant plenty of air and spray in hot weather.

Water: From spring until early autumn keep the centre of the rosette filled with tepid, soft water; also water the compost fairly frequently, but be judicious for the plant can rot as the result of excessive watering. For the rest of the year do not water into the rosette and water the compost only occasionally.

Feed: Give a weak feed once a month from spring until early autumn.

Repot: Not necessary in the ordinary sense since the old plant dies after flowering. Take the whole plant out of the pot, cut away the old shoot, and repot one of the young shoots (if there are more than one) along with the root.

Propagate: When replanting the one chosen offset along with the old root remove the other offsets and plant them in a mixture of loam (which must be lime-free), peat and leaf mould.

Ananas comosus

This is the pineapple, a plant with a five-hundred-year history. It came from Brazil and was first heard of in Europe soon after the discovery of America in 1492. It is terrestrial, not epiphytic, and the version usually grown as a houseplant is *A.c.* 'Variegatus', which has attractive green and white to yellow foliage. The long, narrow leaves, which are menacingly serrated, grow in the form of a rosette. From the centre of it a spike of purple flowers appears and is followed by the fruit. It never ripens, unfortunately, and is therefore inedible. After flowering, the parent plant dies, but its offshoots can be potted.

The Doctor Says—

Environment: From autumn until early spring the temperature must not fall below 60°F (16°C), and a considerably higher temperature is far better. For the

remainder of the year keep the temperature between 65 and 75°F (18 and 24°C). This plant requires as much light as you can give it and full sunlight if the bright colouring of the leaves is to be maintained. During the summer months spray occasionally.

Water: From spring until early autumn water frequently, but only occasionally the rest of the year. How occasional this is will depend on the temperature in which the plant is kept; the higher the temperature, the more often you will have to water.

Feed: Every two or three weeks from spring until early autumn.

Repot: Each spring in a loam-based or a peat-based compost. If the plant fruits, the parent plant will die off and you will have to plant the suckers.

Propagate: From side suckers when repotting.

Billbergia leptopoda

The billbergias are terrestrial bromeliads from South and Central America—Brazil and Mexico in particular. *B. leptopoda*, the permanent wave plant, grows to about twelve inches (30 cm) tall, producing a rosette of broad green leaves, which are banded and spotted with cream and have curling tips. From the rosette emerge pink bracts with blue and green flowers. The most popular billbergia is *B. nutans*, known as angel's tears or queen's tears. The narrow, arching leaves, about twenty inches (50 cm) long, are dark green and have a metallic sheen. From early winter, green and blue flowers and pink bracts are carried on long, slender stems. *B. pyramidalis*, the foolproof plant, also flowers in the winter months. The broad, bright green leaves form a very pronounced rosette and scarlet bracts and red flowers emerge from its centre. *B. saundersii*, the rainbow plant, is low-growing with a few broad, grey-green leaves and a mixture of red, green and blue flowers.

The Doctor Says—

Environment: All billbergias are best kept at a fairly consistent temperature throughout the year—between 60 and 65°F (16 and 18°C). Certainly the temperature must never fall below 55°F (13°C) or the plant will be damaged. Keep it in a good light, but shade from the sun is essential.

Water: Frequently from spring until autumn, occasionally for the rest of the year, keeping the compost just moist.

Feed: Once a month from spring until early autumn.

Repot: Each spring in a peat-based compost.

Propagate: By division when repotting.

Bromeliads

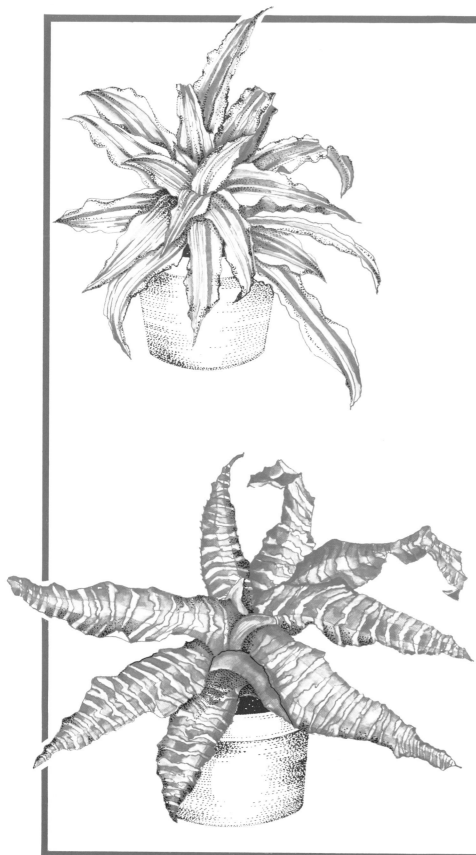

Cryptanthus acaulis

The patterned and coloured foliage is the attraction of these Brazilian bromeliads, most of which are terrestrial. *C. acaulis*, the earth star or starfish, is low-growing, forming a rosette about five inches (12.5 cm) in diameter. The sharply-toothed leaves are bright green on top, with a whitish colouring on the undersides. The white flowers, which appear throughout the year, are insignificant. *C. bromelioides* 'Tricolor', the rainbow star, grows to about twelve inches (30 cm), and the broad leaves have wavy edges and grow from a central rosette. They are strikingly striped with green, yellow and white, and edged with pink. *C. bivittatus* has broad, wavy-edged leaves with bands of deep green and salmon pink. *C. fosterianus* gets its common name, pheasant leaf, from the horizontal bands of brown and grey which make the leaves look like pheasant feathers. The rosette grows up to twenty-four inches in diameter (60 cm)—showiness with which the insignificant white flowers cannot compete. *C. zonatus*, the zebra plant, has leaves which are only about nine inches (22.5 cm) long, wavy-edged, spiny, with horizontal markings of silver and browny-green. The white flowers are produced from the leaf axils and are small and almost unnoticeable.

The Doctor says—

Environment: From autumn until early spring, temperatures should be in the range of 60 to 65°F (16 to 18°C), but *C. bromelioides* 'Tricolor' will do better if the temperature is about 70°F (21°C). For the rest of the year the temperature should be between 65 and 75°F (18 and 24°C). Plenty of light is required, especially by the variegated plants if they are to retain their strong colouring, but shade them from brilliant sunlight during the summer months. They like a humid atmosphere; it helps if the pot is surrounded by moist peat or stands on a dish of wet pebbles.

Water: Frequently from spring until early autumn, keeping the compost moist all the time, but not sodden. For the rest of the year keep the compost just moist by occasional watering.

Feed: Once a month from spring until early autumn.

Repot: Each spring in a peat-based compost.

Propagate: From offsets removed in spring when repotting.

Guzmania lingulata

These bromeliads come from the tropical rain forests of Central and South America and the West Indies. Most of them are epiphytic, but there are some terrestrials. They are notable for the brilliance of their bracts. *Guzmania lingulata*, the scarlet star, has mid-green leaves tinged with red. They grow to about eighteen inches (45 cm) long from a central rosette. Yellowish flowers are carried on long stems from bright red bracts. The flowers live briefly, but the bracts last for many weeks. *G. berteroniana*, with leaves about eighteen inches (45 cm) long, has showy, orange-red bracts and yellow flowers. *G. zahni* has delicate-looking leaves, about twenty inches (50 cm) long, striped with reddish brown. The scarlet bracts, with white flowers, may last as long as two months.

The Doctor Says—

Environment: From autumn until early spring the temperature must not fall below 60°F (16°C). For the rest of the year it should be a few degrees higher—in the range of 65 to 70°F (18 to 21°C). Guzmanias require a rather shady position, direct sunlight being avoided at all costs. High humidity is also essential; plunging the pot in damp peat or standing it on wet pebbles will help; also spray frequently during the growing period.

Water: Frequently from spring until early autumn, keeping the centre of the rosette filled with water. For the rest of the year water occasionally so that the compost is just moist, but keep the rosette dry.

Feed: Once a month from spring until early autumn.

Repot: The parent plant dies after flowering, but until that happens repot the plant every other year in spring, using a peat-based compost. On the death of the parent plant, pot the offsets which appear from the central rosette.

Propagate: From offsets removed after flowering is over.

Neoregelia carolinae 'Tricolor'

The remarkable feature of the neoregelias is the way in which the leaves surrounding the rosette change from shades of green to brilliant shades of red when the plant is about to flower. The flowers themselves, mostly shades of blue, are not particularly noteworthy. The leaves of *N. carolinae* 'Tricolor' are about twelve inches (30 cm) long, a glossy, bright green striped with white, but those around the centre turn brilliant crimson in readiness for the plant's flowering.

The Doctor Says—

Environment: From autumn until early spring the temperature is best kept within the range of 60 to 65°F (16 to 18°C) and should certainly fall no lower than 55°F (13°C). For the rest of the year the ideal range is 65 to 70°F (18 to 21°C). *N.c.* 'Tricolor' needs some light to maintain its variegations, but never expose any neoregelia to direct sunlight. Fortunately, these bromeliads are tolerant of a dry atmosphere, but an occasional spraying in summer is welcome.

Water: Fairly frequently from spring until early autumn and keep the centre of the rosette filled with water. For the rest of the year keep the compost just moist and the rosette dry.

Feed: Once a month from spring until early autumn.

Repot: Every other spring in a peat-based compost.

Propagate: By removing offsets in late spring or when the flowering has finished and the parent plant is dying.

Bromeliads

Nidularium innocentii

This plant gets its Latin name (*nidus* means nest) and its common name, bird's nest, because looked at from above, given a certain degree of imagination, it does look like a nest. *N. innocentii* has narrow, strap-shaped leaves edged with tiny teeth. The tips of the leaves are tinged with purple and the undersides are red. Before and after the white flowers appear the central leaves of the rosette turn orange. The whole rosette can reach about two feet (60 cm) in diameter. There is, however, a smaller version, *N.i.* 'Nana', and a popular American strain *N.i.* 'Paxianum'. *N. fulgens* has shiny, mid-green leaves spotted with a darker green and they grow to about twelve inches (30 cm). Blue flowers are produced from the centre of the rosette which turns red before and after flowering.

The Doctor Says—

Environment: From autumn until early spring maintain a temperature in the range of 60 to 65°F (16 to 18°C), although *N. fulgens* will probably tolerate a temperature as low as 55°F (13°C). For the rest of the year the range should be 65 to 70°F (18 to 21°C). Place the plant in partial shade and always out of direct sunlight. Surrounding the pot with damp peat or standing it on wet pebbles, plus frequent spraying, will help to give the plant the humidity it requires.
Water: Fairly frequently from spring until early autumn and keep the centre of the rosette filled with water. For the rest of the year keep the rosette dry and water the compost occasionally just to keep it moist.
Feed: Once a month from spring until early autumn.
Repot: Every other spring in a peat-based compost.
Propagate: From offsets in late spring.

Tillandsia lindeniana

Tillandsias are to be found growing in the wild all the way from the United States through Central America down to Chile. There are more than five hundred species, but few take to the indoor life. *T. lindeniana*, the blue-flowered torch, is rather palm-like with its narrow, arching leaves, the undersides tinged with purple. From the rosette the flower spike bears overlapping pink bracts from which blue flowers emerge. *T. cyanea* is similar in general appearance to *T. lindeniana*, but the leaves are marked with reddish brown. The flower spike has pink bracts and blue flowers. *T. punctulata*'s long, narrow leaves are tinged with silvery grey; the bracts are red and the flowers white and purple. *T. usneoides*, well known as Spanish moss, is entirely different in appearance, a true epiphyte. It has wiry, grey-green stems which are densely intertwined. During the summer yellowish flowers are produced.

Environment: The suitable temperature range from autumn until early spring is 60 to 65°F (16 to 18°C), and for the rest of the year 65 to 70°F (18 to 21°C) is ideal. A tillandsia needs plenty of light, but not direct sunlight. It also needs a situation which is both airy and humid, a rather difficult climate to maintain. The best you can do is to put the plant in a well-ventilated room and to stand the pot on wet pebbles or surround it with always damp peat and spray it often.
Water: From spring until early autumn water fairly frequently, checking the compost regularly in hot weather to make sure that it is not drying out. For the rest of the year, water occasionally to keep the compost just moist.
Feed: Once a month from spring until early autumn.
Repot: Each spring in a peat-based compost with added sharp sand.
Propagate: From offsets removed during the summer.

Vriesia splendens

Spectacular bromeliads from various parts of Central and South America, many vriesias are epiphytes. *V. splendens*, known as the flaming sword, has dark green, strap-shaped leaves with brownish-red horizontal bands which grow about twelve inches (30 cm) long in rosette formation. The flower spike grows up to fifteen inches (37.5 cm) and is covered with overlapping bright red bracts for much of its length. From these, small yellow flowers appear during the summer months. *V. psittacina*, the dwarf painted feather, has narrow, yellowy-green, strap-shaped leaves which are about eight inches (20 cm) long. The flower spike, about ten inches (25 cm) long, is a striking combination of colours – overlapping red bracts with yellow edges from which emerge green and yellow flowers. The Latin name of *V. hieroglyphica* refers to what look like hieroglyphs formed on the bright green leaves by the dark green bands on their underside. The common name, king of the bromeliads, probably reflects its size; the leaves are about twenty inches (50 cm) long and the flowering spike, up to two feet (60 cm), produces yellow flowers in spring.

The Doctor Says—

Environment: From autumn until early spring it is best not to let the temperature fall below 65°F (18°C), although the plant will tolerate a lower temperature. For the rest of the year a range of 65 to 75°F (18 to 24°C) will be necessary if the colourful bracts are to last for long. The plant must never be put in direct sunlight, but although it needs a degree of shade it must also have enough light to maintain its variegation and to produce flowers. Standing the pot on wet pebbles, or surrounding it with moist peat, and frequent misting in summer will contribute to the essential humidity.
Water: Frequently from spring until early autumn and keep the rosette filled with water. For the rest of the year water the compost occasionally, but keep the rosette dry.
Feed: Once a month from spring until early autumn.
Repot: Every two or three years should be enough. Use a mixture of equal parts of spagnum moss, sand and peat.
Propagate: In spring from offsets.

117

Flowering Plants

As a general rule, you can expect flowering plants to need more care than foliage plants. Many of them are fussy about the conditions in which they will form flower buds. Good light is necessary to bring them into bloom, but not too much warmth and light if the flowers are to last. And pests find them desirable. The investment is more than worthwhile, however, in those plants which flower over a long period and look attractive for the rest of the year.

Abutilon megapotamicum

Although often called a flowering maple, this rapidly growing shrub from Brazil is a member of the mallow family. The elongated, heart-shaped leaves are bright green, a striking background for the lantern-shaped, red and yellow flowers which appear from spring until autumn. It grows to about four feet (1.20 m).

The Doctor Says—

Environment: From autumn until early spring, when the plant is dormant, the ideal range of temperature is 45 to 55°F (7 to 13°C); in summer it is 55 to 65°F (13 to 18°C). Needs good light all year, but in summer should be shaded from direct sun and given plenty of air.
Water: Frequently from early spring until early autumn, but very occasionally for the rest of the year.
Feed: Weekly from early spring until early autumn.
Repot: Each spring in a loam-based compost.
Propagate: By taking stem cuttings in summer.
Special Instructions: To encourage bushiness, prune back hard in spring.

Acalypha hispida

The chenille plant, or red hot cat's tail, comes from the steamy forests of New Guinea, indicating the conditions in which it flourishes. It is capable of growing to twelve feet (3.60 m) and the showy red tassles it bears from late spring until early autumn may be more than fifteen inches (38 cm) long.

The Doctor Says—

Environment: This plant needs warmth and humidity. A minimum winter temperature of 60°F (16°C) is a must, and a few degrees higher are better. In summer, temperatures in the range of 65 to 70°F (18 to 21°C) are required. To help provide a humid atmosphere around the plant, surround the pot with moist peat or stand it on a tray of wet pebbles. Keep it in a good light all year, but in summer protect it from direct sunlight.
Water: Frequently all year so the compost is always moist.
Feed: Every two weeks from spring until early autumn.
Repot: Each spring, preferably in a peat-based compost.
Propagate: By stem cuttings in spring, but they need considerable heat—about 75°F (24°C) in a heated propagator.
Special Instructions: If the plant is getting out of hand cut it back in early spring. Lack of humidity will make the leaves curl and will encourage red spider mites and aphids.

Achimenes longiflora

The long, trailing stems of the Central American hot water plant, or magic flower, make it very suitable for a hanging basket; otherwise it will need some support. It is a seasonal plant; the hairy, dark green leaves die down when flowering is finished and the tuber is then stored until the following year. The flowers, usually purple with white centres, appear from early summer until early autumn.

The Doctor Says —

Environment: When potted in early spring, the tuber needs a temperature around 65°F (18°C). Thereafter until early autumn it should be kept in the range of 55 to 65°F (13 to 18°C), in a humid atmosphere and good light, but out of direct sunlight. When the plant has finished flowering in early autumn and the stems have died, cut them off cleanly at soil level. The tuber may either be left in the compost if it is thoroughly dried off, or stored in dry sand at a temperature of about 50°F (10°C).
Water: Occasionally from early until late spring and then frequently throughout the summer. Stop watering after the plant has flowered.
Feed: Every two weeks from early spring until early summer.
Repot: Each spring in a peat-based compost.
Propagate: By dividing the tuber when repotting.

Anthurium andreanum

This exotic-looking plant is, not surprisingly, a native of the tropical rain forests of Central and South America. *A. andreanum*'s dark green leaves are an elongated heart shape, up to eight inches (20 cm) long. Carried on a long stem, the red bract is a plumper heart shape (hence one common name, painter's palette) from which protrudes a yellow spadix (hence another name, tail flower). The smaller *A. scherzerianum*, the flamingo flower or pigtail plant, often proves to be a more successful houseplant. It has dark green leaves and the waxy flowers, which appear from early spring until summer, are scarlet with a reddy orange spadix.

The Doctor Says —

Environment: Anthuriums need warmth and humidity; a minimum temperature of 60°F (16°C) from autumn until early spring, and around 70°F (21°C) for the rest of the year. *A. andreanum* is most likely to succeed in the humid air of a greenhouse, but if it is indoors the pot should be plunged in moist peat or stood on a tray of wet pebbles.
A. scherzerianum makes a better houseplant if it is given a light situation, but with shade from direct sun in summer.
Water: From early spring until late summer water frequently, and for the rest of the year keep the compost just moist between waterings. Use lukewarm, soft water if possible.
Feed: Every two weeks from early spring until early autumn.
Repot: Each spring in a peat-based compost to which a little sphagnum moss has been added.
Propagate: By division in spring or from seed in a heated propagator.
Special Instructions: There is a risk of attack by red spider mites if the air is dry.

Flowering Plants

Aphelandra squarrosa

The Brazilian aphelandra gets its common names—tiger plant and zebra plant—from the prominent markings formed by the veins of the leaves. On the glossy, dark green leaves of *A.s.* 'Louisae', which grows about eight inches (20 cm) long, the markings are white. *A.s.* 'Brockfeld' is more attractive; the markings are cream and the leaves do not droop like those of the 'Louisae' variety. Yellow flowers appear from pyramid-shaped bracts, which are yellow edged with red. The plants flower for about three weeks during the period from late spring until late summer. After flowering the bracts turn green.

The Doctor Says—

Environment: From autumn until early spring the temperature should be at least between 55 and 60°F (13 and 16°C), and better if somewhat higher. For the rest of the year keep the temperature between 65 and 70°F (18 and 21°C). The plant needs a well-lit position out of hot, direct sunlight. The atmosphere should be humid while the plant is growing; spray frequently as well as surrounding the pot with moist peat or standing it on wet pebbles. But drier air is better while the plant is in flower.

Water: From autumn until early spring water occasionally. Frequent watering will be necessary for the rest of the year.

Feed: Every two weeks from spring until late summer.

Repot: Each spring in either a loam-based or a peat-based compost.

Propagate: From stem cuttings in spring, but a temperature no lower than 65°F (18°C) will be needed.

Special Instructions: When the plant has finished flowering, prune back the top growth by about a quarter to just above a good pair of leaves. This will promote new growth for the following year. Leaves drooping or dropping off may be a sign that the plant is not getting enough water. If the air is too dry the edges of the leaves are liable to turn brown.

Beloperone guttata

The shrimp plant, which comes from Mexico, is a comparative newcomer as houseplants go, having been in cultivation only since the 1930s. It grows about twelve inches (30 cm) tall. The small, slightly shiny leaves are mid green in colour. White flowers appear between late spring and late autumn, emerging from the pinky-brown bracts which resemble shrimp.

The Doctor Says—

Environment: From autumn until early spring the temperature should not fall below 50°F (10°C) and the plant does best in the range of 55 to 60°F (13 to 16°C). The summer temperature should

be between 60 and 65°F (16 and 18°C). This plant needs a light airy position, protected from direct sun during the summer.

Water: Frequently from spring until autumn. For the rest of the year only as often as necessary to keep the compost just moist.

Feed: Every two weeks from spring until early autumn.

Repot: Each year in spring in a loam-based or a peat-based compost.

Propagate: By stem cuttings in spring.

Special Instructions: To keep the plant bushy, cut it back when the flowering has finished or in early spring before the new growth has begun.

Browallia speciosa

The browallias are annual plants which will grow outdoors, but because they flower so generously they also make excellent pot plants. *B. speciosa* grows to about two feet (60 cm), has small leaves and large flowers which are star-shaped and purple with white centres. *B. viscosa* 'Sapphire' is more compact, about nine inches (22.5 cm) tall and the flowers are blue.

The Doctor Says—

Environment: This relatively hardy plant needs temperatures in the range of 45 to 55°F (7 to 13°C) from spring until early autumn. It needs good light but with little exposure to direct sunlight.

Water: Frequently enough to keep the compost moist, but not sodden, at all times.

Feed: Once every two weeks beginning when you see flower buds forming.

Repot: Not necessary, as it is better to raise new plants from seed each year.

Propagate: From seed—successional sowings will provide flowers for much of the year. If you sow seed in autumn and early winter, however, temperatures of between 65 and 70°F (18 and 21°C) will be needed to raise them properly, and even then they will not flower for as long a period as plants from seed sown in spring and summer.

Special Instructions: Pinch out the growing tips of young plants to make them bushy. To encourage the production of fresh buds remove flowers as soon as they begin to shrivel.

Brunfelsia calycina

This evergreen shrub from Brazil has acquired the name yesterday, today and tomorrow because it flowers profusely for such a long time—from spring until early autumn. The delicate-looking flowers are about two inches (5 cm) in diameter, deep purple with white centres when they open, but growing gradually lighter. The leaves, which may be as long as four inches (10 cm), are shiny and leathery.

The Doctor Says—

Environment: It is probably best to keep this plant always in the temperature range of 60 to 70°F (16 to 21°C). Certainly from autumn until early spring the temperature should not fall below 55°F (13°C). A light position is essential to get plenty of flowers, but the plant must be protected from hot sunlight in summer. Occasional spraying is beneficial.

Water: Frequently from spring until early autumn; occasionally for the rest of the year.

Feed: Every two weeks from spring until early autumn.

Repot: Brunfelsia does not grow quickly so repotting need only be done every two or three years in early spring. Use a peat-based compost with, if available, a little added leaf mould.

Propagate: By stem cuttings in summer, but a temperature of around 70°F (21°C) will be needed.

Special Instructions: There is the risk of greenfly if the atmosphere is too dry.

Flowering Plants

Calceolaria x herbeohybrida

The calceolaria is a showy plant which hybridization has made even more flamboyant. The flowers, which go through the whole gamut of reds, yellows and oranges, are produced from late spring until summer. They are curiously shaped, each one forming a pouch with a slipper-shaped lip—hence its common name, slipper plant. The rounded green leaves are soft to the touch and covered with minute hairs which give a velvety texture. The plants grow about eighteen inches (45 cm) tall.

The Doctor Says—

Environment: Calceolarias are usually bought in spring when they are coming into bud. If they are to flower well they must not be exposed to strong sunlight, nor kept too warm. The ideal temperature is between 50 and 55°F (10 and 13°C); a higher temperature will result in fewer flowers. Good light is necessary, but not bright sunlight.
Water: Plants which are growing strongly and flowering will need watering frequently from late spring until summer.
Feed: Every two weeks after the flower buds have started forming.
Repot: There is no occasion to repot since the common practice is to buy new plants or raise them from seed each year.
Propagate: To raise your own plants, sow seed from early summer until early autumn to flower in spring and early summer of the following year. Water the compost occasionally to keep it just moist.
Special Instructions: Keep a careful watch for aphids.

Camellia japonica

Early flowering—from late winter until late spring—is the great virtue of the camellia, an evergreen shrub with glossy, dark green leaves. The camellia originated in Japan, arrived in Europe at the beginning of the nineteenth century, but was not widely grown in the United States until the 1930s. It is usually grown as a pot plant until it is about three feet (90 cm) tall and then it is planted outdoors. The rose-like flowers may be single, semi-double or double. The choice is wide and includes 'Adolphe Audusson', which has semi-double, blood red flowers, 'Alba Simplex', with single, white flowers, 'Mathotiana Rosea', with double, orange red flowers and 'Chandleri', which bears semi-double, deep red flowers streaked with white.

The Doctor Says—

Environment: *C. japonica* requires cool conditions all year. That means a temperature range of 45 to 55°F (7 to 13°C). Coolness is vital from late autumn until mid-winter when the flower buds are forming; otherwise the buds will simply drop. A light position, out of direct sun, is also necessary all year. If possible, put the plant outside in the garden or on a balcony from spring until autumn. The next best position is near a window where it will get plenty of air.
Water: Frequently from spring until summer, and always with lime-free water. For the rest of the year only as often as necessary to keep the compost barely moist.
Feed: Every two weeks from early winter until early summer with an acid fertilizer.
Repot: In spring, or when flowering is over, using a peat-based compost.
Propagate: From cuttings in late summer.
Special Instructions: Never use hard water. It can make the leaves turn yellow.

Campanula isophylla

The bell flower from northern Italy may be grown trailing from a basket or climbing up a trellis. The blue, star-shaped flowers are about one inch (2.5 cm) across when they appear in late summer and early autumn. They almost completely hide the small, pale, grey-green leaves. *C.i. alba* has white flowers. The blue and the white campanulas planted together in the same pot make an effective contrast.

The Doctor Says—

Environment: From autumn until early spring provide a temperature of about 45°F (7°C), and between 45 and 55°F (7 and 13°C) for the rest of the year. Campanulas like as much light and air as possible. A window sill provides an excellent position as long as the plant is not exposed to scorching sunlight.
Water: From autumn until late spring keep the compost barely moist, especially if conditions are as cool as they should be. For the rest of the year water frequently.
Feed: Every two weeks from spring until early autumn.
Repot: Each spring in a loam-based compost.
Propagate: From cuttings in spring.
Special Instructions: The plant usually dies down in the winter. In spring when there are signs of new growth remove the old shoots and increase the frequency of watering.

Clerodendrum thomsonae

The bleeding heart vine from West Africa is a climbing evergreen which grows to about six feet (1.80 m). It has glossy, dark green leaves and the flowers, small, red, star-shaped and surrounded by white calyces, appear in showy clusters from early summer until early autumn. Another showy species is *C. speciosissimum*, the Java glorybean, It grows about three feet (90 cm) tall, and carries large mid-green leaves and scarlet flowers in clusters on a long stem.

The Doctor Says—

Environment: This is a plant for a fairly warm room. From autumn until early spring the temperature should fall no lower than 55°F (13°C), and for the remainder of the year it should be between 65 and 70°F (18 and 21°C). Good light is needed all year, but with shade from hot summer sun. The plant will be grateful for regular spraying in the period before flowering.
Water: During the dormant period, from autumn until early spring, water only occasionally. Frequent watering will be necessary the rest of the year.
Feed: Every two weeks from spring until early autumn.
Repot: Each spring in either a loam-based or a peat-based compost.
Propagate: Take stem cuttings or sow seed in spring.
Special Instructions: Before repotting in spring cut the plant back to about a quarter of its size to encourage vigorous new growth.

Flowering Plants

Clivia miniata

Named after Lady Clive, Duchess of Northumberland, the clivia is a native of Natal, South Africa, so it is also known as the Kafir lily. The strap-shaped, glossy, deep green leaves are produced in pairs from the centre of the plant and often grow twenty-four inches (60 cm) long. The trumpet-shaped flowers, usually orange, but occasionally yellow, are carried in a cluster on a long, thick stem; there can be between twelve and twenty-four individual flowers on one stem. Usually the flowers, which last about a month, appear in early spring, but sometimes a plant will not flower until late summer.

The Doctor Says—

Environment: This plant is remarkably easy to look after, but to flower well it does need a dormant period. So from autumn until late winter it should be kept in a temperature of 50 to 55°F (10 to 13°C). In spring and summer the temperature can go up to 65°F (18°C). A well-lit position is needed, but out of hot direct sunlight.
Water: From autumn until late winter, water very occasionally, and only if the compost has almost dried out completely. For the rest of the year water fairly frequently.
Feed: Once a month from spring until late summer.
Repot: This plant does best when it is potbound. Potting on is necessary only when roots appear above the surface of the compost. When repotting is necessary do it after flowering, using a loam-based compost.
Propagate: By offsets when repotting.
Special Instructions: When the last flower has dropped off, cut off the flower head near the top of the stalk. Let the stalk wither before removing it. Regularly wipe dust off both sides of the leaves.

Columnea microphylla

The so-called goldfish vine comes from the tropical rain forests of Costa Rica where it grows epiphytically high up in the trees. In the house it looks best in a hanging basket, with the stems trailing down as much as three feet (90 cm). The small, hairy, dark green leaves grow in pairs along each side of the stems. From late autumn until spring they are also covered with red flowers, two-lipped and yellow-throated.

The Doctor Says—

Environment: The columnea likes a fairly warm room, but not a dry one, a dislike it will demonstrate by refusing to flower. From autumn until early spring the temperature should be around 60°F (16°C). The rest of the year 65°F (18°C) is ideal. If you put the plant near a window see that it is shaded from direct sunlight.
Water: Fairly frequently from spring until early autumn, but never let the compost become waterlogged. For the rest of the year, when the plant is not in flower, keep the compost barely moist between waterings; if it is too wet the next flowering may be affected.
Feed: Every two weeks from late spring until early autumn.
Repot: Every other year will probably be sufficient. Repot when flowering is over, using a peat-based compost.
Propagate: Take stem cuttings after flowering has finished.

Cyclamen persicum

In the wild, cyclamen is found in the area around the eastern Mediterranean. It is very common, for example, in Greece. It became popular as a greenhouse plant early in the nineteenth century and since then innumerable cultivars have been raised. The leaves are heart-shaped, either light or dark green and marbled with silver. From among the leaves, from autumn until late winter, there emerge masses of flowers, their shape often compared to a shuttlecock. Colours range from white, through pink to deep red.

The Doctor Says —

Environment: The reasons so many cyclamen die prematurely are that they are given too much warmth and too much water, and they are given as presents at the wrong time of the year. This is not a plant for centrally heated rooms, since it requires a temperature throughout the year in the range of 45 to 55°F (7 to 13°C)—uncomfortably cool for living in. In addition, it flourishes best in slightly humid, fresh air and needs good light in winter if it is to flower well. There is a better chance of meeting some of these requirements in a cool bedroom than in a living room. Cyclamen are usually bought around Christmas when they are already starting to flower. They are then put in rooms far too warm for them, usually with the result that the leaves turn yellow and the buds droop and die. If a plant has to go in a living room give it the coolest, lightest position you can. A window sill might do because a cyclamen does not mind direct winter sun, but it must be removed at night if there is any danger of frost.

Surrounding the pot with moist peat will help to increase humidity. Any spraying should be confined to the leaves for the flowers are easily damaged by water.

Water: During the growing season the compost should be kept just moist; if it is always wet the corm and roots are liable to rot. Never water directly on the corm. If you water from above pour the water carefully on the compost between the corm and the sides of the pot. Alternatively, water from below by standing the pot in shallow water for about twenty minutes. Never leave it standing in a saucer of water.

Feed: Every two weeks when new growth appears after dormancy.

Repot: Each year in late summer, and although a special cyclamen potting soil may be used by nurserymen, a peat-based compost is satisfactory. When planting leave the corm showing just above the surface of the compost.

Propagate: From seed sown in autumn or spring.

Special Instructions: The drying off period of the corm is important. When flowering ceases the plant will for a time go on producing leaves to build up the corm for the next crop of flowers. During this time keep the compost just moist. When leaf growth slows down reduce the frequency of watering. When the leaves begin to turn yellow stop watering altogether. Break off the dead stems cleanly from the corm, leaving no little bits behind which would set off rotting. Place the corm—in its pot—in a cool, dark place, bringing it back into the light in summer, and giving it only a little water. As new leaves appear, gradually increase the amount of water given to keep the compost just moist, not sodden. Too dry an atmosphere is bad for the plant and encourages red spider mites.

Flowering Plants

Euphorbia pulcherrima

This plant began its houseplant life early in the nineteenth century as *Poinsettia pulcherrima*, in honour of the American diplomat Dr. J. R. Poinsett who brought it back to the United States from Mexico. When it was later discovered to be a spurge it had to change its generic name to *Euphorbia*. No matter, we all know it, and either love or hate it, as poinsettia. It is popular because it is one of the few plants that will provide a lot of colour around Christmas without dying as soon as it gets into a heated room. Many people throw the plant away when the brilliantly coloured bracts die, but it will give repeat performances if the hours it is made to spend in the light are limited for two months in the autumn.

The leaves of the poinsettia are mid green, the yellow flowers are unmemorable, but they are surrounded by striking bracts which may be bright red, pink or white, depending on the cultivar.

Another Mexican euphorbia is the shrub *E. fulgens*, known as scarlet plume. Long, narrow, pointed leaves grow on arching stems and the flowers are orange.

The Doctor says—

Environment: If you buy or are given a poinsettia in winter when it is already in flower, keep it in a light position at a temperature around 65°F (18°C) and never much below that. A similar temperature is needed for the rest of the year, as well as good light but not direct sunlight. *E. fulgens* is particularly resentful of draughts, which cause it to drop its leaves.

Water: From late spring until late autumn keep the compost just moist. If the plant is not getting enough moisture, however, it will point out the fact by drooping leaves. Cut down the frequency of watering when the plant has finished flowering and water it only occasionally until late spring.

Feed: Once a week from early summer until autumn.

Repot: In late spring in either a loam-based or a peat-based compost. Before repotting, prune back hard to six inches (15 cm), leaving the sturdiest shoots.

Propagate: By cuttings in early summer.

Special Instructions: *E. pulcherrima* is a short-day plant; if it is denied an adequate ration of darkness it will not produce the red bracts which are the whole point of growing it. To ensure that they do appear, and do so around Christmas, put the plant somewhere in mid-autumn where it will have ten hours of light and fourteen hours of total darkness each day. After eight weeks the plant can be put back into the light and the red bracts should appear in about four weeks.

Fuchsia magellanica

This curiously attractive plant was discovered by a Frenchman, Charles Plumier, in Peru, but it was named after a German botanist, L. Fuchs, by the Swedish naturalist Count von Linne (or Linnaeus). *F. magellanica* can be grown as a standard shrub or used as a trailing plant in a hanging basket. The slender stems carry oval, mid-green leaves. The flowers are bell-shaped and carried in clusters from late spring until autumn. Many of the cultivars bear flowers which are a combination of two colours—white and pink, red and white, purple and red—or they may be simple reds and pinks. There are thousands of cultivars and some have flowers more than two inches (5 cm) long.

One of the problems of growing *F. magellanica* indoors is that it likes a cool, moist atmosphere. But *F. triphylla*, the very popular honeysuckle fuchsia, comes from the West Indies and is more at home in higher temperatures. The long, oval leaves are green on the upper surface and purple underneath. Thin tubular red flowers appear from summer until autumn.

The Doctor Says—

Environment: From autumn until early spring the temperature in which *F. magellanica* is kept should not fall below 45°F (7°C). *F. triphylla*, not quite as hardy, needs at least 50°F (10°C). These are minimum temperatures and both species will thrive better if the temperature is in the low 50sF (10 to 12°C). For the rest of the year the temperature should be 55 to 65°F (13 to

18°C). Fuchsias need to be in a light position all year, but protected from direct sunlight. In the summer growing season they benefit from being in an airy situation, if possible with a period outdoors. Also spray frequently during the summer months.

Water: From autumn until early spring the compost is kept just moist, but for the rest of the year water frequently. Buds are likely to fall if the plant is allowed to become dry.

Feed: Once a week from spring until early autumn.

Repot: Each year in early spring, using either a loam-based or a peat-based compost.

Propagate: From cuttings taken in spring and summer.

Special Instructions: To keep the plant bushy, cut it back hard in early spring before repotting. Fuchsias are favourite targets for aphids and red spider mites if the air is dry.

Flowering Plants

Hibiscus rosa-sinensis

This evergeen shrub, commonly called rose of China, grows up to six feet (1.80 m) tall. The dark green leaves with slightly serrated edges are pleasant enough, but it is the flowers which are striking. They are funnel-shaped with long protruding stamens, and those of some of the new hybrids and cultivars are of a staggering size and are even double, The colours range through yellow, orange, red and pink. The flowers do not last long, but they appear in great profusion from early summer until autumn.

The Doctor Says—

Environment: From autumn until early spring keep the plant in a temperature range of 55 to 60°F (13 to 16°C); at lower temperatures leaves will fall. Temperatures for the rest of the year between 60 and 65°F (16 and 18°C) should ensure plenty of flowers. Keep the plant in good light, but not exposed to direct sunlight. Spray occasionally.
Water: Frequently from spring until early autumn, Fairly frequently for the rest of the year.
Feed: Every week from early spring until late summer.
Repot: Each year in early spring in a loam-based compost.
Propagate: From cuttings in summer in a heated propagator.
Special Instructions: Cut back the plant in early spring to keep its size under control.

Hoya bella

The wax plant from India gets its common name from the texture of the flowers. They are star-shaped, white with reddish centres, fragrant and borne in large clusters from late spring until early autumn. The leaves, about one inch (2.5 cm) long, are dark green, sometimes spotted with white. *H. bella* grows to about eighteen inches (45 cm).

The Doctor Says—

Environment: From autumn until early spring a temperature between 50 and 55°F (10 and 13°C) is required. The temperature for the rest of the year should be in the range of 60 to 65°F (16 to 18°C) to ensure a good show of flowers. Hoyas need fresh air, plenty of light—but not direct sunlight—and a humid atmosphere in the period before flowering; spray frequently.
Water: From spring until late summer water frequently, but for the rest of the year only occasionally. As the time of dormancy approaches begin watering less frequently, increasing it gradually when the plant starts into growth again.
Feed: Every two weeks from spring until late summer.
Repot: Every other year in spring in a loam-based or a peat-based compost.
Propagate: From stem cuttings in summer, but heat and humidity will be needed for them to take.
Special Instructions: As flowers fade do not remove the stalks on which they were growing because new flowers will appear on the same stalks. Keep a careful watch for aphids and mealy bugs.

Impatiens wallerana 'Holstii'

Well named busy Lizzie, indeed, for this plant goes on and on producing its small red flowers from spring until autumn. The plant may grow to about two feet (60 cm), but quickly looks straggly if the growing shoots are not pinched out to make it bushier. The fleshy stems are light green and so are the leaves, which feel rubbery.

The Doctor Says—

Environment: From late autumn until early spring the ideal temperature is around 60°F (16°C), but the plant will survive considerably lower temperatures. For the rest of the year the ideal temperature range is 60 to 65°F (16 to 18°C). Keep the plant in good light all year, but never exposed to direct hot sunlight.
Water: Very frequently from early spring until autumn, especially in hot weather when the plant uses up water at a great rate. For the rest of the year water only occasionally.
Feed: Weekly from spring until early autumn.
Repot: In spring in a peat-based compost.
Propagate: From seed sown in spring or from cuttings, which root readily.
Special Instructions: After repotting prune the plant to encourage bushy growth. Regularly inspect it for aphids and red spider mites.

Jacobinia carnea

A shrubby evergreen from South America, *J. carnea* has glossy, dark green leaves and clusters of pink or red, tubular flowers borne on stems from late summer until early autumn. It may grow up to five feet (1.50 m).

The Doctor Says—

Environment: From autumn until early spring *J. carnea* requires temperatures around 60°F (16°C). For the rest of the year it needs to be warmer—60 to 65°F (16 to 18°C). It needs a good light, but not direct sunlight.
Water: Frequently from spring until early autumn and occasionally for the rest of the year.
Feed: Weekly from spring until early autumn.
Repot: In spring in a peat-based compost.
Propagate: From cuttings in spring.

Flowering Plants

Medinilla magnifica

The rose grape from the Philippines is usually grown in a warm greenhouse because of the high humidity it requires in summer. With care, however, you may be successful with it indoors. The broad, oval, shiny, dark green leaves are up to ten inches (25 cm) long. They are borne on long stems forming a freely branching shrub which grows up to five feet (1.5 m) tall. From spring until late summer, pink and purple flowers are carried on arching stems up to twelve inches (30 cm) in length. Altogether, this is a plant that will need plenty of room.

The Doctor Says—

Environment: From late autumn until early spring, the dormant period when flower buds are set, a temperature in the range of 60 to 65°F (15 to 18°C) must be maintained. for the rest of the year a temperature between 70 and 75°F (21 and 24°C) is necessary. Plenty of light is needed all year, but shade the plant from hot direct sunlight. A high degree of humidity is required during the summer months. This you can provide by plunging the pot in moist peat or by standing it on a tray of wet pebbles. Frequent spraying will also help.

Water: Frequently from spring until autumn. For the rest of the year water occasionally.

Feed: Every two weeks from spring until autumn.

Repot: Once every two years in spring using a loam-based or a peat-based compost.

Propagate: From cuttings taken in spring, but heat will be needed.

Special Instructions: Watch for red spider mites which may attack if the air is too dry.

Myrtus communis 'Microphylla'

The myrtle comes from around the Mediterranean and there grows wild to about twelve feet (3.65 m). In a pot it usually stays around two feet (60 cm). The small, leathery leaves give off the distinctive scent. The flowers appear from late spring until early autumn and are white with thick clusters of stamens at their centres. Berries may follow in the autumn.

The Doctor Says—

Environment: From autumn until early spring the temperature should be only 40 to 45°F (5 to 7°C), and for the rest of the year no higher than 55°F (13°C). This plant's other requirement is an airy, well-lit position out of direct sun.

Water: Frequently from spring until early autumn; occasionally for the rest of the year. The lower the temperature in which the plant is kept through the winter months the less it will need watering. Myrtus is a lime-hater, so use either rain water, if it is unpolluted, or distilled water.

Feed: Weekly from early spring until late summer.

Repot: Each spring in a peat-based compost.

Propagate: From cuttings in summer.

Oxalis deppei

This wood sorrel is also called lucky clover for the leaf has four leaflets and looks like a four leaf clover, which is said to bring good luck. The red flowers with yellow centres are carried on long stems and appear from early until late summer. *Oxalis pes-caprae*, from South Africa, but called the Bermuda buttercup, has leaves of three not four leaflets and the bell-shaped flowers are bright yellow. Both leaves and flowers close up when darkness falls.

The Doctor Says—

Environment: Throughout the year the ideal temperature range is 50 to 55°F (10 to 13°C). Good light is a necessity, but direct hot sunlight will be harmful.
Water: Frequently from early spring until late summer, occasionally the rest of the year.
Feed: Every two weeks from early spring until late summer.
Repot: Each spring in a peat-based compost.
Propagate: When repotting, by removing and planting the bulblets which grow on the main bulb.
Special Instructions: When the plant has finished flowering the leaves will wilt, turn yellow and die. Do not worry, this is the nature of the plant and the leaves will start into growth again.

Pachystachys lutea

Not surprisingly this plant has been given a simpler name—the lollipop plant, although it arrived from Brazil long before lollipops arrived on the scene. It is shrub-like and grows up to eighteen inches (45 cm) tall. The bright green leaves grow in opposite pairs. Between early spring and autumn, yellow, cone-shaped bracts appear and from these white, lipped flowers emerge.

The Doctor Says—

Environment: The minimum temperature from autumn until early spring should be between 55 and 60°F (13 and 16°C), rising for the rest of the year to between 60 and 65°F (16 and 18°C). Plenty of light, but not direct sunlight, is needed. During the growing period increase humidity by plunging the pot in moist peat or by spraying the plant regularly.
Water: Frequently from spring until early autumn, and occasionally at other times.
Feed: Every two weeks from spring until early autumn.
Repot: Every spring, in a loam-based or a peat-based compost.
Propagate: In spring from stem cuttings.
Special Instructions: Cut back the plant in spring to promote bushy growth.

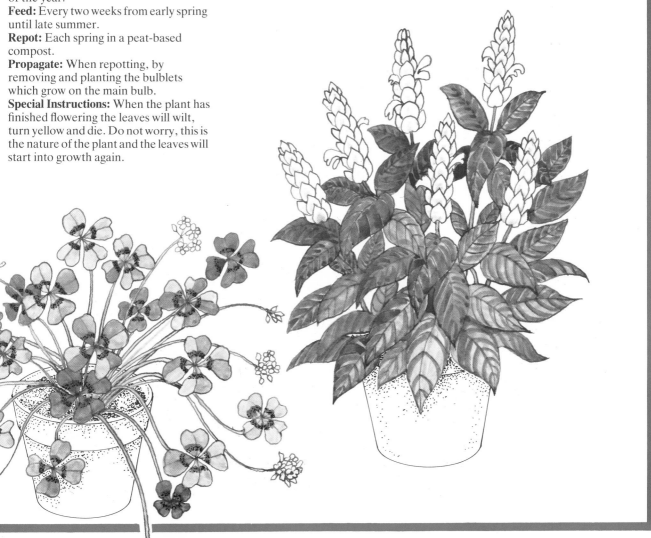

Flowering Plants

Plumbago capensis

This South African climber is also known as *P. auriculata*, or commonly as the blue Cape plumbago or Cape leadwort. Its stems may grow four feet (1.20 m) and tend to become straggly. The leaves are oval and the five-petalled, light blue flowers appear in clusters from spring until autumn. The cultivar *P.c.* 'Alba' has white flowers.

The Doctor Says—

Environment: This plant needs a fairly even and not very high temperature all year; from autumn until early spring not below 50°F (10°C), and for the rest of the year a temperature between 50 and 55°F (10 and 13°C) is quite high enough for growth. It cannot have too much sun, so it will do well on a window sill—except that before long it will be blocking out the light. An alternative is to grow it in a hanging basket. During the winter months, when it is not looking its best, it still needs good light.

Water: Frequently from early spring until autumn, but only occasionally for the remainder of the year.

Feed: Every two weeks from spring until autumn.

Repot: Each year in late winter in a loam-based compost.

Propagate: From cuttings in early summer.

Special Instructions: Before repotting cut the plant back to two-thirds or one-half of its size.

Rhododendron simsii

The Indian azalea in fact comes from China and arrived in the West early in the 1800s. The evergreen leaves are dark green and leathery, but when the plant is in bloom, normally in late spring, they will scarcely be seen for the profusion of flowers. There are double and single flowers and their colour range is from bright red and purple through white.

The Doctor Says—

Environment: The Indian azalea does not like too much warmth, especially from autumn until early spring when it should be kept between 45 and 55°F (7 and 13°C). For the rest of the year the temperature should, ideally, not go above 65°F (18°C). An azalea suffers particularly from heat if it is put in a warm living room after being bought in flower in winter. Buds drop and leaves fall at an alarming rate. The plant also needs partial shade.

Water: Frequently from early spring until early autumn, and fairly frequently for the rest of the year. Azaleas are avid lime-haters, so do not use hard water.

Feed: Every two weeks from early spring until late summer with an acid fertilizer.

Repot: Each year after flowering is over, using a peat-based compost.

Propagate: From cuttings in summer in a heated propagator.

Special Instructions: Clip off all dead flower heads. If the plant is too warm its performance will be poor and it will be susceptible to attack by red spider mites.

Saintpaulia ionantha

The African violet was discovered at the end of the nineteenth century in the high rocky areas of tropical East Africa. It grows a rosette of fleshy, heart-shaped leaves on short stalks which are even fleshier. The leaves are hairy and velvety to the touch. The flowers may be single or double and they range in colour from purple, red and pink to white. They can be reasonably relied on to appear from spring until early autumn, but with good light and management they can be induced to flower almost all year round.

The Doctor Says—

Environment: Throughout the year temperatures between 60 and 70°F (16 and 21°C) are needed. If kept much cooler than that the plant will certainly be reluctant to flower and may die. Neither will it flower if the light is not good. But direct sunlight will cause yellow blotching of the leaves. In addition, African violets need humidity, and surrounding the pot with moist peat or standing it on a tray of wet pebbles will be of some help.

Water: The aim is to keep the compost moist all year round. This will involve watering fairly frequently, usually once a week; judgement and discretion will be necessary. It is best to water the compost from below, standing the pot in shallow water for an hour or so, until beads of moisture appear on the surface of the compost. Never leave the pot standing in water for longer. If you have to water from above avoid pouring water on the stems and crown of the plant.

Feed: Once a month from spring until early autumn.

Repot: Every two or three years in spring in a peat-based compost.

Propagate: From leaf cuttings in spring.

Sinningia speciosa

The gloxinia, from Brazil, is of the Gesneriad family to which belong such other popular houseplants as saintpaulia, streptocarpus, columnea, achimenes, smithiana and episcia. The gloxinia is a low-growing plant which forms a rosette of leaves on hairy, fleshy stems. The leaves are mid green with a velvety surface. The flowers, which appear from late spring until autumn, are tubular in shape and may be dark red, violet, white or pink, while some are combinations of these colours.

The Doctor Says—

Environment: In late winter the corm starts growth when brought into a temperature between 65 and 70°F (18 and 21°C). Once it is growing, a temperature between 55 and 65°F (13 and 18°C) will be high enough. From autumn until late winter the corm should be kept at about 55°F (13°C), whether it has been removed from the pot after drying out or it stays in its pot. While shading the plant from direct sunlight give it good light. Another need is humidity—fulfilled by plunging the pot in peat, or standing it on a tray of wet pebbles. If you spray do so only above or around the plant for direct spraying of the leaves may damage them.

Water: Watering should be stopped after the plant has finished flowering. Give no further water from autumn until late winter. When starting the corm into growth in late winter water only occasionally, increasing to fairly frequently when growth is under way.

Feed: Every two weeks from the start of growth until summer.

Repot: Each year in late winter, in a peat-based compost.

Propagate: Raising from seed in spring is possible but not easy; the alternative is to take stem cuttings in summer.

Special Instructions: Watch for greenfly.

133

Flowering Plants

Smithiana zebrina

The exotic-looking smithiana, or temple bells, comes from Mexico. The velvety leaves are dark green, but mottled with reddish brown. The plant is in bloom from early summer until autumn, and the small, bell-shaped flowers are carried on long stems. A common combination of colours of the flowers is red on the outsides and yellow on the insides, but there are many cultivars with yellow, orange, pink or white flowers.

The Doctor Says—

Environment: The rhizome is started into growth in late winter by bringing it into a temperature between 65 and 70°F (18 and 21°C). When growth is established, a temperature between 55 and 65°F (13 and 18°C) is adequate. After flowering, when the compost has dried out keep the rhizome at about 55°F (13°C) until late winter; it may be left in its pot or taken out ready for replanting. Overhead misting will help to provide a humid atmosphere, but water sprayed directly on the leaves may damage them. Keep the plant in good light, protected from direct sunlight.
Water: Only occasional watering is needed when starting the rhizome into growth, but before long water fairly frequently. Stop watering when flowering is over and give none until late winter.
Feed: Every two weeks from the start of growth until summer.
Repot: Each year in late winter in a peat-based compost.
Propagate: Either by dividing the rhizome before repotting or by leaf cuttings in summer.

Spathiphyllum wallisii

The more attractive common names of this Colombian plant are peace lily or white sails. The leaves are lance-shaped, bright green and glossy. The plant grows only about twelve inches (30 cm) high, but the yellow flowers, surrounded by white oval spathes, are carried on long stems. (The hybrid 'Mauna Loa' has larger spathes.) The flowers appear from late spring until late summer.

The Doctor Says—

Environment: From autumn until early spring keep in a temperature between 60 and 65°F (16 and 18°C); lower temperatures may result in fewer flowers. For the rest of the year, to ensure good growth, the temperature should be between 65 and 70°F (18 and 21°C). Always have the plant in a good light, but during the summer shade it from direct sunlight. Frequent misting, standing the pot on a tray of wet pebbles or plunging it into moist peat will help to keep the air humid around the plant.
Water: Fairly frequently from autumn until early spring and frequently for the rest of the year.
Feed: Every two weeks from spring until early autumn.
Repot: In spring, either in a loam-based or a peat-based compost.
Propagate: By division in spring.
Special Instructions: Red spider mites may strike if the air is dry.

Stephanotis floribunda

The Madagascar jasmine growing in a greenhouse can put out stems up to ten feet (3 m) long. It is less exuberant indoors, but will still need training. It is usually bought twining around a circle of wire, but you can vary this cliché as you wish. The leaves are dark green, leathery and glossy and the five-petalled flowers are a waxy white and fragrant; they appear from late spring until autumn.

The Doctor Says—

Environment: From autumn until early spring a temperature around 55°F (13°C) is required; anything higher will produce lanky growth and encourage all manner of pests. But for the rest of the year the plant needs warmth, around 70°F (21°C). Keep in good light all year, but out of direct summer sunlight. Frequent spraying will help to meet the plant's need of a humid atmosphere, but also surround the pot with moist peat or place it on a tray of wet pebbles.

Water: Occasionally from autumn until early spring, but frequently from spring until early autumn.

Feed: Every two weeks from spring until early autumn.

Repot: Each spring in a loam-based or a peat-based compost.

Propagate: From cuttings in spring, but a temperature of about 85°F (30°C) will be necessary.

Special Instructions: Watch for scale insects and mealy bugs, especially if the plant is in a warm room during the winter.

Strelitzia reginae

Deservedly called bird of paradise, this relative of the banana is a native of South Africa and needs warmth. The plant has grey-green leathery leaves about two feet (60 cm) in length, not unlike those of the banana. Between spring and early summer the dramatic flowers are produced on stems three feet (90 cm) long. From a horizontally growing green bract edged with red, the long, thin, blue and orange petals of the flower emerge.

The Doctor Says—

Environment: Throughout the year a temperature between 60 and 70°F (16 and 21°C) is desirable. The plant can, for a short time, tolerate a fall to 55°F (13°C), but if it is kept as cool as that for very long flowering will suffer. Plenty of light and sunshine are needed all year, with shade only from the hottest sun. A strelitzia also needs a well-ventilated room.

Water: Occasionally from autumn until early spring; frequently at other times.

Feed: Every two weeks from spring until early autumn.

Repot: Each spring in a loam-based compost.

Propagate: By division in spring. Raising the plant from seed will require considerable heat (70°F, 21°C) and three to four years will pass before the first flowers appear.

Begonias

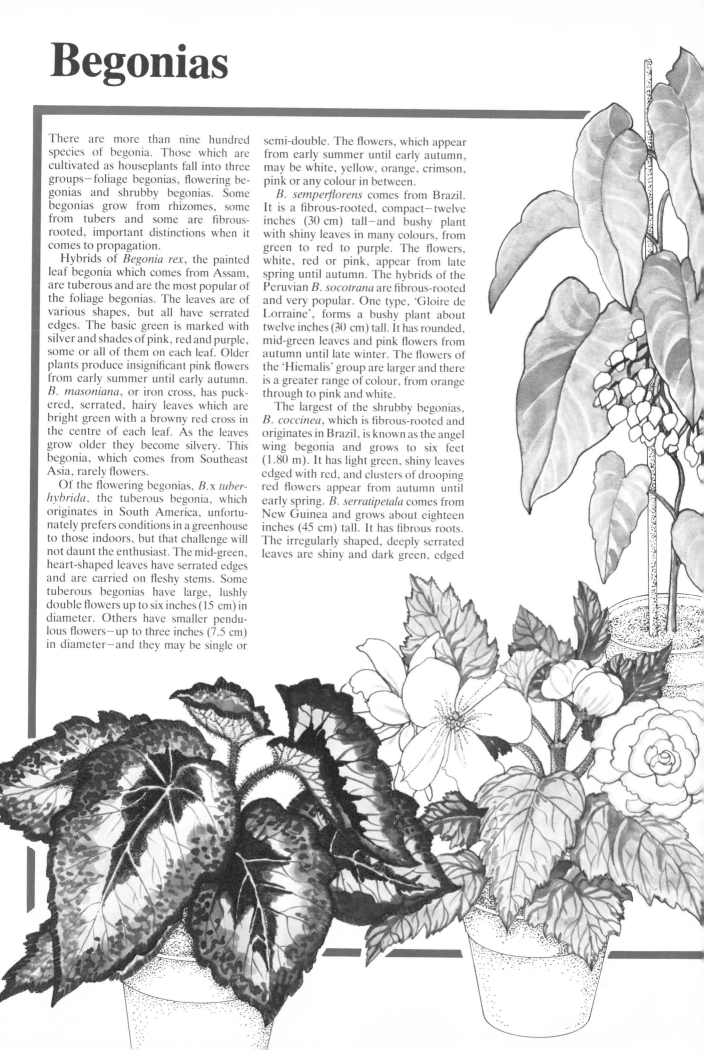

There are more than nine hundred species of begonia. Those which are cultivated as houseplants fall into three groups—foliage begonias, flowering begonias and shrubby begonias. Some begonias grow from rhizomes, some from tubers and some are fibrous-rooted, important distinctions when it comes to propagation.

Hybrids of *Begonia rex*, the painted leaf begonia which comes from Assam, are tuberous and are the most popular of the foliage begonias. The leaves are of various shapes, but all have serrated edges. The basic green is marked with silver and shades of pink, red and purple, some or all of them on each leaf. Older plants produce insignificant pink flowers from early summer until early autumn. *B. masoniana*, or iron cross, has puckered, serrated, hairy leaves which are bright green with a browny red cross in the centre of each leaf. As the leaves grow older they become silvery. This begonia, which comes from Southeast Asia, rarely flowers.

Of the flowering begonias, *B.*x *tuberhybrida*, the tuberous begonia, which originates in South America, unfortunately prefers conditions in a greenhouse to those indoors, but that challenge will not daunt the enthusiast. The mid-green, heart-shaped leaves have serrated edges and are carried on fleshy stems. Some tuberous begonias have large, lushly double flowers up to six inches (15 cm) in diameter. Others have smaller pendulous flowers—up to three inches (7.5 cm) in diameter—and they may be single or semi-double. The flowers, which appear from early summer until early autumn, may be white, yellow, orange, crimson, pink or any colour in between.

B. semperflorens comes from Brazil. It is a fibrous-rooted, compact—twelve inches (30 cm) tall—and bushy plant with shiny leaves in many colours, from green to red to purple. The flowers, white, red or pink, appear from late spring until autumn. The hybrids of the Peruvian *B. socotrana* are fibrous-rooted and very popular. One type, 'Gloire de Lorraine', forms a bushy plant about twelve inches (30 cm) tall. It has rounded, mid-green leaves and pink flowers from autumn until late winter. The flowers of the 'Hiemalis' group are larger and there is a greater range of colour, from orange through to pink and white.

The largest of the shrubby begonias, *B. coccinea*, which is fibrous-rooted and originates in Brazil, is known as the angel wing begonia and grows to six feet (1.80 m). It has light green, shiny leaves edged with red, and clusters of drooping red flowers appear from autumn until early spring. *B. serratipetala* comes from New Guinea and grows about eighteen inches (45 cm) tall. It has fibrous roots. The irregularly shaped, deeply serrated leaves are shiny and dark green, edged with red. Pink flowers are produced from spring until autumn. The Brazilian *B. metallica* grows to three feet (90 cm) and is also fibrous-rooted. The many coloured veins on the hairy leaves produce a shiny, metallic, dark green effect on the surface and red underneath. There are pink flowers in early autumn. *B. boweri* comes from Mexico and is rhizomatous. It is known as the miniature eyelash begonia because it grows only about nine inches (23 cm) tall. The bright green, hairy leaves have brown markings on the edges. Tiny white or pink flowers appear from late winter until late spring.

The Doctor Says —

Environment: The ideal temperature range from autumn until early spring for *B. rex*, *B. masoniana* and *B. boweri* is 55 to 60°F (13 to 16°C). For *B. socotrana*, 'Hiemalis' and 'Gloire de Lorraine' the winter temperature should be between 65 and 70°F (18 and 21°C) when they are in flower, but in the period immediately before flowering they are best kept at 55°F (13°C). The dried-off tubers of

B. x *tuberhybrida* should be stored at 45°F (7°C). For the rest of the year the temperature range of all begonias, except *B.* x *tuberhybrida*, is 55 to 65°F (13 to 18°C). The tuber of *B.* x *tuberhybrida* is brought into growth in early spring or spring in a temperature of 70°F (21°C). Once it has sprouted it can be grown on in the range 60 to 65°F (16 to 18°C). All begonias like a humid atmosphere and plenty of light, but not direct hot sunlight.

Water: Most begonias need frequent watering from spring until early autumn and occasional watering for the rest of the year. When *B.* x *tuberhybrida* finishes flowering stop watering. Cut off the foliage when it has died down (not before), remove the tuber and store it through the winter, keeping it

completely dry. *B. socotrana*, 'Gloire de Lorraine' and 'Hiemalis' need frequent watering from the time they start into growth until after flowering. Then water only occasionally until spring when the plants are brought into higher temperatures.

Feed: Every two weeks from spring until early autumn. Continue feeding the *B. socotrana* types until late autumn.

Repot: Each year in spring in a peat-based compost.

Propagate: *B. boweri* by division in spring. *B. rex* and *B. masoniana* by leaf cuttings in summer. *B.* x *tuberhybrida* by dividing the tuber in spring, making sure there is a shoot on each piece or by cuttings from tubers. *B. socotrana*, 'Hiemalis' and 'Gloire de Lorraine' from new shoots in spring. After flowering, prune back the plant and keep it around 45°F (7°C). In spring the temperature should be 60 to 65°F (16 to 18°C). When new shoots appear remove them and pot in a peat-based compost. This gives better results than keeping the plant for a second year. Other begonias can be propagated by stem cuttings in summer.

Special Instructions: All begonias are susceptible to mildew and botrytis. Underwatering causes the flowers to drop.

137

Pelargoniums

All pelargoniums are commonly known as geraniums and all of them come from South Africa. While many of them are grown for their brilliant flowers, others—although they do flower—are cultivated mainly for their foliage. *P.* x *domesticum* is the regal pelargonium, with almost circular, tooth-edged, mid-green leaves. The flowers are large—up to two inches (5 cm) in diameter—and are borne in clusters from the leaf axils. The colours range from purple through reds to pinks and some flowers are two colours. In addition, each flower has darker colouring either along the veins or in blotches. The flowers are produced from late spring until early autumn, quite a long period, but shorter than that of *P.* x *hortorum*, which, consequently, has become more popular.

P. x *hortorum*, usually referred to simply as the geranium, is developed mainly from *P. zonale*, the zonal geranium. The round leaves are mid-green, but have distinctive circular markings. The colour range of the flowers is from white through innumerable shades of pinks and reds. The plants are in flower from spring at least until autumn, but may go on until the frost gets them. *P. peltatum* is the ivy-leaved geranium, a trailing plant with stems up to two feet (60 cm) long, and is often grown in a hanging basket or window box. The thick, fleshy leaves are ivy-shaped. The flowers appear from spring until autumn or later, may be single or double, and are as variously coloured as those of *P.* x *hortorum*.

The attractiveness of the foliage geraniums is not only in the form of the leaves but also in their scent. *P. crispum*, which grows to about two feet (60 cm), has lemon-scented foliage. The leaves are bright green, crinkly, deeply toothed and slightly hairy. The variegated version has cream edges to the leaves. Pinkish flowers appear from late spring until autumn. *P. tomentosum*, the peppermint geranium, has leaves which smell stongly of peppermint. It is by nature a climber, but grows to only about two feet (60 cm). The bright green leaves are large, lobed, flat and slightly hairy. The white flowers, produced from late spring until autumn, are insignificant.

The Doctor Says—

Environment: From autumn until early spring the temperature range for pelargoniums is between 45 and 50°F (7 and 10°C). Any frost will kill the plants immediately. A slightly higher temperature range—between 50 and

55°F (10 and 13°C)−is best for
P. x *domesticum*. A satisfactory summer
temperature for all of them is around
60°F (16°C). They all need plenty of air,
so should be kept in a well-ventilated
room. They thrive on sunshine and given
it will flower exuberantly.

Water: Frequently from spring until
early autumn, without making the
compost permanently sodden. Use the
finger test to decide whether the plant
needs watering again. For the rest of the
year water only occasionally, especially
when the plants are kept at low
temperatures.

Feed: Every two weeks from spring until
early autumn.

Repot: In early spring each year in either
a loam-based or a peat-based compost.

Propagate: From stem cuttings taken
either in spring or late summer.

P. x *hortorum* may be raised from seed
sown late in winter.

Special Instructions: Prune back the
plants in spring and as they grow pinch
out the tips to promote bushy growth.
Although pinching out will delay
flowering at first, you will have a much
more attractive plant and plenty of
flowers later.

Bulbs

Although bulbs, which have only a brief flowering period, are part-time houseplants, some of them are so stunningly beautiful—as well as easy to grow—that any failing must be forgiven. Moreover, a bulb is one of the most exciting of plants to watch as it grows and flowers.

Amaryllis belladonna
Hippeastrum hybrids

There is understandable confusion between an amaryllis and a hippeastrum, not least because a hippeastrum is usually sold under the name of amaryllis. Actually, both belong to the Amaryllidaceae family. They look much alike and both often produce leaves only after flowering. There are differences. The hippeastrum comes from Brazil and Mexico and flowers on a long two-foot (30-cm), hollow stem from midwinter until early spring. *A. belladonna*, often called the belladonna lily or Cape belladonna, comes from South Africa. The flower stems are solid and the pink or red flowers appear from late summer until autumn. The many hippeastrum hybrids have larger flowers ranging from deep reds to pinks and whites.

The Doctor Says—

Environment: *A. belladonna* is usually started into growth in early autumn, and the hippeastrum from autumn until late autumn. They need a temperature between 65 and 70°F (18 and 21°C) or even a little higher. When the shoots begin to appear a temperature between 55 and 60°F (13 and 16°C) is needed until the dormant period—for *A. belladonna* from early summer until early autumn and for the hippeastrum from late summer until autumn. During these periods the bulbs should be stored at around 50°F (10°C). They need light at all times, but should be shaded from the sun when flowering.
Water: Occasionally between starting the bulbs into growth and the appearance of the first shoots and frequently thereafter. Stop watering when the foliage dies down or as the dormancy period approaches.
Feed: Weekly from the appearance of the first leaves until they die.
Repot: Every three years, since they do best when potbound, towards the end of the dormant period. Use a loam-based compost and bury the bulb to only half of its depth.
Propagate: From offsets when repotting.
Special Instructions: Cut off the dead flowers and seed pods, but leave the stalk and leaves until they have completely shrivelled.

Lilium longiflorum

The white, trumpet-shaped flowers of the beautiful Easter lily, a native of Japan, appear in spring and often measure six inches (15 cm) in diameter. The stem may be three feet (90 cm) long and almost its whole length may be covered with five-inch (12 cm), dark green leaves, some curving up, others down.

The Doctor Says—

Environment: In autumn pot the bulb in a loam-based or a peat-based compost with the bottom of the bulb set two-thirds into the pot. Keep the pot in a frost-free place between 35 and 40°F (2 and 5°C) until late winter or early spring. Then bring it into the warmth (about 60°F, 16°C) and it can be expected to flower in spring. If you want later flowers keep the bulb in a cool place longer.
Water: After potting the bulb keep the compost moist at all times. Water frequently after the shoots appear, but only occasionally after flowering when the stems and leaves begin to yellow.
Feed: Every two weeks from the appearance of shoots to the end of flowering.
Repot: When the stem has completely died and will break easily from the bulb. A second year's flowering cannot always be relied on.
Propagate: From offsets when repotting.

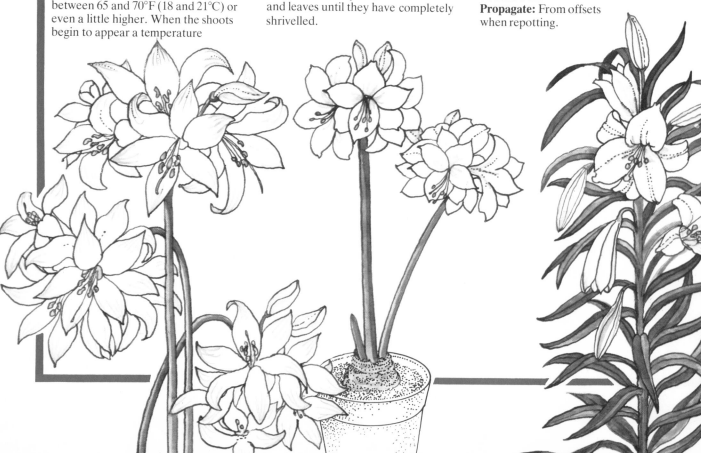

Ornithogatum thyrsoides

The so-called chincherinchee, from the Cape Province of South Africa, is said to get its name from the noise the wind makes when it blows through the flowers. It is unlikely that you will have the chance to put this to the test indoors. The plant is, however, worth growing for its clusters of white, star-shaped flowers carried on eighteen-inch (45-cm) stems from late spring until summer.

The Doctor Says—

Environment: In autumn, plant three or four bulbs in a pot in a loam-based compost, burying them below the surface. Keep them in a well-lit position with a minimum temperature of 50°F (10°C). In late winter or early spring move them to a temperature of 60°F (16°C) to bring them to flowering.
Water: After potting keep the compost just moist, watering frequently when flowers appear. After flowering, gradually reduce water until the bulbs are left completely dry for the dormant period from summer until early autumn.
Feed: Every two weeks from the appearance of flower shoots until flowering is over.
Repot: Every other year in autumn in a loam-based compost.
Propagate: From offsets when repotting.

Veltheimia viridifolia

The forest lily (syn. *V. capensis*) originated in South Africa. The glossy, bright green, crinkly-edged leaves, which are about ten inches (25 cm) long, grow in the form of a rosette. From its centre grows a brownish-red, mottled stem about eighteen inches (45 cm) long, carrying a cluster of pink, tubular flowers that are remarkably long lasting.

The Doctor Says—

Environment: In early autumn plant the bulb in a loam-based or a peat-based compost, and keep it in a temperature about 55°F (13°C) or a little higher, but not lower. It needs good light, but not sunlight, especially when flowering. If the plant is kept at 55°F (13°C) the flowers can last up to eight weeks.
Water: Occasionally from potting until the foliage appears, increasing it then, and on to frequent watering when the plant is in full growth. When the foliage wilts after flowering stop watering to allow the bulb its dormant period from early to late summer.
Feed: Every two weeks from the start of growth until the end of flowering.
Repot: Every other year in autumn in a peat-based or a loam-based compost.
Propagate: By offsets when repotting.

Zephyranthes grandiflora

The zephyr lily is found in Central America and the West Indies. It flowers from late summer through to early autumn. The pink, funnel-shaped flowers have spreading petals and are carried on eight-inch (20-cm) stems. The very narrow leaves may appear at the same time as the flowers or after the flowers die.

The Doctor Says—

Environment: In early spring plant four or five bulbs in a pot in a peat-based compost so that the tips of the bulbs are level with the surface of the compost. Keep them for several weeks in a light room in a temperature about 50°F (10°C). In late spring bring them into more warmth, but not exposed to hot sunlight. In winter the temperature should be around 55°F (13°C).
Water: Occasionally from potting until shoots appear, then watering will have to be frequent. After flowering the foliage should die down, but may have to be helped on its way by a drastic cut in watering; the bulbs need a dormant period. Little or no water need be given after the foliage has died until growth starts again in late spring.
Feed: Every two weeks from the time the shoots appear until the flowers die.
Repot: In early spring once every three or four years, as they thrive when potbound. Use a peat-based compost.
Propagate: From offsets when repotting.

Orchids

Not many years ago, it would have been almost impossible to grow orchids in a living room. Today, it is possible, if not easy, for enthusists to succeed with some of the newer varieties. The greatest problem is to provide enough humidity and at the same time adequate ventilation to avoid mildew and botrytis.

Cattleya bowringiana

During most of the year, the cluster cattleya, an epiphytic orchid from Central America, is not a very prepossessing plant with its single leathery leaf about five inches (12.5 cm) long. But when it is in flower in autumn it is most striking, with clusters of up to twenty pinky-purple, maroon-lipped flowers.

The Doctor Says—

Environment: The optimum daytime temperature range for this orchid throughout the year is between 65 and 75°F (18 and 24°C). At night the temperature should be somewhat lower than during the day, but it should never fall below 60°F (16°C). A cattleya responds to as good a light as it can get most of the year, but needs to be partly shaded from spring until summer and also when it is in bloom, if the flowers are to last. It requires a humid atmosphere in a well-ventilated room, one of the most difficult combinations to achieve in a living room. Frequent misting will help.
Water: Only occasional watering is needed from the time flowering has ceased in autumn until early spring. Water frequently the rest of the year, especially during the hot summer months. The best method is to immerse about two-thirds of the pot in water. Let the compost almost dry out before watering again.
Feed: Once a month from spring until early autumn is enough.
Repot: Every two or three years in late spring in a mixture of osmunda fibre, peat and sphagnum moss.
Propagate: By division when repotting or from seed sown in spring.

Cymbidium x *Rosanna* Pinkie

This is one of the many hybrids derived from the cymbidiums which grow in the mountains of northern India and its Himalayan neighbours. The mountains are more than four thousand feet (1,200 m) high and the cymbidium, therefore, needs cooler conditions than most orchids and is often suggested as the best choice for a beginner. Long, narrow, evergreen leaves surround the flower spike which may be twenty-four inches (60 cm) long. The white flowers, tinged with pink and tipped with deep pink, are produced in spring.

The Doctor Says—

Environment: From autumn until early spring it is best if the temperature is between 50 and 55°F (10 and 13°C); at

night the temperature should be at the bottom end of the range; a temperature as low as 45°F (7°C) will be tolerated. For the rest of the year a daytime temperature between 60 and 70°F (16 and 21°C) is needed for good growth, but the night temperature should be down to 50°F (10°C). Cymbidiums need plenty of light, but must be shaded from direct, hot sun. Standing the pot on wet pebbles will help to provide the vital humid atmosphere. Spray frequently from spring until late summer. The plant will grow more sturdily if it is placed outdoors in the summer months, somewhat shaded from the sun.

Water: Occasionally from autumn until early spring and frequently the rest of the year. Immersing about two-thirds of the pot in water is the best watering method.
Feed: Every two weeks from spring until early autumn.
Repot: Once every two years when flowering is over, using a mixture of peat, osmunda fibre and sphagnum moss.
Propagate: By division when repotting.

Dendrobium nobile

One of the less demanding species of dendrobium is *D. nobile*, from India. The strap-shaped leaves and the flowers are borne on three-foot (90-cm), bamboo-like stems, which are actually pseudobulbs. Some of the leaves are likely to fall during the dormant period. The flowers appear from late winter through spring. They are about three inches (7.5 cm) across, white flushed with pink or purple, with a yellowish tip and a maroon-blotched throat.

The Doctor Says—

Environment: From autumn until midwinter the ideal temperature range is between 50 and 55°F (10 and 13°C), but a temperature as low as 45°F (7°C) can be endured. For the rest of the year the temperature must be around 75°F (24°C). Keep the plant in good light, but shaded from hot direct sun. During the summer months spray frequently.
Water: Occasionally from autumn until midwinter. When the flower spikes begin to develop, gradually increase the frequency until you are watering very often in the summer months. To water, immerse the pot to two-thirds of its depth.
Feed: Once a month from spring until early autumn.
Repot: Once every two or three years after flowering, using a mixture of peat, osmunda fibre and sphagnum moss. Do not use too large a pot; the dendrobium does best when it is somewhat potbound.
Propagate: By division when repotting.

Miltonia vexillaria

The pansy orchid comes from Colombia where it is found growing at heights up to six thousand feet (1,800 m), but the climate is nonetheless warm and humid. Flowering occurs in late spring, but the twenty-four-inch (60-cm) long flower spikes appear some time before there is any sign of the flowers. When they appear they are pansy-like, rose-coloured with yellow markings radiating from the lips.

The Doctor Says—

Environment: The daytime temperature throughout the year should be between 60 and 70°F (16 and 21°C), and the nearer the top end of the range the better. The temperature at night should be a little lower than during the day, but never below 55°F (13°C). This orchid needs a slightly shaded position, especially in summer when the strong sun is positively harmful. But good light is needed in the winter months when the plant is in full growth before flowering. During the summer months spray frequently, but provide good ventilation to prevent fungus diseases from developing.
Water: The compost should be kept just moist all the time. Too much water may cause the roots to rot.
Feed: Once a month from late autumn until early spring.
Repot: In summer when flowering is finished, in a mixture of peat, osmunda fibre and sphagnum moss.
Propagate: By division when repotting.

Orchids

Odontoglossum grande

This is commonly known as the clown orchid or tiger orchid—and it is one of the odontoglossums less difficult to grow indoors. A native of Guatemala, the plant is not overlarge—the flower spikes are about twelve inches (30 cm) tall—but the long-lasting flowers, which appear in autumn, may be six inches (15 cm) across. The petals are yellow with bands of reddish brown.

The Doctor Says—

Environment: This orchid does not like great heat and though it will tolerate a daytime temperature up to 70°F (21°C), if necessary, it is happiest at only a little above 60°F (16°C). At night the temperature should drop to about 50°F (10°C). While the plant needs good light, it must be protected from direct sunlight, especially because of its dislike of high temperatures. It wants a humid atmosphere, but unless it is also cool there is a risk of disease.
Water: Occasionally from late autumn until early spring, letting the compost dry out between waterings. For the remainder of the year water frequently. Spray often in summer.
Feed: Once a month from spring until early autumn.
Repot: Each year when flowering is over in a mixture of peat, osmunda fibre and sphagnum moss.
Propagate: By division when repotting.

Oncidium varicosum

The butterfly orchid from Brazil has been in cultivation for almost two hundred years. Its greatest attraction is the profusion of the delicate flowers. Eighty or more yellow, red-tipped blooms appear in autumn on stems up to three feet (90 cm) long. The evergreen leaves are broad and leathery.

The Doctor Says—

Environment: Throughout the year the temperature during the day must be between 65 and 75°F (18 and 24°C), and down to between 55 and 60°F (13 and 16°C) at night. The plant will revel in plenty of sunlight, needing to be shaded only from the hot midday sun. Frequent misting, especially during the summer months, will contribute to the high humidity it needs. Good ventilation is also vital.
Water: Very frequently from spring through to the end of flowering. For the remainder of the year water occasionally to keep the compost just moist. Overwatering at this time will rot the plant.
Feed: Once a month from spring until early autumn.
Repot: In spring every two or three years, in a mixture of peat, osmunda fibre and sphagnum moss.
Propagate: By division when repotting.

Paphiopedilium insigne

This terrestrial orchid from Nepal and Assam is best known as the slipper orchid or lady's slipper. The broad, strap-shaped leaves are bright green. The flowers, which appear singly on ten-inch (25-cm) stems from early winter until spring, are yellowish green with purple-brown blotches and a yellow lip shaded with brown.

The Doctor Says—

Environment: Throughout the year the ideal daytime temperature is between 60 and 65°F (16 and 18°C), although this orchid will tolerate a temperature a few degrees lower. To induce the plant to flower it must have slightly lower night temperatures in the range of 55 to 60°F (13 to 16°C). *P. insigne* grows wild on forest floors and, therefore, needs comparable shade indoors at all times. Too much sun makes the leaves turn yellow. Humidity is not as great a problem as with other orchids and too high a level of humidity may encourage fungal diseases. Nevertheless, spray regularly while providing very good ventilation.
Water: At all times keep the compost moist, but never sodden.
Feed: Give a weak solution of fertilizer once a month from late spring until early autumn.
Repot: In spring every two or three years, in a mixture of peat, osmunda fibre and sphagnum moss.
Propagate: By division when repotting.

Vanda tricolor

This is a vigorously growing epiphyte from Java; the name vanda derives from the Sanskrit word for epiphyte. It grows six feet (1.80 m) tall, with layers of thick, strap-shaped leaves, and puts out aerial roots. The creamy, brown-spotted flowers are borne on long stems from autumn until late winter.

The Doctor Says—

Environment: This orchid requires considerable heat. Throughout the year the temperature during the day should be in the range of 70 to 75°F (21 to 24°C) falling at night, but not below 60°F (16°C). It also needs plenty of sun, with shading only from the hot midday sun. During the growing period especially, high humidity is required so spraying must be frequent, but good ventilation is also vital.

Water: Frequently from spring until autumn. For the rest of the year water only occasionally, allowing the compost almost to dry out between waterings.
Feed: Once a month from spring until autumn.
Repot: In spring every two to three years, in a mixture of peat, osmunda fibre and sphagnum moss.
Propagate: From offshoots taken in spring.

Fruiting Plants

A plant which not only flowers, but also produces brightly coloured berries or fruit has undeniable appeal. Unfortunately, only a few fruiting plants are suitable for growing indoors, and they will not keep their fruit long unless they are in a cool room—probably too cool for human habitation. But nevertheless the brightness they bring, even if it is short-lived, makes them worth growing.

Ardisia crispa

The main attraction of the coral berry, or spear flower, are its red holly-like berries which may last more than six months. Some species grow to forty feet (12 m) in their native haunts, which extend from the East Indies to Japan. As a house-plant, however, *A. crispa* slowly reaches about two feet (60 cm), but it will flower and fruit while it is still quite small. The small, fragrant, red flowers appear in clusters in summer. The evergreen leaves are dark and glossy, with wavy margins.

The Doctor Says—

Environment: During the dormant period, from autumn until late winter, try to maintain a temperature about 50°F (10°C), for the higher the temperature goes the sooner the berries will drop. In summer keep the plant in good light, but out of direct sunlight, in a temperature range of 55 to 65°F (13 to 18°C).
Water: Frequently from early spring until late summer. Spray the leaves often using lukewarm water. As the dormant period approaches, gradually cut down the frequency of watering and during the winter months water only occasionally.
Feed: Every two weeks from spring until late summer.
Repot: In spring in a loam-based compost enriched with leaf mould.
Propagate: By cuttings from late spring until early autumn, or by seed in early spring.
Special Instructions: When the plant grows old it will need hard pruning in spring.

Capsicum annuum

Paprika and cayenne pepper are derived from some varieties of *Capsicum annuum*, or chilli peppers. The smaller cultivars, however, which are grown as house-plants have been bred only for their looks. Many of them are hybrids of *C. annuum* and *C. frutescens*, both of which originate in South America. The white flowers appear from early summer until early autumn, but you may never see them unless you grow your own plants, since they are usually put on sale after they have flowered. The fruit of the different cultivars vary considerably in shape and colour—green before they ripen and then yellow, orange, red or even violet or black. *C. annuum*, in spite of its name, is a perennial, but it loses its interest when the fruits have shrivelled, so it is invariably treated as an annual.

The Doctor Says—

Environment: If it is to thrive *Capsicum annuum* must have plenty of light in summer and winter. In summer the temperature should be in the range of 55 to 65°F (13 to 18°C). From late autumn until late winter, when it will be fruiting, the plant should be kept cooler—about 55°F (13°C).

Water: Frequently from early spring until early winter, and spray the plant occasionally in summer. In winter keep the compost moist.
Feed: If you do possess the plant when it is starting to flower give it a weekly feed.
Repot: Hardly worth it, since the plant looks rather pathetic once the fruit has gone.
Propagate: From seed in spring.
Special Instructions: Do not allow the compost to dry out. And remember that unless it is kept in a somewhat cooler position in winter both fruit and leaves are liable to drop.

Citrus mitis

Many citrus fruit trees make delightful houseplants in their infancy, but only for their foliage; before they fruit most of them must mature and then require greenhouse conditions. *C. mitis*, the calamondin orange from the Philippines, is an exception; it will flower and fruit while it is still quite small and will often continue in flower most of the year. The sweet-smelling, white flowers frequently appear along with the orange-coloured fruit.

The Doctor Says—

Environment: Good light is a necessity all year round. In winter the temperature should not drop below 50°F (10°C), but no harm is done if it goes higher. In summer the warmer and lighter the position the better. *C. mitis* also likes plenty of air and in a warm summer it would benefit by being outdoors, although not in strong sunlight.
Water: Frequently from spring until late summer, especially when fruit is developing. Spraying from time to time when there are flowers will help the fruit to set. In winter infrequent watering will be needed.
Feed: Every two weeks from late spring until late summer.
Repot: Since the plant is slow-growing, repotting will not be necessary every year, but when it is, repot in spring, using a loam-based compost to which a little bonemeal has been added.
Propagate: In spring from cuttings or from seed, which will germinate quite readily. Whichever method you choose, a temperature of 70 to 75°F (21 to 24°C) will be needed.
Special Instructions: Watch for attacks from red spider mites.

Duchesnea indica (Fragaria indica)

The Indian strawberry has delighted Western gardeners since it was brought from India nearly two hundred years ago. In many ways it resembles the garden strawberry, but the flowers are bright yellow, rather than white, and the fruit has no taste; this may be no disadvantage since they are more likely to be left on the plant. Flowers and fruit appear in succession from spring until autumn. The plant is particularly attractive when it is grown in a hanging basket with the long stems trailing over the sides.

The Doctor Says—

Environment: In summer the best temperature for this plant is around 55°F (13°C), with good light, but not in direct sun. In winter it should be cooler, about 45°F (7°C), or even lower as long as there is no danger of frost.
Water: Frequently in spring and summer; occasionally in winter, keeping the compost just moist.
Feed: Every two weeks from spring until early autumn.
Repot: In winter or early spring. The plant soon becomes straggly, however, and it may be better to replace it each year by taking runners from it in late summer.
Propagate: By runners in late summer, or by division when repotting.

Fruiting Plants

Fortunella margarita

The kumquat is not a true citrus fruit, although it looks as though it should be. It was discovered in China in the middle of the nineteenth century by the great English plant hunter Robert Fortune, who introduced it to the Western world. Easy to grow, it is also an attractive plant with glossy, green leaves, small, fragrant, white flowers in spring and summer followed by small orange-like fruit in autumn and winter. It usually stays bushy, but if it does get out of hand the growing shoots can be cut back in spring.

The Doctor Says—

Environment: The aim should be steady growth throughout the year if the plant is to have time to flower and then ripen its fruit. This is possible only if the winter temperature does not fall below 50°F (10°C); if it is colder than that the plant will not die, but neither will it grow. From spring until early autumn give it an airy, light position, preferably in the sun.

Water: Frequently in hot weather from spring until late summer, but beware of overwatering. To help set the fruit, spray lightly every few days when flowers appear. During the winter months water only as often as necessary to keep the compost moist.

Feed: Every two weeks from spring until late summer.

Repot: Each spring in a loam-based compost with added leaf mould.

Propagate: By cuttings, or by sowing the seeds taken from the fruit.

Nertera granadensis

For its size the bead plant is astonishingly showy, and the bead-like berries it carries last for months well into the winter. It is a creeping plant, a native of South America and New Zealand, and is best grown in a wide, shallow pot, so that it can form a decent-sized mound of leaves and berries. Small, white flowers appear in spring and are followed in late summer by bright orange berries in such profusion that they almost hide the leaves. When the berries fall many people throw the plant away, but this is quite wrong, for it should be treated as the perennial it is.

The Doctor Says—

Environment: The bead plant needs plenty of light all year round, but in summer it must be protected from direct hot sunlight. Beginning in mid-autumn it should be kept in a temperature of about 50°F (10°C) if you want the berries to stay on the plant as long as possible. Even when the berries have fallen this

temperature should be maintained until early spring.

Water: Throughout the summer water quite frequently, and spray the plant often before and after flowering. The plant should be watered fairly frequently from autumn until early spring.

Feed: Monthly only from spring until early autumn, but use a weak fertilizer solution in order not to encourage too lush a growth of leaves.

Repot: In early spring when the pot becomes overcrowded, using an all-peat compost.

Propagate: By division in early spring or from seed (around 70°F, 21°C).

Solanum capsicastrum

Because of its brilliant berries *S. capsicastrum* rates high among the plants that lighten the gloom of winter. It has several common names, winter cherry, Christmas cherry and false Jerusalem cherry—to distinguish it from the Jerusalem cherry (*S. pseudocapsicum*), which is a similar but more robust version. *S. capsicastrum*, a native of South America, is a bushy plant with dark green, oval leaves, small, white flowers which appear in late spring and early summer, followed by berries which start green, turn yellow and then become bright red. They will last for many weeks in the winter months if the plant is not kept in too warm a room.

The Doctor says—

Environment: From autumn until late winter, when the plant is fruiting, try to keep the temperature a little below 50°F (10°C) to prevent all the berries from dropping off. In spring the plant can be moved to a warm, sunny position, but not in hot direct sunlight. It would benefit from a spell outdoors in summer, if that is possible.

Water: Frequently throughout the summer. From autumn until late winter keep the compost just moist.

Feed: Every two weeks from spring until late summer.

Repot: In early spring each year, using a loam-based compost. When repotting, cut back the plant to almost half its size so that it will put out new shoots. This is far better than following the common custom of throwing the plant away and buying another.

Propagate: By seed in early spring.

Carnivorous Plants

There are sixteen genera of carnivorous plants, covering more than four hundred species. Most have evolved and live in swampy areas. They absorb carbon dioxide through their leaves as other plants do, but because the impoverished medium, such as peat, in which they are growing is lacking in nutrients the carnivorous plants have taken to eating flesh, mainly insects, to provide the nitrogen they need for a balanced diet. The plants catch their prey in a variety of ways—jaws which snap shut, sticky surfaces like fly paper, and holes for the insects to fall in and drown. Carnivorous plants are becoming increasingly fashionable as houseplants. The three chosen here require the same care, but will only thrive if the proper microclimate around them is maintained.

Dionaea muscipula

The best known carnivorous plant is the Venus fly trap, which comes from the coastal swamps of North and South Carolina. The "trap" consists of two hinged jaws with rows of teeth along their edges, carried on the end of tri-angular green leaves which are two inches (5 cm) long. Insects are attracted by the bright red colour and the nectar which the trap secretes. When an insect alights in the trap tiny hairs set off a trigger mechanism and before you can say *Dionaea muscipula* the jaws with their long interlocking teeth have snapped shut and the hapless insect is inside. The plant then produces enzymes to soften and digest the insect. After a few days the trap opens to let the next shower of rain flush away the indigestible bits of the victim. White flowers appear during the summer months.

Drosera rotundifolia

The sundew, indigenous to Europe and North America, depends for its food on the fly-paper technique. The upper surface of the small, round leaves are thickly carpeted with reddish hairs which secrete a sticky substance from their tips. As the sun catches the leaves they glisten, hence the name sundew. The insects are attracted and get stuck. The more they thrash about the more they are caught and eventually they drown in the goo. The enzymes the plant produces break down the body of the insect and digest the edible parts. What is left is blown away by the wind. White flowers are produced during the summer months.

Sarracenia flavia

The yellow pitcher plant is a trap to fall into and drown. Its tubular pitchers grow about two feet (60 cm) long and some two inches (5 cm) wide at the top, ending in a flaring lid. Insects are attracted to the plant by the bright greenish-yellow of the pitcher and the nectar which is released inside. Once the insect has entered it is tempted by the smell of nectar to explore further, but slips on the smooth surface into a pool of enzymes and water below, where it is consumed. To prevent any chance that it might escape, the sides of the pitcher are covered with downward pointing hairs. The yellow pitcher plant, which comes from boggy areas in eastern parts of North America, bears large yellow flowers in summer.

The Doctor Says—

Environment: From autumn until early spring a temperature between 45 and 50°F (8 and 10°C) is necessary; this is the dormant period when the flowers are set. For the rest of the year the temperature should be kept in the range of 50 to 55°F (10 to 13°C). The plants need plenty of sun and high humidity all year.

Water: Very frequently from spring until early autumn to keep the compost always wet, indeed the pots can be left standing in saucers of water. For the rest of the year, when the temperature is lower, cut down the frequency of watering, but keep the compost always damp. Always use rain water or distilled water.

Feed: Once a month from spring until early autumn.

Repot: Every two or three years in spring. Use a mixture of equal parts of peat, sand and sphagnum moss.

Propagate: By division in spring. Sarracenia can be grown from seed sown in spring.

Special Instructions: The humid conditions may encourage fungus and botrytis. Also watch for aphids.

Glossary

Aerial root. A root that grows above ground level on the stems of such plants as the climbing philodendron, through which the plant absorbs moisture and food.

Aggregate. An inert medium—gravel, small pebbles, coarse sand or vermiculite—used to anchor a plant grown hydroponically.

Air layering. Also called Chinese layering, this is a method of propagating such single stem plants as *Ficus elastica decora*, the rubber plant, which have grown too tall and spindly and have long, bare stems. An incision is made in the stem just below the leafy top of the plant. When roots have appeared from this incision the stem is cut and the newly rooted plant is potted.

Alkaline medium. A growing medium which contains lime and has a pH value above 7.5.

All-peat compost. A potting mixture which contains peat, fertilizers and, sometimes, sand.

Annual. A plant which lives for only one year.

Anther. The part of the stamen which bears pollen.

Anthracnose. A fungal disease which may affect ficus, palms, avocado and kalanchoe.

Aphids. Green, black, brown or yellow squashy insects which are found in clusters and suck the sap from the tender growth of a plant. Some aphids also attack roots.

Areole. The small protuberances on cacti, from which flowers and spines grow.

Basal offshoot. A shoot which grows from the base of a plant, puts out roots and forms a plantlet.

Bonemeal. A fertilizer made from ground or crushed bone.

Botrytis. A fungal disease which attacks flowers and foliage.

Bract. A modified leaf, often vividly coloured and surrounding insignificant flowers. Some plants, such as *Euphorbia pulcherrima*, the poinsettia, are cultivated for their bracts rather than for their flowers.

Bromeliad. A member of the *Bromeliaceae* family. Most bromeliads are epiphytic and one of their main characteristics is a rosette of leaves which collects and holds water to supply the plant's needs.

Bulb. A swollen underground bud which stores food, enabling it to survive out of the soil through the winter. The bulb also protects the next season's embryo shoot and flowers.

Bulbil. A small, immature bulb which forms above ground on the stems of some plants. It may be removed carefully and repotted.

Bulblet. A small bulb which grows at the base of a larger bulb and may be used for propagation.

Calyx. A ring of modified leaves which protects the flower bud. The calyx can consist of separate organs called sepals, or be fused into a cup or tube.

Capillary action. The way in which, under certain conditions, a liquid is drawn upwards.

Capillary mat. Absorbent matting that will hold thirty ounces of water to one square yard (1 sq. m). Such a mat is often used to keep plants supplied with water during the owner's absence.

Capillary wick. Frequently used for absent plant care. One end dangles in water, while the other is pressed through the drainage hole of the plant pot, into the compost. The plant can take up moisture through the wick as needed.

Compost. (Potting soil in the United States.) The medium in which houseplants are grown, it provides a reservoir for nutrients and water. Compost can be loam-based or peat-based. Proprietary mixtures are available.

Corm. A swollen stem base that usually grows underground and stores food.

Crocks. Pieces of a broken clay pot (shards). They are placed over the hole in the bottom of a plant pot to ensure good drainage.

Crown. The point at which the stem and the root of a plant meet.

Crown and stem rot. Fungal disease, often caused by overwatering, which results in the crown and stems of a plant turning mushy.

Cultivated variety. Also called cultivar. A hybrid, or mutant form of a species, grown in cultivation.

Cutting. A piece of a plant used to grow a new plant. Depending on the plant, the cutting can be a stem with a growing tip, a piece of stalk, a leaf and its stem, or a piece of leaf.

Cyclamen mites. Tiny insects which flourish in cool, humid conditions. Not only cyclamen, but also saintpaulias, gloxinia, pelargonium, begonia, azalea, impatiens and fuchsia are prone to attack.

Cythion. A non-persistent insecticide similar to malathion, but without its strong odour.

Damping off. A fungal disease carried in the soil where it attacks seedlings.

Deciduous. Describes plants which drop their leaves in the autumn, remain dormant through the winter and burgeon in the spring.

Derris. A non-persistent insecticide made from derris root and containing the poison rotenone. It is known in the United States as rotenone.

Division. A way to propagate plants which have several stems.

Dormant period. The annual resting period all plants must have, when their growth slows down and they need less light, warmth, water and no food.

Epidermis. A plant's thin, protective outer skin.

Epiphyte. A plant which grows above ground on another plant, but does not live off it parasitically. Epiphytes obtain nutrients and water from rain, falling debris or insects. Many bromeliads, cacti and orchids are epiphytic.

Evergreen. A plant which stays in leaf all year.

Fibrous roots. The small, fine, lateral roots branching off the main roots.

Floret. One of the individual flowers in a composite flower head such as that of the geranium.

Flower spike. A flower head consisting of one straight central stem with flowers growing directly from it.

Foliar feed. A fertilizer solution that is sprayed directly on the leaves of a plant and is absorbed immediately.

Forcing. Inducing a plant to grow faster or flower earlier than it would do naturally by giving it extra heat or light or both.

Fungicide. A chemical which destroys fungi.

Fungus. A plant which has no chlorophyll and which feeds on dead or living organic matter. Mushrooms, moulds and mildew are all fungi.

Fungus gnats. Small black flies, harmless themselves, which produce root-eating maggots.

Genus. A botanical category, describing plants which have common characteristics distinct from those of all other groups. A genus usually contains several species.

Germination. The sprouting of a spore or a seed.

Glochids. Short, bristly hairs growing from the areoles of some cacti.

Grey mould. A fungal disease that attacks stems and leaves. It can be caused by too much humidity in winter during a plant's dormant period.

Growing shoot. The growing tip of a stem.

Hardening off. Acclimatizing a young plant, which has been grown under glass, to colder conditions by gradually reducing the temperature.

Hard wood pruning. Cutting back into old wood to stir into growth the dormant buds under the bark.

Hardy. A description of a plant that can remain outdoors all year and even withstand a certain amount of frost.

Heel. The base of a soft wood cutting that retains some of the old, hard stem from which it was taken.

Honeydew. The excrement of such pests as aphids and scale insects.

Hormone rooting powder. An organic compound that encourages cuttings to form roots.

Humidifier. A device used to maintain or increase the humidity in the air.

Hybrid. A plant produced by crossing different varieties, species or genera.

Hydroponics. A method of growing plants without soil. The plants are given their nutrients in liquid form, rather than through the potting mixture.

Hydropot. A special pot used for growing plants hydroponically.

Hygrometer. An instrument that measures the relative humidity of the air.

Ion exchange fertilizers. Synthetic resins which release the nutrients slowly as they are used up by the plant. Such fertilizers are used when growing plants hydroponically.

Lateral shoot. A side shoot growing from the main stem of a plant.

Leaf-bud cutting. A cutting which includes a leaf, a leaf bud and a portion of the stem from the parent plant.

Leaf cutting. A whole leaf or piece of leaf used as a cutting. The cutting is pressed into the compost and plantlets appear at the base of the leaf or from shallow cuts in the veins on the underside. Begonias can be propagated by this method.

Leaf hoppers. Aphid-like pests, with a taste for fuchsia, calceolaria and pelargonium.

Leaflet. One of the individual leaf-like lobes which make up a compound leaf.

Leaf miners. The larvae of certain moths, flies and beetles, which burrow into and devour leaves.

Leaf mould. Partly decayed leaves.

Leaf spot. An umbrella name for various fungal or bacterial diseases which cause discoloured patches on leaves.

Loam-based compost. A potting mixture typically consisting of sterilized loam, granulated peat and sharp sand, with fertilizers added to provide nitrogen, phosphorus and potassium.

Loamless compost. A potting mixture composed of peat, fertilizers and sand.

Long-day plant. A plant which forms its flower buds only if it has more than twelve hours of daylight each day.

Lux. The scientific unit in which levels of light are measured.

Malathion. A synthetic, non-persistent insecticide effective against most plant pests. It can, however, also harm such plants as ferns, cacti and other succulents.

Mealy bugs. These pests, which are related to scale insects, have a white, waxy coating. White fluff on stems or leaves is the first sign of an attack.

Metaldehyde. A chemical used, in pellet form, to kill slugs.

Methiocarb. A chemical used in pellet form for killing slugs.

Microclimate. The atmosphere immediately around a plant, which can be made more humid, drier, warmer or cooler than the rest of a room, according to the plant's needs.

Mildew. A fungal disease to which begonias, codiaeum and *Euonymus japonica* are susceptible.

Mineral salts. The nutrients a plant requires for healthy growth—nitrogen, potassium, phosphorus and various trace elements.

Miticide. A preparation which kills mites and their eggs.

Molluscicide. A preparation used to kill slugs and snails.

Nematode. Also known as an eelworm, this pest attacks leaves and stems and sometimes destroys the roots of plants by sucking the sap.

Neutral medium. A growing medium neither too acid nor too alkaline, being only a little above or below the neutral point of pH 7.

Nicotine sulphate. An organic substance made from tobacco, which effectively destroys foliage pests.

Node. A joint in the stem of a plant, from which leaves, buds or side shoots spring.

Offset. A small plant produced naturally by the parent plant. It can be removed and potted.

Offshoot. Side shoot or branch.

Organochloride pesticides. Extremely persistent insecticides, many of which (notably DDT) have been banned.

Osmosis. The process which enables water to be drawn into the root hairs.

Osmunda fibre. Made from the matted roots of *Osmund regalis*, the royal fern, this is an ingredient in a potting mixture recommended particularly for epiphytic orchids.

Peat. (Peat moss in the United States.) Partly decomposed vegetable matter used for potting plants. It drains well but is difficult to moisten again once it has dried out.

Peat-based compost. A potting mixture composed of granulated peat and sharp sand. It is without nutritional value, so fertilizers have to be added.

Perennial. A plant which can live for more than two years and flowers annually.

Persistent. Term used to describe insecticides which remain in the plant or in the soil for a long time after use.

Petiole. The stalk which joins a leaf to the main stem of a plant.

pH indicator. Special paper or liquid used to measure the degree of acidity or alkalinity of water or compost.

pH value. The degree of alkalinity or acidity in water or compost. Above pH 7 is alkaline, below pH 7 is acid.

Photosynthesis. The process by which a plant uses light to manufacture food in its leaves.

Phototropism. The tendency of a plant to bend or turn towards the source of light.

Phyllode. A flattened leaf stalk which resembles a leaf.

Pinching out. Also called stopping. Removing the growing tip of a stem to encourage the growth of side shoots.

Pistil. The female reproductive organ of a flower.

Plantlet. A small plant, or offset, produced by the parent plant, which can be removed and potted.

Potbound. Term used to describe a plant whose roots have grown too large for its pot.

Potting on. Moving a plant to a larger pot because the roots need more room or because the plant looks top heavy.

Potting soil. Compost or potting mixture.

Propagating case. A heated box. It maintains humid, warm conditions in which seeds will germinate and cuttings will put down roots.

Pruning. Cutting a plant back to make it grow bushy and flower or to keep it a manageable size.

Pseudo-bulb. A bulb-like swelling in the joint of an orchid stem, which stores water.

Pyrethrum. An organic, non-persistent insecticide made from the flower heads of various species of pyrethrum (chrysanthemum). It is particularly effective against aphids.

Red spider mites. Tiny, sap-sucking insects which flourish in hot, dry rooms. The leaves of an infected plant become speckled with yellow spots and start to fall.

Relative humidity. The amount of water actually in the air measured against the

Glossary

maximum amount the air could hold at that temperature.

Repotting. Putting the plant in a new container of the same size and giving it a change of compost.

Respiration. The process by which a plant converts food into energy, using the oxygen absorbed in its leaves.

Rhizome. A horizontal stem which can grow either underground or on the surface, and which acts as a storage organ.

Root ball. The complete mass of roots belonging to a plant.

Root hairs. Fine hairs which grow near the tips of most roots and through which a plant absorbs nutrients and water from the compost.

Root pruning. Cutting back the roots all around the root ball to encourage the renewal of root hairs.

Root rot. A fungal disease to which begonias, gloxinias, saintpaulias, palms, cacti and succulents are susceptible.

Rotenone. A non-persistent pesticide made from derris root. It is known as derris in Britain.

Runner. A long shoot sent out by such plants as chlorophytum, the spider plant. When the runner comes into contact with the soil, it puts down roots and forms a new plant.

Rust. A fungal disease.

Scale insect. A little sucking insect, hard to detect, which is found on the undersides of leaves. It attacks codiaeum, dieffenbachia, *Laurus nobilis*, schefflera, stephanotis, ficus, cacti, bromeliads and *Chamaedorea elegans*.

Self-watering pot. Also called a hydropot, it is very useful for absent care, and consists of two pots, one suspended inside the other. The plant grows in the inner pot. The outer pot has water at the bottom, from which a capillary wick takes up moisture into the plant pot as needed.

Sepal. One of the modified, petal-like leaves of the calyx.

Setting. The swelling of a flower ovary after it has been fertilized, resulting in a small fruit, or seed pod.

Sharp sand. Coarse river sand.

Short-day plants. Plants which will flower only after a period in which they have more hours of darkness than of daylight —about fourteen hours of darkness to ten hours of daylight.

Shrub. A plant with woody stems arising from ground level, but with no central trunk.

Soft wood pruning. Pruning by removing not only a growing point, but also some new, non-woody growth below it, to encourage growth from the normally dormant axil leaf buds.

Soil ball. The compost surrounding the roots of a plant.

Sooty mould. A fungus which lives on honeydew, the excrement of such pests as aphids and scale insects. Plants which are infested by these insects are susceptible to attack.

Spadix. A fleshy flower spike, such as that of *Spathiphyllum wallisii*, the peace lily, usually enclosed in a spathe, and whose flowers are embedded in little pits in the stem.

Spathe. A large bract, or modified leaf, which envelops the flower spike of certain plants, such as *Spathiphyllum wallisii*, the peace lily.

Species. A group of closely related plants within a genus.

Species plant. A plant which retains its original form as it grew in the wild, i.e., it is not a variety or a cultivar.

Sphagnum moss. Spongy bog mosses of the genus *Sphagnum*, which can hold a lot of water.

Spore. A single reproductive cell, the equivalent of a seed, which is produced by ferns, mosses and fungi.

Springtails. Minute insects which chew roots and stems of young plants, especially those growing in damp conditions. The aerial roots of orchids growing in damp moss are susceptible to attack.

Stamen. The pollen-bearing part of a flower (the male reproductive organ).

Stem cutting. A piece of the stem of a plant which can be induced to grow roots.

Stem-tip cutting. The tip of a young stem which is removed and used as a cutting.

Stigma. The part of a flower pistil (the female reproductive organ), on which the pollen must be deposited before fertilization can take place.

Stomata. The pores on the epidermis of a leaf through which the plant absorbs and gives out water vapour and gases.

Stopping. See pinching out.

Succulent. A plant which is able to store water in its thick fleshy stems or leaves. Cacti are succulents, but not all succulents are cacti.

Sucker. A shoot springing from an underground part of a stem, or root, or from an axil.

Symphalids. Pests which are related to millipedes, but cause much more damage. They burrow into the compost, eat root hairs and small roots, and damage larger roots, making them susceptible to rot.

Systemic insecticides. These chemicals are taken up through the roots to all parts of a plant, killing pests which are sap suckers or chewers. They have a long-lasting effect and the poison can build up in the plant and in the compost. Systemic insecticides should not be used if there is any possibility of children or pets nibbling the leaves.

Tap root. A plant's main root.

Terminal. Describes the bud or shoot at the tip of a stem.

Terrarium. A glass case in which small plants that enjoy a humid atmosphere can be grown. The moisture evaporates through the plant's leaves, condenses on the inside of the container, seeps back into the compost, and is thus continually recycled.

Terrestrial. Growing on the ground.

Thrips. Flying insects which suck the sap of plants. Their offspring at the nymph stage eat the leaves. Susceptible plants include avocado, azalea, codiaeum, begonias, citrus, fuchsia, orchids, gloxinia and stephanotis.

Transpiration. The process by which water is drawn up the stem of a plant and evaporated through the stomata, or pores, of the leaves.

Trifoliate. A leaf which consists of three separate leaflets.

Tuber. A swollen underground stem or root which stores food.

Umbel. A flower cluster in which the individual flower stalks all spring from the same point at the tip of the stem.

Variegated. Term used to describe leaves or petals with two or more colours.

Variety. A group of plants which in nature have developed some minor variations from the species to which they belong. A variety which has been artificially cultivated is called a cultivar.

Vermiculite. An inert growing medium used in hydroponics.

White flies. Minute moths. Both they and their nymphs are sap-suckers

Xerophytic. Describes a plant which is able to survive very dry conditions.

Index of Plants by Common Names

Index of Plants by Common Names

General Index

Page numbers in **bold face** type denote illustrations.

General Index